*Leading Representatives*

INTERPRETING AMERICAN POLITICS

*Michael Nelson, Series Editor*

# *Leading Representatives*

## The Agency of Leaders in the Politics of the U.S. House

RANDALL STRAHAN

The Johns Hopkins University Press

*Baltimore*

© 2007 The Johns Hopkins University Press
All rights reserved. Published 2007
Printed in the United States of America on acid-free paper
2 4 6 8 9 7 5 3 1

The Johns Hopkins University Press
2715 North Charles Street
Baltimore, Maryland 21218-4363
www.press.jhu.edu

Library of Congress Cataloging-in-Publication Data

Strahan, Randall.
Leading representatives : the agency of leaders in the politics of the U.S. House /
Randall Strahan.
p.   cm. — (Interpreting American politics)
Includes bibliographical references and index.
ISBN-13: 978-0-8018-8690-4 (alk. paper)
ISBN-13: 978-0-8018-8691-1 (pbk. : alk. paper)
ISBN-10: 0-8018-8690-2 (alk. paper)
ISBN-10: 0-8018-8691-0 (pbk. : alk. paper)
1. United States. Congress. House—Leadership. 2. United States. Congress.
House—Biography. I. Title.
JK1319.S78 2007
328.73′0762—dc22
2007006286

A catalog record for this book is available from the British Library.

Special discounts are available for bulk purchases of this book. For more information,
please contact Special Sales at 410-516-6936 or specialsales@press.jhu.edu.

*For my teachers: Charles O. Jones and James W. Ceaser, and to the memory of Ross M. Lence*

# CONTENTS

Richard Nixon frequently drew a sharp distinction between people who seek political office to "be somebody" and people who seek office to "do something." (He said he was against the former and for the latter.) In this wonderfully readable, theoretically rich, historically sound, and acutely perceptive book on congressional leadership, Randall Strahan quotes the late nineteenth-century Speaker of the House of Repesentatives, Thomas Reed, to similar effect. "Office as a ribbon to stick in your coat is worth nobody's consideration," said Reed. "Office as opportunity is worth all consideration."

Reed is one of three Speakers whom Strahan treats in riveting chapter-length case studies. The first, Henry Clay, led the House nearly a century before Reed and the third, Newt Gingrich, led it nearly a century after. Outside the narrow bounds of contemporary political science, all three have been regarded as historically important figures ("consequential leaders," in Strahan's phrase) who led the House in directions it otherwise would not have gone for the sake of enacting public policies or institutional reforms that each speaker held dear.

Within those disciplinary bounds, however, the importance of congressional leaders has recently been discounted. The subfield of legislative studies has been in thrall to "contextual" approaches to congressional leadership that regard the speaker of the House as a be somebody, ribbon-wearing politician who wants only to hold onto the speakership. When the Speaker's party is united, he or she will appear to lead, but it's only an illusion—the Speaker is merely an agent carrying out the will of his or her principal, the party's members of Congress. When the party is divided, the Speaker won't even try to lead for fear of alienating a large number of members and thus losing the speakership.

In *Leading Representatives,* Strahan takes up the burden of demonstrating anew the importance of Speakers in particular and congressional leaders in general. Far from caring only about hanging on as Speaker, he shows, Clay, Reed, and Gingrich all had other important goals. They cared deeply about enacting certain policies (for example, internal improvements for Clay, the gold standard for Reed, and a balanced budget for Gingrich) and reforms of the House itself (a partisan speakership for Clay, responsible party government for Reed and Gingrich). Further, each wanted to be president.

Because these leaders were risk-taking pursuers of new policies, institutional reforms, and higher office, Strahan finds, each made his mark as a leader in precisely that situation when contextual scholars rule out—that is, when their party was divided and therefore could be turned in one direction or another by vigorous leadership. Strahan calls his theory of congressional leadership, which accommodates the goals and ambitions of leaders, "conditional agency." In other words, under the right conditions—a risk-taking leader, a divided party, and a party new to majority status—leaders really do lead.

Michael Nelson

This book is a study of leadership in the U.S. House of Representatives. Although the focus of the study is on speakers of the House, for the purposes of this study leadership is defined as a mode of political action rather than an institutional position. Other scholars have provided excellent accounts of the development of congressional leadership offices and of the activities of the legislators who have occupied those positions over the history of the House.[1] My purpose is different. The objective of this book is not to describe or explain what members of Congress call "the leadership" but instead to look specifically into the question of whether congressional leaders *lead*. Leadership as a mode of political action occurs when a leader acts independently of followers to cause an important political outcome that is different from what would have likely occurred without the action by the leader.

More times than I could count, when telling friends or relatives the subject of the book on which I was working, I heard: "Leadership? In Congress?" or "That's going to be a very short book, isn't it?" Exactly what leadership of Congress involves is not well understood by most Americans outside the circle of professional Congress-watchers. Part of the reason for this lack of understanding may be that some of the most influential recent scholarship in political science tells us that leadership rarely, if ever, occurs in Congress. Congressional leadership studies have generally found that changes in leaders' "styles" and in leadership institutions in Congress tend to follow broaderchanges in political conditions; the actions of leaders thus appear to reflect rather than shape political currents in American politics. This view of congressional leadership has been reinforced by the popularity among political scientists of economic principal-agent theories for explaining leadership politics. As these theories have been applied to Congress, leaders are usually viewed as self-interested "agents" who win and hold their leadership positions by supplying what their followers want. From this perspective, congressional leadership is mostly followership.

The argument of this book is that viewing congressional leaders as agents who "lead" by doing what their followers want is not so much wrong as it is incomplete. The principal-agent perspective on congressional leadership is correct in implying that congressional leaders must always lead with an eye to retaining the support of their followers. Leadership as defined here—acting independently to influence political outcomes—is not the most common mode of action for congressional leaders. Within the American constitutional system, the institutional capacity for leadership is found primarily in the unity of the executive. But even if leadership is normally an executive function in the American political system and congressional leaders ultimately depend on support from their followers, it does not follow that consequential leadership does not occur in the legislative branch as well. One goal of this book is to show that consequential leadership occurs in Congress and in some important cases has been a major factor in the development of congressional institutions and in shaping the direction of national governance in the United States. The House speakerships of Henry Clay, Thomas Reed, and Newt Gingrich provide the main focus of the book and supply the main evidence in support of this claim.

A second goal is to look closely at the interplay between leaders and the political conditions or contexts in which they work in Congress. Leadership in Congress occurs within an institutional context that imposes political limits on leaders. But I will argue that those limits can change as political conditions change and that opportunities arise for congressional leaders to shape or even decide outcomes in Congress. A question that has not been given sufficient attention by political scientists who study Congress is why some leaders take advantage of those opportunities and others do not. Leadership involves not only the conditions that make leadership possible but also the choice of the leader to act. The conditional agency framework proposed in this book focuses attention on the conditions that provide opportunities for leaders to shape outcomes in Congress, as well as how individual leaders' goals incline some but not others to take advantage of these opportunities. Neither approaches that focus on political context alone nor so-called great man theories of leadership, in which extraordinary individuals break free of contextual or institutional constraints, can explain leadership politics in Congress. The challenge, as I see it, is to understand how these two key factors in leadership politics—political context and the characteristics of individual leaders—interact to produce consequential leadership in Congress.

It is a pleasure to acknowledge those who have supported this project or given of their time in ways that made it better. Support for the research on which the book is based was provided by the Dirksen Congressional Center, the Faculty of Social Sciences and Center for American Studies of the University of Southern Denmark, the Emory University Research Committee, and an Emory College Research Completion Leave. Excellent research assistance provided by a long line of Emory graduate students was indispensable to the completion of this project. I especially want to thank Maryann Gallagher for her assistance in preparing the final manuscript and a group of students—some now launched on their own academic or research careers—who began as research assistants and ended up my coauthors on articles related to this project: Matthew Gunning, Moshe Haspel (Spelman College), Vincent Moscardelli (University of Massachusetts–Amherst), Richard Vining (University of Georgia), and Richard Wike (Pew Research Center for the People and the Press).

I have also benefited greatly from many conversations with other scholars about questions addressed in the book as well as comments some have provided on earlier versions of parts of this project. In particular I wish to thank Alan Abramowitz, John Aldrich, Robert Bartlett, Merle Black, William Buzbee, James Ceaser, Roger Davidson, Richard Doner, Richard F. Fenno, Jr., Ronald Formisano, Gerald Gamm, Micheal Giles, Susan Hammond, Jeffery Jenkins, Steven Kautz, Samuel Kernell, Mathew McCubbins, Iain McLean, James Mahoney, David Mayhew, Poul Erik Mouritzen, Mogens Pedersen, David Robertson, David Rohde, Byron Shafer, Kenneth Shepsle, Joel Silbey, Barbara Sinclair, Charles Stewart III, Richard Valelly, Rick Wilson, and Donald Wolfensberger. More than a few of these people took issue with aspects of my work. It is always encouraging to hear that people like your work, but it gets better because people criticize it and challenge you to think harder. I am grateful both for the encouragement and the criticism. I am also grateful to Ed Kutler, both for taking time to share his knowledge of congressional politics in a series of interviews and for helping to arrange interviews with others in the Washington community.

I also benefited from opportunities to present work related to the book at Nuffield College, University of Oxford, the Institut for Staskundskab at the University of Southern Denmark, and the Department of Politics at the University of Virginia, and at conferences or symposia organized by Ronald M. Peters, Jr., at the Carl Albert Center at the University of Oklahoma, David Brady and Mathew McCubbins at Stanford University, Samuel Kernell at the University of California–San Diego, and Donald Wolfensberger at the Woodrow Wilson International Center for Scholars.

Another group of scholars was especially generous with their time in reading and commenting on the book manuscript. Joseph Cooper read the chapters on leadership theories and on the nineteenth-century speakers and saved me from a number of errors. William F. Connelly, Jr., Charles O. Jones, Michael Nelson, Daniel J. Palazzolo, and Ronald M. Peters, Jr., all read the entire manuscript and inspired many improvements. Henry Y. K. Tom and Claire McCabe Tamberino of the Johns Hopkins University Press and series editor Michael Nelson have all demonstrated a remarkable mix of patience and efficiency and have made the process of getting this book into print virtually painless.

The love and support of my family sustained me over the considerable time this project was in the works. I can no longer blame glacial progress in writing on my children; while this book was being written Andrea and Alex have gone off into the world. I could not be prouder of you two. To my wife Annie I owe more than I can ever repay.

I have been extraordinarily fortunate to have the privilege of studying with three remarkable teachers. I hope those two who are still with us see something in this book that shows I learned something they were trying to teach. Neither the teachers to whom the book is dedicated nor anyone else mentioned above should be held responsible for the limitations of the author. With agency comes responsibility.

*Leading Representatives*

# CHAPTER ONE

# Leading Representatives

Henry Clay's career as one of the most important congressional leaders in American history began in 1811 with his election as speaker of the House and a public profession of his dependence on his fellow legislators: "Gentlemen. In coming to the station which you have done me the honor to assign me—an honor for which you will be pleased to accept my thanks—I obey rather your commands than my own inclination. I am sensible to the imperfections which I bring along with me, and consciousness of these would deter me from attempting a discharge of the duties of the chair, did I not rely confidently upon your generous support" (*Annals of Congress,* 12th Cong., 1st sess., 330).

Some years later, after he had been reelected speaker four times—and in a less public setting—Clay offered a different view of leading Congress. "Looking at Congress," he told John Quincy Adams in 1821, "they were a collection of *materials,* and how much good and how much evil might be done with them, accordingly as they should be well or ill-directed" (Adams 1875, 5: 324, emphasis in the original).

Speaker Clay's public speech and private observation provide us with two very different perspectives on congressional leadership. In his first speech to the House, the newly elected speaker presents himself as the servant of his fellow members of the House of Representatives. He obeys his followers' commands rather than his own inclinations. This perspective on political leadership is immediately recognizable to political scientists. Clay's profession of dependence on his followers bears a close resemblance to principal-agent theory, a theory of political leadership that has gained wide acceptance in the field today. Clay's inaugural speech has even been cited in a text by a leading political scientist as "the statement of the quintessential agent" (Shepsle and Bonchek 1997, 382). In the principal-agent framework, political leaders are understood as "agents" to whom authority is delegated to oversee tasks that advance their followers' or "principals'" goals. First advanced by scholars of the rational choice school in economics and political science as a general theory of political and organizational leadership, this perspective has been especially influential in studies of legislative leadership.

Clay's later, less public comment suggests a very different understanding of leadership. Whether this divergence reflects the normal differences between pieties uttered on ceremonial occasions and frank private conversations between experienced politicians, or Clay's experience of leading the House of Representatives over almost a decade, or perhaps some other motive on Clay's part, is difficult to say. But the contrast is striking. In place of the speaker as an agent of others, in the later statement Clay characterizes the leader more as an architect or builder, whose purpose and skill in using a particular set of "materials" are crucial in determining what occurs within the legislative body. Clay's private observation suggests that congressional leaders may indeed be agents, but in a very different sense from the agent who acts at the direction of others. Clay implies that leaders can cause important things to happen in Congress. This view of political leadership may even recall nineteenth-century historian and critic Thomas Carlyle's claim that the "history of the World . . . was the biography of Great Men" (Carlyle 1901, 15). While variations on the "great man" view of leadership still appear in popular accounts of politics, such a view strikes most political scientists today as naïve, almost certainly overstating the political influence of any particular individual in relation to institutions, interests, ideas, or other more general causes.[1]

This tendency to downplay the importance of individuals and focus instead on more general causes to explain leadership politics has been especially characteristic of recent scholarship on the politics of the U.S. Congress. Principal-agent theories, in which leaders' power, style, strategies, and influence are explained primarily in terms of causes arising from institutional and political context have become the predominant approach in scholarly work on this subject by political scientists. As political scientists have come to view leaders as agents whose actions primarily reflect the collective interests or expectations of their followers, individual leaders have received scant attention in some of the most influential recent studies of Congress (for example, Cox and McCubbins 1993, 2005; Sinclair 1995). However, other scholars question whether this contextual orientation may have gone too far and have focused attention on individual leaders as well as contextual factors in explaining congressional leadership politics (for example, Palazzolo 1992; Peters 1997; Zelizer 1998; Mayhew 2000; Schickler 2001; Green, forthcoming).

Newt Gingrich's meteoric career as speaker of the U.S. House during the last decade has contributed to a renewal of interest in understanding the contributions leaders make in congressional politics. According to David Mayhew, politically consequential moves by congressional leaders, such as Gingrich's orchestration of the

"Contract with America" in advance of the Republican takeover of the House of Representatives in 1994, are part of "a world of politics that we experience in our lives, but for some reason, tend to skirt in our scholarship" (Mayhew 2000, xi). As a result, Mayhew contends: "Key aspects of congressional politics, including analytically orderable ones that anyone trying to understand American politics and government should be interested in, are being downplayed or ignored" (Mayhew 2000, x). Ronald M. Peters, Jr., likewise observes in his study of the history of the House speakership: "There exists no clearer example in the history of the House of Representatives of a political leader who created the conditions of his own leadership . . . The independent force of Newt Gingrich's leadership must be acknowledged" (Peters 1997, 318).

This book addresses the question of how individual leaders matter in congressional politics by examining Speaker Newt Gingrich's leadership of the House of Representatives, alongside that of two of his most interesting predecessors in the speaker's chair: Henry Clay and Thomas Reed. Clay was the first American political figure to gain national prominence as speaker of the House, serving as speaker for most of the period between 1811 and 1825. He led the movement within the House to take the country to war with Britain in 1812 and was the first to demonstrate the full potential of the office of speaker as a position from which to influence both domestic and foreign policy. Thomas Reed was a cerebral, quick-witted, sometimes acerbic representative from Maine who served as speaker from 1889 to 1891 and again from 1895 to 1899. He was the principal architect of a system of party government that brought the speakership to its highest peak of influence in American history. Yet even though the Republican Party had established a dominant position in the House and the country by the late 1890s, Reed ended up resigning in disgust at his party's embrace of an expansionist foreign policy. And Newt Gingrich was, well, Newt Gingrich: a tireless organizer and partisan firebrand who led the Republicans out of "permanent minority" status in the House, used the speakership to move the national agenda rightward in the mid-1990s, and helped to create a new type of congressional party government that has outlasted his own brief hold on power in the House.

Not only is each of these figures interesting in his own right, but when examined closely, the politics of each of their speakerships at times look quite different from what we would expect in light of the contextual approaches that have come to define the way political scientists usually explain leadership in Congress. These leaders acted as agents not only in the sense of exercising power delegated and controlled by others but also in the more active sense of an agent as "something that produces or is capable of producing a certain effect: an active or efficient cause: a force effecting or facilitating a certain result" (*Webster's Third New International Dictionary, Unabridged*). Each of these leaders at times acted independently of his followers in leading the House toward important institutional innovations, new departures in public policy, or in some cases both.

No claim will be made anywhere in this book that these leaders should be understood as "great men" whose "charisma" or "force of personality" made it possible for them to reshape the House or public policy in their own images. By design, the U.S. Congress is an institution that is highly resistant to such heroic modes of leadership. Leading a body of representatives in a constitutional system of separated powers necessarily involves responding to political, economic, and social forces over which congressional leaders have limited control. Even when leaders have succeeded in centralizing power in the House, the Senate and the presidency present independent centers of power that must concur for important policy changes to occur. Contextual factors must be given substantial weight in explaining congressional leadership. The central question addressed in this book is how characteristics of leaders matter *along with* contextual factors for understanding leadership in Congress. Congressional leaders have different goals they care about and different orientations toward leadership. Some are clearly more willing than others to push hard or get out in front of their followers and take risks to advance the goals they care about. Do these differences among leaders matter for what happens in Congress? If so, when and why do they matter?

The central thesis of this book is that major policy and institutional changes in Congress can occur as a consequence of actions taken by leaders who take political risks to advance goals about which they care deeply. I propose a "conditional agency" approach as the framework for examining both the political conditions under which leaders encounter opportunities to lead and how individual leaders' goals and willingness to take risks to achieve those goals incline some but not others to take advantage of these opportunities. The most important proposition implied by this framework is that consequential leadership—leaders acting as *causal* agents rather than agents of their followers—occurs when a leader who is willing to take risks to advance some strongly held goal encounters a political situation in which his or her followers are undecided or even deeply divided about some policy or institutional decision that presents an opportunity to advance the leader's goal.

Even if constrained by congressional rules and procedures, developments within political parties, issues on the national agenda, the preferences of presidents and members of the other chamber, and other important contextual factors, leaders matter in congressional politics because leaders sometimes shape or determine how these broader political causes play out in decisions about how Congress operates or what legislation it enacts. As Nelson Polsby observes in his recent study of the institutional changes that transformed the House of Representatives over the period from the 1960s to the 1990s, "To make the claim that institutional evolution is founded upon social and demographic changes is not to claim that there is anything simple or automatic about the influence of these changes on political institutions" (2004, 154). Broader political causes define parameters or possibilities for institutional and policy developments in Congress, but opportunities often arise for leaders to play an independent role in determining the specific path that gets chosen. Evidence from the three cases examined in this book will show that leaders have at times acted independently of their followers to influence important institutional and policy developments in Congress and that the best explanation of leadership politics is one that includes both characteristics of individual leaders—specifically their goals and tolerance for risk—and institutional context or other general causes. This book seeks to advance our understanding of how leaders' personal qualities and contextual conditions can interact to make the agency of leaders an important causal factor in congressional politics.

Before taking up the analysis of these three House leaders it will be helpful first to step back and consider the distinctive tasks involved in legislative leadership and how other scholars have approached explaining the politics of leadership in Congress. The remainder of this chapter will examine the first question: what are the main challenges involved in leading a body of representatives? This discussion will show how legislative leadership differs from political leadership in other settings and also why contextual explanations of leadership have such strong appeal to political scientists. The chapter will conclude by introducing the conditional agency framework for explaining leadership politics in Congress. In chapter 2 I provide an overview of the scholarly work on congressional leadership and discuss how the three cases of Henry Clay, Thomas Reed, and Newt Gingrich will be explored in light of the conditional agency framework.

## Leadership in Legislatures

In a 1975 essay that remains one of the best introductions to the study of legislative politics, Nelson W. Polsby defines a legislature as follows: "The term legislature . . . refers to an organizational form. A legislature can be identified in the first instance by certain of its structural properties: it has more than one member and they meet, deliberate, and vote as equals as a way of doing their business." Along with these organizational characteristics, legislatures are also defined by the capacity to enact laws that are "officially binding on some meaningful population" and by the fact that their authority is grounded in their status as representative bodies. "What they do receives ultimate support because they are in some sense the embodiment of the people governed by their decisions" (1975, 260).

This distinctive organizational form poses distinctive challenges for leaders. How does one lead a body whose members are formally equal, that is expected to deliberate before acting, and whose authority rests on representing the views of a larger political community? As Joseph Cooper (1977, 147) has observed in the case of the American national legislature: "In contrast to bureaucratic organizations, Congress has a low tolerance for hierarchy . . . [It] accordingly cannot be run like an army or even a business corporation. Members formally must have equal standing and decision making must be collegial, even if such collegiality in turn must be limited by the majority principle." As Cooper explains, the formal equality of members implies that majority rule should serve as the normal basis for the legislature's acts and as its internal governing principle.[2] Legislative leaders may exercise considerable powers over organization and procedures, but these must usually be based on the continuing approval of a chamber majority, most often in the support of a partisan majority or coalition of parties. As representatives, members of most legislatures are also responsible to an electoral constituency or subsidiary governmental unit. As a result legislative leaders may have limited control over the recruitment and retention of members of the body (although they may have some say in these matters in their capacities as party leaders).

However, in most legislatures, including the U.S. Congress, the members of the legislature have control over the selection and retention of their leaders. The fact that legislators choose their own leaders and can alter the leaders' powers is one reason for the strong appeal to political scientists of contextual approaches such as principal-agent theory for explaining legislative leadership. In economic principal-agent theories, principals delegate authority to an agent to carry out some task under terms defined by the principals (think of hiring a lawyer or a real estate agent). In this respect leaders do resemble agents of the members of the legislature to whom power is delegated under terms defined by the members.

The distinctiveness of legislative leadership consists in the challenge of orchestrating action in a collectivity 1) that is engaged in the tasks of representation, deliberation, and lawmaking, 2) whose members are usually elected representatives responsible to some external constituency, 3) that requires agreement among a majority of the members for action to occur, and 4) that requires continuing support of a majority of the members for the leader and the powers he or she exercises. Leaders have primary responsibility for ensuring that the legislature acts, as the authors of the *Federalist* put it, "where justice or the general good might require new laws to be passed, or active measures to be pursued" (*Federalist 58:* 361).[3] But if the legislature is to maintain its authority as a representative body, legislative enactments cannot occur without first allowing expression of the full range of interests and opinions present in the political community. Leadership in a legislature must "provide for both consent and action" (Cooper 1977, 155; see also Cooper 1970, 92–98). Nor should action orchestrated by leaders eclipse deliberation, which requires the gathering of information and time for legislators to consider that information and weigh competing arguments about appropriate action.[4] The more numerous the opinions and interests concerned and the more complex the issues involved, the more difficult may be the task of leading the body to a decision.

As Charles O. Jones describes these essential tasks of legislative leadership: "The expressive function is crucial to the work of a representative legislature and so it is not in the least unnatural to expect leadership to facilitate its realization. At the same time, expression alone will not necessarily lead to conclusions. Making law requires drawing conclusions. Thus integrative mechanisms, too, are required to meet the condition of leadership. The combination of expressive and integrative functions appears essential to the working of a democratic legislature" (1981, 119). In practice, most modern legislatures are organized along political party lines and political party organization is crucial in helping to resolve these dilemmas. Parties provide majorities or building blocks of majorities needed for the legislature to act and supply the main justification for establishing hierarchies among legislators, as well as providing many of the rewards and punishments—"carrots" and "sticks"— used by legislative leaders (Cooper 1977, 150–151). In many legislatures the formal leaders are also party leaders, and politically speaking, their followers are primarily their fellow partisans. An additional set of tasks comes with being party leader. These include advancing the party's policy goals, looking out for the party's reputation with the voters, and supporting its candidates in elections. But the leader of the majority party or majority coalition in the legislature remains a legislative leader with responsibilities to the entire legislative body and political community as well as his or her party.[5]

To summarize, legislative leadership involves more than just organizing or orchestrating action by the legislature. Taking responsibility for the passage of laws or carrying out other collective tasks legislators or legislative parties may value is only one aspect of leadership in the legislature. If the legislature is to maintain its authority in a democratic political community, the pursuit of efficient collective action must be undertaken in a way consistent with institutional responsibilities to represent and deliberate.[6] As some of our most thoughtful scholars of legislative politics have emphasized, legislative leadership always involves striking a balance—between expression and integration as Jones puts it, or for Cooper, between gaining consent from representatives and orchestrating action by the legislature. And leaders must maintain ongoing support among the members of the body for the balance they strike.

In this institutional setting the courses of action open for leaders will always be defined in part by what their followers want and what is occurring outside the legislature, in the political community it represents. If, as I will argue, there remain situations in which the agency of leaders (understood in the sense of an independent cause) has important consequences for institutional and policy outcomes, leaders are always constrained to some degree by the political and institutional setting within which they work. Context matters a great deal for understanding leadership in a legislature, but it is not the entire story. The subject of this book is leadership in a particular national legislature, the U.S. House of Representatives. Leadership in the House involves features common to all legislative bodies but also has some distinctive features arising from the design of the American constitutional system. I turn now to that institutional design and its implications for leadership in the House.

## Leadership in the U.S. House of Representatives

The designers of the American constitutional system understood the distinctive contributions of legislative institutions, especially the importance of the legislature for providing deliberative capacity and the representational linkages needed for actions by government to embody popular consent. The modes of leadership considered appropriate to different institutions in the American constitutional system are discussed in the *Federalist 70*. Unity and energy, Alexander Hamilton explained in that essay, are capacities best supplied by a single executive. Legislatures, on the other hand, are "best adapted to deliberation and wisdom, and best calculated to conciliate the confidence of the people and to secure their privileges and interests" (424). While leadership marked by "decision" and "dispatch" are essential to the exercise of executive power, "In the legislature, promptitude of decision is oftener an evil than a benefit. The differences of opinion, the jarring of parties in that department of the government, though they may sometimes obstruct salutary plans, yet often promote deliberation and circumspection, and serve to check excesses in the majority" (ibid., 426–427). As Joseph M. Bessette (1994, 31–32) characterizes this view of legislative organization: "If the legislature tries too hard to emulate the executive's capacity for quick, decisive, and often secret action, it endangers its capacity for wide-ranging and public deliberation."

Of course, the American Founders' constitutional design attempted to secure institutional capacity for representation, deliberation, and effective lawmaking by means of not one but two legislative bodies, each intended to contribute different strengths and capacities. The Senate was to provide permanence, stability, and expertise; the House to be the most direct embodiment of "the genius of republican liberty" (*Federalist 37:* 227).[7] With shorter terms, smaller electoral constituencies, and less-stringent qualifications for membership, the House was to be "open to merit of every description" and its members to have "an immediate dependence on, and an intimate sympathy with, the people" (*Federalist 52:* 326–327).

Little is to be found in either the U.S. Constitution or the *Federalist* on the specific matter of leadership of the House of Representatives. The Constitution provides that the members of the House "shall chuse their own Speaker and other Officers" but otherwise simply grants to each chamber responsibility to "determine the Rules of its Proceedings" (Article 1, sections 2, 5). Still, from the institutional analysis in the *Federalist* and the underlying logic of the constitutional design, some reasonably clear inferences about leadership of the House of Representatives follow. Most importantly, as Ronald M. Peters, Jr., has noted in his account of the development of the House speakership, "[The Founders'] desire to foster the conditions of deliberation required that the speaker's first obligation was to manage the House so that deliberation could take place"(1997, 23).

Other inferences about the politics of House leadership follow from the institutional design of the chamber and the Founders' understanding of lawmaking. The House would be the most accessible of all national institutions to the broad range of interests, opinions, and popular moods that would be present in an extensive republic. The leadership of the chamber would therefore potentially play an important role in the "regulation of . . . various and interfering interests [that] forms the principal task of modern legislation." Also, while the Founders attempted to design legislative institutions that would foster deliberation, they were well aware that these "various and interfering interests" would not always be reconciled through disinterested reason or deliberation about the public good; modern lawmaking involves "the spirit of party and faction in the necessary and ordinary operations of government" (*Federalist 10:* 79). Negotiation and bargaining would also be involved in assembling House majorities among legislators whose motivations would often be narrower than considerations of the public good.[8]

Finally, it appears that the Founders expected the House's larger size to cause leadership to be more important in its operation than would be the case in the Senate. "In all legislative assemblies," Hamilton observed, "the greater the number composing them may be, the fewer will be the men who will direct their proceedings" (*Federalist 59:* 360). Two principal arguments are made in support of this view: that a greater proportion of legislators are likely to be inexperienced or of modest talents in a large assembly; and the greater propensity of large bodies "to yield to the impulse of sudden and violent passions, and to be seduced by factious leaders" (*Federalist 62:* 379; see also *53:* 335, and *65:* 400–401). The latter argument is a reminder both that the Founders recognized the potential for leaders to have great influence in the politics of the House and that they did not view "leadership" as an unalloyed good. Leadership in Congress and elsewhere was understood to have the potential either to advance or to undermine good governance, depending on the motives of leaders and the incentives different institutional arrangements create for officeholders to advance broader or narrower interests.[9]

As Peters (1997, 23) notes, "The exact contours" of how leadership would operate in the House "were left by the Founders to history." Still, the analysis provided by the authors of the *Federalist* makes it clear that the most thoughtful of the Founders believed the quality of House leadership could turn out to be either a significant strength or a serious weakness of the constitutional structure they had designed. Talented and public-spirited leaders could help establish conditions within which deliberative majorities would decide matters in the most open and democratic branch of government. Conversely, irresponsible or narrowly self-interested leaders might bring out the considerable potential for impulsive or unjust action that would always be present in a large assembly designed to be sensitive to popular moods and sentiments. Revisiting the logic of the original constitutional design also helps clarify the tasks involved in leading the House and the importance of leaders in carrying out those tasks. From whatever quarter exercised, if House leadership is to contribute to effective governance, it must be attentive to the representative and deliberative responsibilities of the legislative branch, all the while incorporating closer popular connections than any other national political institution. Not an easy task, to be sure, and the high probability of failures or lapses in the quality of leadership in the House was an important reason for the countervailing institutional design of the Senate and the creation of an independent executive.

A feature of American political development unforeseen by the Founders, the emergence of political parties, added a dimension to congressional leadership that was not contemplated in the original constitutional design. Reflecting that development, studies of congressional leaders by political scientists have focused primarily on congressional leaders in their roles as party leaders. The central theme of recent political science scholarship in this area is that conditions in the political and institutional context, particularly developments within political parties, are the key to explaining congressional leadership politics. What individual leaders contribute to congressional politics or how the characteristics of individual leaders matter for understanding important institutional or policy changes in Congress are questions that have received much less attention by political scientists.

## A Conditional Agency Approach to Leadership in Congress

In contrast to studies that emphasize various aspects of the political context in explaining what leaders do in Congress, this study begins from the premise that understanding leadership politics in Congress also requires understanding more about leaders. As will be explained in more detail in chapter 2, contextual approaches usually view congressional leaders as agents who have limited autonomy because they are chosen by party followers and need majority support for their actions. From this perspective, a necessary condition for strong or active leadership in Congress is a high level of agreement—homogeneous preferences—among followers on the issue being decided. Who the leader is matters much less than what the followers want. This book will propose an alternative perspective on congressional leadership, a *conditional agency* framework. An important difference between these two perspectives is that the conditional agency framework proposes that leaders exercise agency in congressional politics—in the sense of being an important cause in decisions about legislation or organizational changes—under a broader range of political conditions. While recognizing that congressional leaders usually will be active and assertive in political situations in which followers are already in agreement about what they want, the conditional agency framework proposes that leaders can also be influential in political situations in which followers are uncertain or divided about what they want to see happen in Congress.

The conditional agency framework begins with the understanding that congressional leaders have multiple goals and hold those goals with varying levels of intensity. Surely most leaders enjoy the power and prestige that come with holding a leadership position in Congress and, all other things being equal, they prefer to keep it. But wanting to hold on to a leadership position does not provide an adequate account of what motivates congressional leaders; some are also motivated by strongly held views on issues of public policy, on how Congress should operate, or by powerful ambition to hold higher office or even leave a mark on history. Leaders' goals matter for explaining congressional leadership because two leaders with different goals may respond differently to political contexts or situations they encounter in Congress. In particular, leaders who care deeply about policy issues or how the legislature should operate or who possess strong ambitions that reach beyond Congress may be willing to take greater risks as leaders when opportunities arise to advance those goals. All three of the figures discussed in this book were risk-takers who possessed strongly held goals beyond simply remaining a leader in Congress.

A second proposition on which the conditional agency framework is based is that political situations arise with some frequency in Congress that provide opportunities for leaders to lead. If the members of Congress almost always know for certain what policies or institutional arrangements they favor, and leaders are essentially agents of their followers with limited means of getting legislators to change their minds, then it would follow that opportunities for leaders to influence the outcomes of congressional decisions would also be quite limited. The conditional agency framework is based on a different view of how followers and leaders interact in Congress.

In the real world of congressional politics, members are sometimes uncertain about the policies they favor or which way of organizing Congress will work best for them or the people they represent. And although leaders do need followers' support to be elected (and reelected) leader and to pass legislation, congressional leaders still have a variety of means available for influencing the members. The most important of these are persuasion, control over how and when decisions are made in the legislative body, and the meting out of punishments and rewards. By means of these "causal mechanisms" leaders can influence outcomes in Congress—both when their followers are in agreement on where they want to be led and sometimes when they are not.

To summarize, from the conditional agency perspective, opportunities may be present for leaders to influence outcomes in Congress, not only when their followers agree on where they want to be led, but also in some cases when followers are uncertain or unable to reach agreement about what they want. But not all leaders will be inclined to take the lead under these conditions because leadership in these uncertain conditions can involve political risk if the leader fails to persuade enough followers to follow. The leaders most likely to use the prerogatives of a leadership position aggressively in these situations are leaders who care deeply about the issue in question or who see an opportunity to advance some other strongly held goal beyond simply remaining a leader in Congress. The central question to be addressed by this book is whether such a perspective helps us better to understand not only three important congressional leaders—Henry Clay, Thomas Reed, and Newt Gingrich—but also congressional politics more generally and the contributions leaders make to decisions in the legislative branch.

Chapter 2 provides an overview of the most influential scholarship on congressional leadership, a more detailed explanation of the conditional agency framework, and an explanation of the choice of cases for the study. This chapter will be of greatest interest to readers concerned about the theoretical issues involved in the study of legislative leadership in political science and the challenges involved in designing research to explore those issues. After exploring these matters in greater depth in chapter 2, the focus shifts to the three leaders examined in the book, beginning with Henry Clay's leadership in the early decades of congressional politics when some of the most important organizational features of the House of Representatives were taking form.

To return to the contrasting statements by Speaker Clay with which the chapter began, Clay may or may not have been entirely sincere when he claimed in 1811 that he would only follow the commands of his House followers and may have had his own reasons for trying to impress John Quincy Adams with his ability to influence Congress when they spoke privately in 1821; in either case the questions posed by his remarks about the nature of leadership remain important ones for students of Congress to explore, and they provide the focus for what follows.

# CHAPTER TWO

# Explaining Congressional Leadership

Explaining political leadership presents a challenge to political science. As James Q. Wilson (1995, 195) observes, "Finding and explaining uniformities, both trivial and important, is the special competence and perhaps the chief function, of social science." But, as Wilson also notes, leadership often involves "acts representing a break in a prior pattern of behavior" (ibid.). As social science, political science seeks above all to generalize about politics, to identify patterns and develop theories that can bring order to the otherwise daunting complexity of political life. In keeping with this focus on uniformities and patterns, much recent scholarship on Congress explains the behavior of congressional leaders as primarily a reflection of more general causes in the political context. Although some scholars have considered how leaders can act independently to alter the effects of these general causes in congressional politics, theories that assign significant causal influence to actions of individual leaders are less well developed and have been less widely accepted in contemporary political science than the contextual approaches.

In this chapter, I examine the leading theoretical approaches to congressional leadership, then set forth the conditional agency framework in more detail. Contextual approaches focus our attention on the conditions that create opportunities or limits for leadership. Studies highlighting individual leaders have shown that congressional leaders sometimes bring very different goals and approaches to their positions and that some leaders have played crucial roles in particular policy or institutional decisions in Congress. What remains unclear in many theories of leadership are the causal links between contextual conditions, characteristics of leaders, and outcomes in Congress. The conditional agency framework seeks to advance our understanding of leadership politics by specifying more clearly what types of contextual conditions and what characteristics of individual leaders can interact to produce leadership that is consequential for policy and institutional outcomes in Congress. Following this discussion of the conditional agency approach, the final section of the chapter explains the selection of the three cases of Henry Clay,

Thomas Reed, and Newt Gingrich and how each will be explored for evidence regarding how best to understand leadership politics in Congress.

## The Contextual Approach to Congressional Leadership

In one of the earliest attempts to develop a general explanation of the politics of congressional leadership, political scientist Charles O. Jones (1968) has emphasized the "limits of leadership" in the House of Representatives.[1] Drawing on evidence from the cases of early twentieth-century speaker Joseph Cannon and midcentury Rules Committee chair Howard W. Smith, Jones argues that leaders in the House have limited independence because of the need to maintain a "procedural majority" among members of the legislature who will support the rules and organizational arrangements on which the leader's authority is based. Speaker Cannon and Rules Committee chair Smith both provoked major changes in House rules, Jones (1968, 619) concludes, by engaging in "excessive leadership." According to Jones attempts by leaders to shape legislative outcomes in Congress are limited by the majoritarian foundations of authority within the legislature; any leader, regardless of his or her goals or skills must work within those limits or risk action by a chamber majority to reduce the leader's authority or remove him or her from office. It is important to note that Jones did not conclude, as have some more recent studies (see especially Krehbiel 1991) that the majoritarian foundations of congressional rules imply that leaders are of little importance in congressional politics. Jones's (1968, 645) conclusions are that "all House leaders have considerable latitude" but that they must also remain attentive to chamber majorities to retain their authority.

Political scientists who followed Jones in developing explanations of congressional leadership politics were drawn to the puzzle of why the House of Representatives has witnessed such different leadership styles across its history—why it has seemingly been dominated at times by a "Czar" Reed or a "Boss" Cannon while at other times its leaders seemed unwilling or unable to rein in independent-minded factions or powerful standing committees. The most important of these studies was Joseph Cooper and David W. Brady's "Institutional Context and Leadership Style: The House from Cannon to Rayburn" (1981). Seeking to explain why the centralized, "czar-rule" of turn-of-the-century speakers was displaced by the decentralized, brokerage-type leadership exemplified by Texan Sam Rayburn, they conclude: "Institutional context rather than personal skill is the primary determinant of leadership power in the House." And: "Institutional context rather than personal traits primarily determines leadership style. To be sure, style is affected by personal traits. Nonetheless, style must be responsive to and congruent with both the inducements available to leaders and member expectations regarding proper behavior" (1981, 423).

Cooper and Brady define institutional context broadly to include House rules as well as ideas members share about matters such as party loyalty. In their view the most important condition that determines how leaders operate within a given institutional context is party strength, which is determined primarily by electoral politics *outside* the House—specifically the degree of similarity in the types of constituencies represented within and across parties.[2] Rules that concentrated formal powers in the hands of leaders and strong norms of party loyalty are part of their explanation for the powerful leaders and hierarchical leadership styles that emerged in the late nineteenth- and early twentieth-century House. But the most important cause that explains leadership politics in this period is said to be the high level of party unity that arose from polarization of the Democratic and Republican members' electoral constituencies along agricultural-industrial lines. The decentralized, brokerage leadership style of Sam Rayburn and the leaders who followed him up through the late 1970s was in turn primarily the product of the greater heterogeneity of constituency interests represented in the majority party during the more recent period.[3]

Partly in response to the emergence of more active House leadership in the 1980s, a second important wave of congressional leadership studies began to appear. These studies built on the earlier contextual perspectives but incorporated some new elements, most notably the use of principal-agent theories from organizational economics to conceptualize leader-follower interactions. One of the most influential works of this second wave, David W. Rohde's *Parties and Leaders in the Postreform House* (1991), also attributed the more active and centralized House leadership of the 1980s primarily to greater party unity (preference homogeneity) within the majority party, occurring mostly as a consequence of the declining electoral fortunes of the Democratic Party's southern conservative wing. Rohde's perspective on leadership is similar to the Cooper-Brady contextual theory in stressing party unity as the key variable that explains both leadership power and behavior. Synthesizing the earlier contextual perspective with principal-agent theory, Rohde proposes: "[Contemporary leaders] are strong because (and when) they are agents of their memberships, who want them to be strong" (1991, 172).

Rohde also proposed a number of refinements to contextual leadership theory. The first is that unlike the strong leadership that emerged when the majority party was unified in earlier eras, leadership power in the contemporary House is conditional and will vary across issues depending on the level of agreement on the issue among members of the majority party (ibid., 31–34, 35–37). Rohde and coauthor

John H. Aldrich (Aldrich and Rohde 1997–98, 2000) have also argued that this "conditional party government" theory, in which the strength of leadership depends primarily on the level of unity within the majority party and divergence on policy goals from the minority party, also explains the strong leadership that has been witnessed in the Republican-controlled House after 1994.

Second, Rohde (1991, 37) observes that a contextual explanation of the reemergence of strong leadership in the contemporary House, "while basically correct, is not quite complete." Based on comparisons of the Democratic speakers, Thomas P. "Tip" O'Neill, Jim Wright, and Thomas Foley, he argues that under certain conditions, personal characteristics of the individual who occupies a leadership position can be important as well: "There is an asymmetry between the circumstances which constrain leaders and those which are permissive. When conditions won't support strong leadership activity, then leaders who want to exercise power and those who do not will probably yield roughly the same results. When the membership is permissive or demanding of strong leadership, however, leaders who are aggressive and enthusiastic will likely exhibit substantially more activist behavior than will leaders who are reluctant about the exercise of their powers" (ibid., 172).

Elaborating on conditional party government theory in relation to the speakership of Newt Gingrich, Rohde (2000, 5) observes: "The personality and skills of leaders play a significant role, and Gingrich epitomized this aspect of the theory. Just as Democratic speaker Tom Foley's reluctance to use the institutional powers available to him made him a weaker Speaker than he had to be, Gingrich's approach enhanced his power and facilitated its exercise." While calling attention to the importance of individual leaders for understanding House politics under both Democratic and Republican control, Rohde's theory does not address *why* some leaders seek to exercise the powers of the speakership aggressively and others do not.[4] This is an important point to which we will return.

A second political scientist at the forefront of contemporary scholarship on congressional leadership is Barbara Sinclair. In a series of books and articles Sinclair has carefully documented the reemergence of stronger leadership in the contemporary House of Representatives, as well as the strategies that have been employed by leaders over this period (Sinclair 1992, 1995, 1999). Sinclair (1995, chap. 2) also characterizes her theory of leadership as "a principal-agent approach." "Within this framework," she explains, "congressional party leaders are seen as agents of the members who select them and charge them with advancing members' goals, especially (though not exclusively) by facilitating the production of collective goods"(ibid., 9). Along with Rohde, Sinclair contends that increased unity within the majority party was a key factor in the reemergence of stronger House leadership in the 1980s and 1990s.

Sinclair's theory also identifies a number of additional contextual variables that can influence leadership behavior by affecting members' expectations of leaders: the predictability of the law-making process, opposition party control of the White House, availability of opportunities for individual member entrepreneurship, interpretations of electoral outcomes, and confidence in leaders' strategic judgment (Sinclair 1990, 101–105; 1995, chaps. 1–4; 1999, 422–425, 434, 441–442).

However, in contrast to Rohde, Sinclair explicitly rejects the idea that characteristics of individual leaders are an important factor in House leadership politics. She contends that explanations of leadership should "omit personality" and that both the emergence of stronger House leadership under Democratic majorities in recent decades as well as the politics of the Gingrich speakership are explained by changes in the political context (Sinclair 1999, 423). As Sinclair (1990, 99–100) puts it: "Predicting behavior requires some simplifying assumptions . . . It is reasonable to assume that retaining their leadership position is a major goal for party leaders. Since leaders are chosen by their party members, satisfying their members' expectations should be a top priority. Member expectations should be a critical determinant of leadership behavior." Within Sinclair's theory, leaders may be granted considerable latitude to develop the means to advance goals on which their partisan followers agree, but leaders do not differ significantly in their propensity to exercise this latitude. Nor can they act independently in deciding what goals to pursue if their followers are not in agreement (Sinclair 1999, 423, 445–447). From this perspective, party leadership matters in Congress because those in leadership positions can influence how issues get framed and are often in a position to decide which specific alternatives get voted on (Sinclair 2002); however, characteristics of individual leaders are not an important factor because the critical determinant of how leaders actually wield this influence is not who the leader is but what followers want.

A third wave of influential scholarship on congressional leadership has been that developed by Mathew D. McCubbins in collaboration with D. Roderick Kiewiet (Kiewiet and McCubbins 1991) and Gary W. Cox (Cox and McCubbins 1993, 2002, 2005). McCubbins and his coauthors have focused not so much on explaining variations in leadership style or power as on how congressional institutions create incentives for congressional leaders to look out for the collective electoral interests of their fellow party members in the legislature. Principal-agent theory provides the explanatory framework for these studies as well (Kiewiet and McCubbins 1991, chaps. 2, 3; Cox and McCubbins 1993, chaps. 4, 5). Leaders are said to be motivated by "a desire for internal advancement" within the legislature (Cox and McCubbins 1993, 126; see also 2005, 23). The personal interest of the leader in retaining the power and prestige that come with a leadership position—especially with leadership of the majority party—is said to provide the motive for carrying out the central task for which the agent has been delegated authority by fellow party members: protecting the party's collective reputation with the voters. As Cox and McCubbins put it, "By creating a leadership post that is both attractive and elective, a party can induce its leaders to internalize the collective electoral fate of the party" (Cox and McCubbins 1993, 132–133).

The leader's personal interest in using the advantages conferred by chamber rules to protect the collective electoral interests of the party (and the similar interests of "senior partners" in the party to whom other offices are assigned) makes the majority party a privileged group or "cartel" within the legislature. In this theory, the majority party in the modern House always retains the capacity to exercise "negative agenda control" to block measures that divide the party. Party unity or preference homogeneity remains an important factor explaining leadership politics because the degree of party unity is said to determine the scope of issues over which party leaders will attempt to advance new legislation—or exercise "positive agenda control" (Cox and McCubbins 1993, 2002, 2005). The empirical work inspired by this "legislative cartel" theory of party government thus focuses on demonstrating the capacity of the majority party to use chamber rules to maintain its majority status by exerting influence over key committees and controlling the legislative agenda under a variety of political conditions.

Here, at the level of theories developed in the second and third waves of contemporary leadership scholarship, we find one important reason why so little attention is paid to actual leaders in some of the most important recent political science scholarship on Congress. At first glance this might seem paradoxical given that these approaches view party leaders as such important actors in congressional politics. Leaders are said to have primary responsibility for identifying and advancing the collective interests of the majority party in the legislature. Congressional rules, in turn, confer substantial authority on leaders to influence both organizational decisions (who gets appointed to what standing committee, for example) as well as the course of legislation. Choices made by leaders have major consequences for their followers' political careers and for determining what legislation gets enacted or blocked by the chamber, as well as for the electoral strategy and success of the legislative party.

But within neither the party cartel theory nor Sinclair's principal-agent approach does anything of real significance occur when one leader replaces another. In these theories elected leaders such as the speaker of the House are understood to be more or less interchangeable "agents" who will respond in like manner to contextual conditions, the most important being the degree of unity among their party followers.[5] Because leaders are assumed to be motivated primarily by the same self-interested goal—remaining leader—what matters for explaining congressional leadership politics is not who the leader is, what goals or skills or interests he or she brings to the position, but what followers want and how congressional institutions create incentives and tools for advancing the interests of followers. From this perspective, explaining the politics of congressional leadership involves identifying what the collective interests of party followers are, determining why members give their leaders some tools and not others to advance them, and identifying how the use of those tools in service of collective party interests may affect different aspects of congressional politics.[6]

While the contextual theories differ somewhat on the specific contextual factors that may affect what members want of their leaders, they share a central proposition regarding the necessary political condition under which leaders will actively use the prerogatives of office to shape outcomes in the legislature. Note the following statements of this proposition by leading proponents of contextual leadership theories:

- "When there is a high degree of homogeneity of preferences . . . leaders vigorously use the tools they have been granted. As preference homogeneity declines, institutional arrangements tend to be altered to reduce the capacity of leadership for independent and forceful action, and leaders tend to respond with caretaker or housekeeping strategies" (Rohde and Shepsle 1987, 122–123).
- "When the legislative situation involves an issue that party members care about and on which their preferences are homogenous, the stage is set for the maximal use of the leadership's powers. If, however, the party is deeply divided, then leaders will be reluctant to use the tools at their disposal" (Rohde 1991, 172).
- Leaders have "great latitude in the means they employ" when their principals are "homogeneous in what they want to accomplish" but when followers are divided or factionalized, "members' heterogeneity tends to limit them [leaders] more stringently in the means they can use" (Sinclair 1999, 447).
- "The size of the majority party's agenda . . . waxes and wanes, depending on how similar party members' policy goals are, because leaders do not wish to waste their time leading where their followers will not (or cannot be induced to) follow" (Cox and McCubbins 2002, 109).

From the perspective of these contextual theories, then, a necessary condition for congressional leaders to use their prerogatives aggressively to influence outcomes is homogeneous preferences among followers regarding the political ends for which the leader's powers are to be employed.[7] Put simply, in these contextual theories strong legislative leadership occurs when party followers are already in substantial agreement about where they want to go. If that high level of agreement (homogeneity) is not present, according to these theories, leaders will avoid assertive use of the prerogatives of office to shape outcomes in the legislature and will not be consequential for explaining congressional outcomes.[8]

If this perspective accurately captures the most important features of leadership politics, students of congressional politics would indeed be ill advised to focus much energy on studying leaders because knowing more about individual leaders will explain little of importance for what happens in Congress. Because these theories define strong leadership to mean situations in which leaders take the lead in working out the details of legislative or political strategy on issues on which followers are already in substantial agreement, the agency of leaders would seem to operate within very limited bounds in any case. If this view of leadership politics is correct, it seems fair to ask whether a legislative leader is *ever* a consequential agent in the sense of independently influencing outcomes or causing anything of importance to happen in Congress that would not have happened otherwise. Wouldn't a unified majority in a legislature that decides on the basis of majority rule arrive at roughly the same decision regardless of who happened to occupy leadership positions? Or whether the leader chooses to act vigorously or not?[9] However, a closer look at scholarship on Congress shows that both at the level of theory and in light of empirical research by other congressional scholars, there are good reasons to think leaders can be more important in shaping outcomes than implied by the contextual theories and that leaders are consequential in a broader range of political situations than those in which followers are already in substantial agreement about what they want the legislative body to do.

## Why Should Leaders Matter? Theoretical Arguments

Remaining for a moment at the level of theory, why should we expect that leaders matter in shaping outcomes in Congress? First, even within the economic principal-agent theories on which the newer contextual theories of congressional leadership are based, principals can never completely control their agents. Principals delegate authority to an agent within an incentive structure that attempts to align the agent's interests with those of principals (think of a lawyer hired by a group of clients to handle a lawsuit under an agreement where the lawyer receives a substantial share of the settlement if the suit is successful). But as Terry Moe explains:

"There is no guarantee that the agent, once hired, will in fact choose to pursue the principal's best interests or to do so efficiently. The agent has his own interests at heart, and is induced to pursue the principal's objectives only to the extent that the incentive structure imposed in their contract renders such behavior advantageous" (1984, 756). The problem of incomplete control of agents—termed agency loss in economic theories—arises partly because there are almost always conflicts of interest between principals and agents (the clients want their lawyer to leave no stone unturned in pursuing their case, the lawyer seeks to devote the minimum amount of time and energy possible for the maximum fee), and because agents can be difficult to monitor and may exploit asymmetries in the information to which they and their principals will have access.

Some scholars who have applied principal-agent theory to congressional politics acknowledge that the problem of agency loss is never entirely solved by having followers elect leaders, or by other institutional arrangements in Congress. Kiewiet and McCubbins, for example, note that control of agents by principals is especially difficult in settings, as in Congress, where collective principals are involved (1991, 24–27). While observing that members of legislative parties exert control through careful selection of their leaders and by delegating power to multiple agents (i.e., to party *and* committee leaders), Kiewiet and McCubbins also emphasize that congressional leaders retain significant strategic and informational advantages in relation to their followers, including the ability under some conditions to use agenda powers to manipulate decision-making processes (ibid., 27, 48–55). Finally, some have also noted that the main incentive said to tie congressional leaders to followers once the leader is in place—the threat of removal from office—is in practice a fairly blunt instrument for controlling a leader such as the speaker of the House. Regarding a situation where followers might prefer a particular mode of leadership but a leader is unwilling to supply it, Rohde (1991, 38) observes: "The membership's only recourse in such a case would be to depose the leader, a messy prospect to say the least. Such action would likely be taken only if the deviation from members' expectations were extreme."[10] Of course the fact that removing a leader is costly does not mean that leaders have unlimited autonomy. As Jones (1968) has explained, leadership in Congress always has limits. Congressional leaders do get deposed; such was the fate of one of the leaders discussed in this book.

But even if one is persuaded that congressional leadership is best understood from the perspective of principal-agent theory (as many political scientists are today), such an approach does not foreclose the possibility that individual leaders matter for explaining outcomes in Congress. In fact, principal-agent theory supplies some important insights about why legislative leaders *always* enjoy a certain degree of autonomy from their followers. Multiple principals sometimes have difficulty controlling agents because agents can play groups of their principals off against one another, replacing the agent in this setting can be difficult and costly for the principals, and the agent may have a number of important strategic advantages over principals in terms of access to information and control over decision-making procedures.

Beyond principal-agent frameworks, a number of other theoretical approaches to legislative politics also imply that leaders will sometimes be in a position to exert independent influence over decisions. Some of the most innovative recent scholarship on Congress has argued that legislators may have vaguely defined preferences on policy issues that reach the agenda, creating opportunities for leaders to *shape* followers' preferences and leaving a significant range of discretion for leaders to decide what legislative alternatives should be advanced or blocked (Cooper and Hering 2003; Behringer, Evans, and Materese 2006; Weaver 2000). Others have argued persuasively that leaders sometimes determine legislative outcomes by means of persuasion, strategic use of legislative procedures, or by winning over critical members or blocs through the distribution of selective benefits (Arnold 1990, 92–99; Evans 2004). The influential political theorist William Riker (1980, 1986) in particular has argued that leaders can sometimes manipulate the instability of majority coalitions in the legislature to produce the outcomes they favor. Still others have noted that over the longer term leaders in the legislature can have an independent influence by shaping the culture of the institution in ways that affect its politics (Peters 1997).

But if a variety of theoretical approaches imply that opportunities will arise for leaders to exert independent influence over outcomes in Congress, is there reason to expect one congressional leader might act differently from another when those opportunities arise? Is there reason to believe that individual characteristics of leaders will matter? In a word, the answer is yes. Congressional scholars have repeatedly demonstrated through careful empirical research that legislators have multiple goals and that legislators who are pursuing different goals act differently. The pathbreaking work in this area was Richard Fenno's (1973) study of how members pursue different goals—reelection, good public policy, and influence or prestige—through their committee work in the House. Other studies have shown how different goals motivate participation in different types of legislation or different levels of involvement in oversight activity (Hall 1996; Evans 1994, 2004, 31–36).

Related to the work on the multiple goals of members of Congress is Richard Hall's (1996) demonstration that members hold policy preferences with varying levels of intensity. Hall has shown that explaining members' levels of participation in legislative work requires attention not only to members' different goals and interests but also to the strength or intensity with which those interests are held: "Members who wish to affect specific outcomes have much more to invest than their votes. Their legislative time and energy, staff effort, and political capital, borrowed or accrued, can be variously invested or conserved in the legislative competition over the issues that come before the chamber. Members with relatively strong interests in a given issue expect greater benefits from such investments; they are thus more inclined to participate and when participating, to pursue their positions more vigorously" (1996, 6–7).

It therefore seems reasonable to expect that leaders in Congress will also have multiple goals—that is, goals beyond the goal of winning and holding a leadership position as emphasized in the contextual theories. It also seems reasonable to expect that leaders will hold these different goals with varying levels of intensity. As will be explored in more detail below, these goals might include views on public policy or on how Congress should be organized or political ambitions that reach beyond Congress. And to the extent that leaders have intensely held goals other than office-holding ambition inside Congress, it also seems reasonable to expect that leaders will sometimes act independently of followers' expectations in pursuit of those goals. Most importantly, leaders motivated by goals other than ambition to hold a leadership position inside Congress might be inclined to act independently to influence decisions in political situations when their followers' preferences are not homogeneous, that is when followers have yet to decide what they want to happen on legislative issues or proposed institutional changes, or even when followers may know what they want but are deeply divided. In other words, leaders with intensely held goals that reach beyond office-holding ambition in Congress may attempt to *lead*, and actions by these leaders may have important consequences for institutional and policy outcomes in Congress.

## How Individual Leaders Matter: Empirical Evidence

Turning from the realm of theory to evidence from previous studies of congressional politics, quite a few scholars have found that characteristics of leaders matter in explaining important aspects of congressional politics. Regarding leadership style and strategy, we have already seen that Rohde's analysis of House leadership politics, though primarily contextual, recognizes a "personal dimension in leadership style" (1991, 184). Although the political contexts faced by Democratic House leaders during the period he studied were similar, Rohde found that Jim Wright wielded the prerogatives of the speaker's office much more aggressively to shape policy than did Speakers O'Neill or Foley (ibid., 37–39, 105–119, 185–189). Rohde (2000, 5–6) also attributes the remarkable concentration of power achieved by Newt Gingrich during the first Congress he served as speaker in part to Gingrich's aggressiveness and personal willingness to use power. Daniel Palazzolo's analysis of leadership in the congressional budget process during the 1970s and 1980s reached similar conclusions about the importance of personal characteristics: "While O'Neill followed a cautious middleman style of leadership that included responding to the expressed or implied expectations of the party membership, Wright's activist style involved acting before he consulted party members, and then bargaining to achieve his policy goals" (1992, 173). Other scholars have also noted the importance of leaders' personal characteristics for explaining differences in leadership styles and strategies in the modern House (Bader 1996; Owens 1997, 2005; Peters 2004; Strahan and Palazzolo 2004).

Along with identifying effects of individual leaders' characteristics on leadership styles and strategies, a number of scholars have also found important leader effects in studies on the institutional development of Congress and on major policy decisions. In his historical study of the House speakership, Peters (1997, 122) concludes that "the contextual thesis . . . gives insufficient attention to the manner in which a leader can shape the institutional context within which he is called upon to lead." Among the leaders Peters singles out whose personal qualities had important effects on House politics are Henry Clay, Thomas Reed, Sam Rayburn, and Newt Gingrich (ibid., 69–70, 122–125, 142–143, 292–321). Looking at major institutional changes in Congress between 1890 and 1989, Eric Schickler found that independent actions by leaders "were significant in fifteen of forty-two cases" (2001, 250). Among the leaders Schickler found to have exercised significant influence on the institutional development of the House by framing innovations in ways that could win approval by a majority of members are Speakers Thomas Reed, Joseph Cannon, Nicholas Longworth, and Newt Gingrich.[11] Studies of congressional decisionmaking have also found strategies chosen by leaders to be crucial for explaining legislative outcomes in policy areas including energy regulation, federal budgeting, taxation, telecommunications, transportation, and health care (Arnold 1990, 149–261; Evans and Oleszek 1999; Evans 2004, 90–130; Jacobs et al. 1998). Matthew Green (forthcoming) has identified forty-one cases over the period from 1941 to 1999 in which House speakers influenced legislative outcomes while pursuing goals other than advancing the preferences of their party followers. More broadly, David Mayhew has argued recently that leaders as well as other members of Congress have considerable autonomy to take actions that shape both elite and public opinion in the public sphere, where "society's preference formation, politics, and policymaking all substantially take place" (2000, x).

None of the scholars who have found independent leader effects in congressional politics claims that individual leaders alone cause institutional or policy outcomes in Congress.[12] What congressional leaders did in many of these cases was to act in ways that involved using the prerogatives of their positions to amplify certain contextual forces and mute others. Of particular importance were leadership strategies that involved framing choices to appeal to a variety of members' interests and motivations, or through persuasion or control over legislative procedures to encourage or induce members to support the leader's favored alternative over others that could also have attracted majority support. What has not been developed in these previous studies of consequential leadership in Congress is a broader framework that links contextual conditions that create opportunities for leadership with propositions about the specific characteristics of leaders that cause some but not others to assert the prerogatives of a leadership position to influence outcomes in these situations. The conditional agency approach proposed in this book is intended to advance our understanding of leadership politics by supplying one such framework. Before taking up this new framework in more detail, however, an important objection to efforts to develop theories of this type needs to be addressed.

## Political Leadership and Political Science

Even if it is demonstrably true that the agency of individual leaders is consequential in legislative and institutional developments in Congress, for some there remains serious doubt about whether the study of leaders is of importance for political science. While it might seem only common sense that political scientists should focus on leaders' contributions to congressional politics if those contributions are consequential, this is not a trivial objection. The goals of political science are to identify patterns and develop generalizations about regularities in political life and why those patterns occur, not simply to describe individual actions or events. The study of political leaders therefore presents a challenging problem, especially for those political scientists who seek to emulate the natural sciences and develop broadly applicable, lawlike theories of politics. As Arnold (1990, 122) has argued, partly as a consequence of the influence leaders can exert over outcomes, there will always be "a certain indeterminacy" in congressional politics.

If leaders' goals and the intensity with which their goals are held vary, and their actions can result in things happening in Congress that would not otherwise have occurred as a result of more general causes present in the political or institutional context, how can we generalize about when the agency of leaders will matter for influencing outcomes in Congress or how much leaders will matter? One answer is that we probably cannot succeed in doing this. As David Brady and Mathew McCubbins argue: "The desire for parsimony almost unavoidably means that we construct theories that cannot explain some of the variance in which we are interested." In this view, rather than attempt to incorporate the agency of leaders in our explanations of congressional politics, these effects are probably best treated as "idiosyncratic" because they cannot be reliably predicted by (or deduced from) a parsimonious theory (2002, 11).

The alternative view on which this study is premised is that the "variance" that can result from the agency of leaders is of sufficient importance that we need to take it into account in developing our explanations of congressional politics, even if those explanations cannot take the form of lawlike theory from which instances of consequential leadership can always be predicted or deduced. If, for example, developments in congressional politics as important as the emergence of the House speakership as the central leadership institution in the chamber in the early nineteenth century, or the transformation of the House into a truly majoritarian body by the adoption of new rules in the 1890s, or the emergence of a new type of party government regime in the 1990s cannot be explained without taking into account the goals and actions of individual House leaders, then by omitting the agency of leaders from our explanatory theories we gain parsimony at the cost of losing the ability to explain some very important aspects of congressional politics.

As Schickler (2001, 15) argues, "The challenge . . . becomes incorporating leadership into a broader theoretical perspective."[13] We should take up this challenge, in Schickler's view, because "leadership is not an idiosyncratic residual that defies systematic analysis. Strategic innovation by would-be leaders is endemic to legislative politics and rooted in the pluralism of member interests" (ibid.). To which can be added that the independent agency of leaders is also rooted in the pluralism of leaders' goals and interests and certain other recurring political conditions that can be specified. As Arnold has argued, despite the indeterminacy that can be present in congressional politics because of causes such as the agency of leaders, "there is still a large role for theory" (1990, 122). But a theoretical framework that incorporates the agency of leaders will necessarily be typological or conditional in the sense of stating conditions under which leaders are likely to influence outcomes and identifying the causal mechanisms by which this occurs, rather than offering lawlike statements that purport to predict precisely when these leadership effects will be present in Congress.[14]

## The Conditional Agency Perspective on Leadership

Both theoretical reflection and evidence other scholars have found on the influence of leaders in congressional politics suggest that contextual approaches to leadership are incomplete in two important respects. The first is that contextual leadership theories are based explicitly or implicitly on overly simple assumptions about leaders' goals. Leaders are said to be responsive to what their followers want because the followers choose the leader and leaders want to keep their leadership positions. The assumption that leaders will be responsive to followers because leaders want to win and hold power is a useful starting point for understanding the politics of leadership in any democratic institution. However, such an assumption may become misleading if leaders are understood to care *only* about retaining their leadership positions. If some congressional leaders are strongly committed to political goals beyond remaining leader—and we shall see that some are—we would not expect those leaders always to be inclined to take their bearings from what their followers want. When opportunities arise to pursue other intensely held goals, some may be willing to act independently of followers and even risk their leadership positions in pursuit of those goals. If so, leaders who are more risk-tolerant may be consequential for influencing outcomes in a wider range of political situations than just those situations in which their followers are already mostly in agreement.

Second, contextual theories tend to view institutional constraints on leaders as more or less constant across time. In the language of social theory, most contextual theories of leadership view the relationship between structure and individual agency as essentially fixed. While contextual theories do hold that certain political conditions will evoke more active and vigorous legislative leadership (generally, high levels of agreement among followers), institutional arrangements in Congress are usually viewed as constraints that limit congressional leaders to acting in ways consistent with what their followers want. Even the most assertive congressional leaders are understood to be acting in response to followers' expectations and to be advancing objectives on which their followers are already in substantial agreement. If leaders exercise agency in the sense of causing things to happen, they do so only at the margins or in working out the details on issues about which followers have already reached consensus.

But some situations in congressional politics appear to present much greater leeway for leaders. These political situations create opportunities for the agency of leaders to matter in ways that go beyond simply working out details of enacting policy or institutional changes on which followers are already in agreement. The extraordinary authority wielded by Speaker Newt Gingrich over both institutional and policy matters in the initial period after Republicans gained control of the House of Representatives in 1994 is a recent case in point. As Gingrich's predecessor, Speaker Thomas Foley commented: "I don't think any Democratic Speaker could be in quite the same situation as Speaker Gingrich. In addition to whatever talents, abilities, and leadership capacity he brings to the office, he's starting off afresh. There have been no Republican committee chairmen for over 40 years: there is not an established political directorate of committee chairmen in the House . . . So he's had a blank slate on which to write and that has given him a great deal of influence" (quoted in Owens 1997, 263). One of Gingrich's top aides at the time makes the same point: "I was surprised at the extent to which members said Newt could operate with impunity . . . I was just amazed at the amount of freedom he had. [House Republicans were] a group of people who believed he was a hero, a Moses who led them out of the wilderness and he could do what he damn well pleased" (Swinehart 1996).

Leaders matter more in congressional politics than contextual approaches imply for both reasons: because leaders do not all have the same goals or hold those goals with the same degree of intensity and thus should not be expected to respond in the same ways to the political situations they encounter; and because political situations arise in congressional politics that create opportunities for the agency of leaders to have important effects beyond influencing a few members at the margins or carrying out objectives on which followers already are in agreement. Contextual theories of leadership have been very helpful for understanding the broad parameters within which congressional leaders work and identifying central tendencies in leadership politics across different periods in congressional politics. But a different type of framework is needed to explain what leaders actually contribute to institutional and policy outcomes in Congress. Each of the above points merits further elaboration by way of outlining a framework that may help advance our understanding of the contributions individual leaders make.

## Why Lead? Congressional Leaders' Goals

In the contextual theories, leaders are assumed to be motivated primarily by self-interest of a particular type—ambition to retain office within the legislature. To quote Sinclair: "To the extent that leaders value their positions and want to retain them, they have an incentive to try to fulfill members' expectations" (1995, 18; see also Rohde and Shepsle 1987, 113, 128–130; Cox and McCubbins 1993, 126–134). As we have seen, Rohde (1991, 37–38, 172) has noted that some leaders are more willing than others to exercise power when conditions allow for assertive leadership.

Beyond this one qualification, however, how leaders' behavior might be influenced by goals other than retaining office has not been addressed in contextual theories. In these theories, leaders take their bearings from their followers and refrain from attempts at active leadership in political situations where followers are divided to avoid alienating some significant bloc of support in a future leadership contest. The politics of the leader-follower relationship look different if we relax this assumption and entertain the possibility that leaders have multiple goals and hold those goals with varying levels of intensity. If opportunities arise for a leader to pursue intensely held goals beyond getting reelected leader, office-holding ambition inside the legislature would not necessarily induce a leader to take his or her bearings from followers' preferences or to refrain from active use of the strategic advantages of a leadership position because followers are not in agreement on an issue.

Why might an elected legislative leader be motivated to act independently of his or her followers' preferences or expectations? The first possibility is that a leader desires to advance some view of good public policy (lower taxes help create more economic growth, for example), or an opinion on the merits of some existing or proposed institutional arrangement in Congress (control of the legislative process by the majority party is necessary for voters to hold Congress accountable, or changes are needed to strengthen the influence of Congress vis-à-vis the president, for example). It would be naïve in the extreme to assume that principled or public-spirited goals always motivate the behavior of congressional leaders. But is it not equally unrealistic to assume away the possibility that leaders are sometimes motivated by serious concerns about public policy or the institutional capacities of Congress? Empirical research has found repeatedly that concerns with advancing good public policy are an important motivation for legislators and legislative leaders (Bader 1996; Fenno 1973, 1991; Bessette 1994, 106–149; Derthick and Quirk 1985, 102–146; Strahan 1989; Hall 1996). Leaders with intensely held views on policy or institutional matters might act independently of followers' views—even to the point of placing a leadership position at risk—if deferring to followers or taking no action when followers are divided might produce an outcome the leader considers personally unacceptable.[15]

Altruism, or a willingness to sacrifice personal ambition to political principle, is not the only type of motivation that might encourage congressional leaders to act independently of followers. Other motives might also encourage a leader to act independently or take political risks if the result might be some highly visible political achievement that secures a national political reputation. A national reputation as a statesman might be pursued as a means to winning a higher office or as an end in itself—the desire to win the lasting esteem of others and leave a mark on history.

Some of the most thoughtful theorists of modern liberal democracy, including the authors of the *Federalist*, have viewed a concern with historical "fame" as an important motivation for individuals likely to be attracted to leadership positions (see Adair 1974; Manzer 1996; Epstein 1984, 183–185). Contemporary research on Congress has also found concerns about respect and reputation to be important motivations for members' behavior, particularly for those who hold leadership positions (see Derthick and Quirk 1985, 145–146, 239–242; Sabl 2002, 143–200).

In the *Federalist*, Alexander Hamilton proposes that political leaders motivated by this "love of fame" will "plan and undertake extensive and arduous enterprises for the public benefit" if they are allowed sufficient time in office to receive recognition and credit for the success of their efforts (*72: 437*).[16] The logic of Hamilton's analysis of leadership politics is remarkably similar to that employed by modern principal-agent theories: "The desire of reward is one of the strongest incentives of human conduct," and "the best security for the fidelity of mankind is to make their interest coincide with their duty" (*Federalist 73: 437*). Where the two approaches diverge is not so much on the importance of self-interest as a motive for political leaders as in how the self-interest of political leaders is understood. For Hamilton, political leadership involves not only short-term opportunities to enjoy the prestige and power or other psychological or material gratifications that come with office-holding, but also the possibility of establishing a longer-lasting reputation, even a permanent place in history.

For congressional leaders, concern for one's reputation might encourage action independent of followers for a number of reasons. Parochial concerns of rank-and-file legislators may cause them to pay insufficient attention to broader, long-term interests, while advancing these broader interests is precisely what confers lasting "fame" on a leader. Also, gaining recognition and credit for a major reform or for passage of important new legislation requires that a leader be out in front of followers. In either case, a leader concerned with establishing a national reputation might have partly self-interested, as well as principled, reasons to use the prerogatives of a leadership position actively to advance some preferred outcome even when followers are uncertain or deeply divided. The frequency with which presidential ambitions have been visible among speakers, would-be speakers, and former speakers—including Henry Clay, James K. Polk, James G. Blaine, Thomas Reed, William McKinley, Joseph Cannon, James Beauchamp "Champ" Clark, John Nance Garner, Sam Rayburn, Richard Gephardt, and Newt Gingrich—indicates that the office has regularly been sought and held by figures whose political ambitions transcended remaining a leader in the House.[17]

To be sure, some legislators probably do seek out leadership positions such as the House speakership primarily to enjoy the prestige of the office. Others might be inclined toward caution in wielding power for other reasons. These leaders could be expected to act in the ways suggested by the contextual theories. They would avoid using the powers of office in any way that might threaten followers' support for their continuation in office. If concerned primarily with remaining leader, a leader would be more cautious and probably take his or her bearings from followers whenever possible. As one of the congressional leaders discussed later in this book observed: "If a man's object in life is to hold office and to wear decorations, undoubtedly the best course for him is to go softly like a cat on a carpet" (Thomas Reed in 1891, quoted in Robinson 1930, 254). However, the politics of leadership will be better understood if we move beyond thinking of leaders' actions as always motivated by office-holding ambition within the legislature, and consider the implications for leaders' behavior of other goals and the intensity with which they are held.

We need not try to incorporate every possible motivation of leaders or combination of motivations in a theory of leadership. Nor does developing such a framework require that we somehow account for the full range of personality types who might ascend to a position of leadership in Congress. For purposes of generalizing about when the agency of leaders may be an important cause of outcomes in congressional politics, it is sufficient to begin with the simple proposition that holding different goals with varying levels of intensity will cause leaders to vary in their willingness to take risks with their leadership positions. We can then think of congressional leaders as being of two basic types: risk-averse leaders for whom retaining their leadership position in Congress is their most intensely held goal; and risk-tolerant leaders who have other goals that are held with at least the same intensity as the goal of retaining their congressional leadership positions. A variety of intensely held goals (policy concerns, opinions about institutional reform, ambition for higher office, fame) may encourage leaders to tolerate risk with their positions of leadership. Bessette makes the case that "serious lawmakers" in Congress are defined in part by their willingness "to take some political risks for the sake of good public policy" (Bessette 1994, 136).

Leaders with intensely held goals beyond office-holding ambition in Congress will be more risk-tolerant and willing to act independently of followers to influence outcomes in Congress when opportunities arise to advance those goals. In practical political terms this means that leaders who are risk-tolerant will attempt to use the prerogatives of office to influence outcomes in a wider range of political situations than those who are risk-averse. Political actors' goals are always difficult to ascertain with certainty, but close observation of leaders' political careers and actions allows reasonably certain inferences regarding their goals and the intensity with which those goals are held. In addition to paying closer attention to leaders' goals and how different goals and intensities can cause leaders to differ in their willingness to risk acting independently of followers, the conditional agency framework also seeks to identify the political situations that create openings or opportunities for leaders to influence outcomes in Congress.

## Political Opportunities for Leadership

The idea that the influence of individual actors versus those of more general causes can vary across time has a long history in political science, from Machiavelli's treatment of the role of fortune in human affairs, to Tocqueville's account of aristocratic and democratic social states, to works by contemporary social scientists employing punctuated equilibrium theories and concepts of critical junctures and path dependence to explain political and institutional development (see Mahoney and Snyder, 1999; Pierson 2004). One of the most influential contemporary works in this vein is Stephen Skowronek's *The Politics Presidents Make* (1993). Skowronek's analysis of the politics of presidential leadership makes the case that structural constraints on presidential leadership vary across time. Those presidents who assume office in opposition to vulnerable governing regimes (Franklin Roosevelt, for example) encounter "the most promising of all situations for the exercise of political leadership" (1993, 37). These "reconstructive" situations contrast sharply with "the difficulties leaders in all other situations have had in trying to assert authority over their moments in history" (ibid., 39). What these approaches share is the recognition that certain moments in the life of an institution or a regime allow greater scope for the influence of individual agency than others.

Because of the distinctiveness of Congress as an institution, theories developed to explain the varying influence of agency and structure in other political settings may not be directly transferable to this setting.[18] But there is much to be gained in our understanding of congressional leadership by going beyond an essentially static view of the relationship between leaders and institutional context. Certain political situations create greater opportunities than others for actions by leaders to be consequential in institutional or policy decisions in Congress. Again, by consequential leadership I mean influence beyond organizing action or settling details on issues on which followers have already reached consensus or something close to consensus.

Probably the clearest examples of political situations in which the agency of leaders has the greatest scope for influence in the U.S. House have been times when a new majority party has been elected after that party has been in the minority for an extended period of time. As Schickler observes, these have been political situations during which leaders have succeeded "in the wholesale dismantlement of existing institutions" and the enactment of major institutional reforms (2001, 253). In these situations leaders may also encounter greater leeway in leading the House on policy decisions as well as opportunities to shape the institutional context within which they and their successors work. The two clearest examples in the history of the House have been the 51st (1889–1891) and the 104th (1995–1997) Congresses. It is probably not accidental that these two Congresses correspond to the initial years of the speakerships of two figures considered among the most powerful leaders ever to serve in the House, Thomas Reed and Newt Gingrich. To be sure, political situations that create opportunities for the agency of leaders to influence congressional politics on this scale occur infrequently across the history of Congress. However, the underlying conditions that give rise to opportunities for consequential leadership probably occur quite frequently in congressional politics.

The agency of leaders is most likely to be consequential in political situations when followers share dissatisfaction with the institutional or policy status quo in Congress but their preferences regarding new alternatives are ill defined, uncertain, or involve substantial conflict. Contextual theories are correct in stating that leaders will rarely be consequential when their followers' preferences are truly fixed and homogeneous. When a leader's goals encourage him or her to act contrary to the settled, homogeneous preferences of followers, the leader will discover the limits of leadership. The point is that followers' preferences may be unsettled or in conflict on issues even when most are unsatisfied with the status quo. This condition was present across an unusually broad range of institutional and policy issues with newly elected House majorities in 1889 and 1995, but it may be present on a narrower scale more often in congressional politics (see Palazzolo 1992, 218–221).

Along with electorally driven changes in the composition of the majority party or the election of a new majority party, major shifts in any number of contextual factors may give rise to serious dissatisfaction among members with existing organizational arrangements in Congress or with the policy status quo. Cooper identifies changes in the congressional agenda, in the state of relations with the executive branch, and in public and elite opinion about how democratic institutions should operate as additional contextual factors that can give rise to support among legislators for organizational innovations in Congress (Cooper 1981, 331–336; 2001, 346–355). Evans and Oleszek (1997), Forgette (1997), and Schickler (2001) have also shown that a variety of members' interests including reelection, service of clientele groups, congressional capacity, access to institutional power bases, partisan goals, and policy concerns can all underlie coalitions supportive of institutional changes. Causes of support for policy change in Congress are equally numerous.

Here again we encounter contingencies in leadership politics that make highly parsimonious and lawlike generalizations difficult if not impossible to formulate. The sources of discontent with existing institutional arrangements and policies that in turn create leadership opportunities are sufficiently complex to belie prediction in advance. Whether a leader is able to identify or develop a proposal capable of winning sufficient support to prevail in these situations or able to use the tools at his or her disposal to assemble that support are matters of skill that also belie simple generalizations or predictions. Yet specifying the conditions under which the agency of leaders will be most important and identifying the means, or causal mechanisms, through which leaders can influence congressional outcomes advance our understanding of what leaders contribute to congressional politics even though we cannot predict precisely when the agency of leaders will come into play.[19]

## How Legislative Leaders Lead

To lead, legislative leaders usually need majorities to follow. There are three primary ways leaders can assemble the majorities they need to enact legislation or secure organizational changes: persuading followers, framing issues to favor the outcome the leader wants to prevail, and selectively meting out rewards and punishments. These are the main causal mechanisms through which leaders influence outcomes in Congress.

As Richard Fenno (1990, 97) observes, "At some point leadership involves the act of persuasion. Leaders must persuade followers to do something or not to do something."[20] Bessette (1994, 53) offers a helpful definition of persuasion in a legislative setting: "Persuasion occurs when information and arguments on the merits of an issue lead a participant in the policymaking process to take a substantive position that he or she had not taken prior to engaging the process. It thereby involves some kind of change or development in the policymaker's understanding." Arnold (1990, 93) notes that persuasion by leaders may also involve a political dimension: "Leaders seek to persuade legislators that a policy proposal is simultaneously a good idea *and* that is it unlikely to generate electoral problems for them" (emphasis in the original). Leaders' efforts to persuade members to support a proposal the leader favors may also include efforts to shape public debate or understanding of issues (Jacobs et al. 1998; Sinclair 2002). Persuasion may also involve convincing legislators about which of their competing goals (reelection, good public policy, influence in the chamber, the good of the party, etc.) should take precedence in deciding on an issue.

We tend to think of persuasion as changing minds. While leaders sometimes do persuade members to change their minds, persuasion by leaders probably occurs more often in situations where members of the legislature are making up their minds. As Sinclair (1999, 445–446) has observed regarding the situation after Republicans took control of the House in 1994, "Junior members, by and large, did not have well-formed preferences on many of the matters of institutional structure or normal procedure." Cooper and Hering (2003) note that members' views on legislation often involve broad orientations rather than clearly defined preferences for specific alternatives. Based on close observation of how members respond when a new issue arises in Congress, Fenno found that some legislators decide early on the policy alternatives they intend to support or oppose, while others decide later or change their preferences as new information comes out or new issue dimensions emerge (for example, concerns about the president's need for congressional support to conduct foreign policy effectively in addition to the merits of a specific foreign policy issue). "Either way, through the imposition of a new issue or through the addition of information on the old issue, preferences can change as the governing sequence unfolds" (Fenno 1986, 13). Based on archival evidence on House members' positions on legislation as compiled by party whip organizations over a four-year period, Behringer, Evans, and Materese (2006, 22) observe: "Even on major issues toward the final stages of the House legislative process, large portions of the membership remain undecided about how to vote." Comparing House members' positions as recorded in whip polls with their actual votes on legislation, Evans and his colleagues found that party leaders "exert a significant impact on the process through which rank-and-file members develop positions on policy issues on the floor. Much of what constitutes party influence . . . concerns the formation of preferences" (ibid., 22–23).

Members' uncertainty creates opportunities for leaders (as well as others) to persuade. "When legislators develop reasoned judgments on legislative matters about which they originally had no opinion or only broad preferences, they are as much 'persuaded' by the information and arguments brought to their attention as when they change their mind from a previously affirmed position" (Bessette 1994, 55). Leadership through persuasion is most consistent with the responsibility congressional leaders have to the legislative body as a whole to ensure that deliberation occurs within the institution.

Persuasion may take one of two forms. The first involves the leader attempting to persuade and build support among followers before advancing an institutional or policy change. The second approach is to use the prerogatives of a leadership position to advance publicly the leader's preferred alternative, then attempting to persuade followers after the fact to support that position (and presenting followers with the more difficult choice of supporting the leader or having to repudiate him or her publicly). The latter approach obviously involves greater risk because the leader cannot be certain that the majority he or she needs to prevail will be there. We would expect so see this more aggressive strategy of persuasion—publicly getting "out front" of followers then persuading them to follow—more often from risk-tolerant leaders.

The second important means leaders have of influencing outcomes involves their power over the congressional agenda and the framing of issues. Especially in the case of the speaker and majority party leaders in the House of Representatives, leaders can sometimes influence what happens in Congress by determining when and how issues come before the legislature for a decision. Agenda control can be used to block or delay votes on alternatives leaders oppose as well as to structure decisions in ways that maximize support for the alternatives leaders favor (Arnold 1990, 99–108; Cox and McCubbins 1993, 233–273, 2005; Sinclair 1995, 136–162, 1999, 437–438, 2002). The most important instruments leaders have available for controlling the agenda in the modern House are special orders or "rules" written by the Rules Committee that can be used to structure debate and voting on legislation. While House leaders have at times been able to maintain strict control over the Rules Committee, their ability to structure choices through use of rules is never unrestricted: "Every rule must be able to command a majority in the House" (Sinclair 1995, 137).

Opportunities to use agenda control to influence outcomes also arise from the fact that majority coalitions can be unstable in situations when multiple issue dimensions are present. Under these conditions different majorities may be assembled in the legislature depending on how the issue gets framed. Leaders who can influence how issues are presented to the legislature for a decision are in a strong position to influence—or even determine—outcomes.[21] Riker (1986, 129–135) argues that Speaker Reed succeeded in leading the House to adopt pathbreaking procedural reforms in 1890 (discussed in chapter 4) because he brought the most important reforms before the House as rulings in a contested election case, thereby making the critical votes more about whether to support one's party in a pitched battle with the opposition for control of an additional House seat than about the merits of changes in House rules. More recently, Evans and Oleszek (1999, 11) have shown how Speaker Gingrich and the Republican leadership "fundamentally altered the distribution of preferences" during debates over health care legislation in 1996 by broadening the scope of legislation before the House from portability of health insurance—on which there was bipartisan agreement—to a broader array of health policy changes—over which the parties were sharply divided. "This reciprocal relationship between member preferences and leadership behavior should be a central feature of party leadership studies," Evans and Oleszek (ibid., 18) contend, "because framing and agenda control are so integral to legislative leadership in Congress."

Finally, a third important means leaders have to influence outcomes on institutional and policy matters is the use of selective rewards and punishments—carrots and sticks—to induce legislators to follow. As Aldrich and Rohde (2000, 4) argue, "The wider the range of these two kinds of inducements that leaders and parties control, the more likely it is that they will be able to influence members' choices." House leaders' control over rewards and sanctions has varied across the history of Congress, but the most important carrots and sticks have included control over members' assignments to standing committees, the power to recognize members on the House floor, and the ability to advance or block legislation members favor, including provisions that distribute specific benefits, or "pork," to members' constituencies.

The majoritarian basis of authority in Congress requires that the rewards leaders control be granted primarily in support of collective (usually party) goals and that punishments be used sparingly. Congressional leaders cannot force members to follow, or at least not very many members for very long. As Speaker Cannon discovered in 1909–1910 when his use of the prerogatives of the speakership to punish Republican dissidents resulted in major reforms to reduce the speaker's power, overusing sanctions controlled by the leader to secure outcomes the leader favors may result in lost authority when a chamber majority comes to view the punishments as illegitimate (Jones 1968).

During periods when House rules place more control over the agenda of the legislature and more sanctions and rewards in the hands of leaders, opportunities for the agency of leaders to matter are correspondingly greater. As Cooper and Brady (1981, 412) note regarding the late nineteenth and early twentieth centuries, when the powers of the office of speaker were at their zenith: "These prerogatives gave the Speaker great power to control outcomes in the House."[22] In this respect, institutional context should be understood not only as something that constrains or limits legislative leaders but also as providing resources leaders can use to enhance their influence in the legislative process. What Mahoney and Snyder (1999, 24–25) have proposed for conceptualizing "structure" in studies of regime change is also useful for understanding institutional context in legislative politics: "Conceptualizing structures as resources highlights how they simultaneously enable action by providing tools actors use to pursue their political projects and constrain action by delimiting the range of possible projects." Similarly, Hargrove (2004, 580) observes that "agency does not act in a void; it must struggle against something or be lifted by something." Many recent studies of congressional leadership by political scientists approach institutional context as a constraint against which leaders generally choose not to struggle; the conditional agency framework recognizes that institutions and other aspects of the political context can provide resources that enhance the independent agency of leaders, especially leaders who are willing to bring those resources to bear in situations when followers are divided or have not yet made up their minds.[23]

In summary, the conditional agency framework provides a different perspective from the contextual theories that have guided some of the most influential recent scholarship on Congress. The focus of this framework is on identifying conditions under which the agency of leaders is most likely to be an important factor in institutional and policy outcomes in Congress. The first condition is the presence of a leader with intensely held goals that reach beyond office-holding ambition inside Congress. Leaders of this type will be willing to accept risk to a leadership position when opportunities arise to pursue other intensely held goals. The second condition is a political situation in which followers are discontented with the institutional or policy status quo but their preferences for new institutional arrangements or policies are uncertain or seriously divided, making a range of alternate outcomes possible. By either persuading followers, framing issues in ways that favor their preferred alternative, or distributing rewards and sanctions, the conditional agency framework proposes that leaders can play an independent role in determining which alternative is chosen by the legislature.

The contextual approach and the conditional agency framework yield different expectations about when and why leaders are consequential in congressional politics. Contextual theories propose that leaders are active and consequential *only* when followers are in substantial agreement in support of some political or policy goal. Paradoxically, leaders are said to be most important and influential when most of their followers share a clear idea of where they want to be led. When followers disagree about an issue before the legislature, these theories predict that leaders will refrain from aggressively using their prerogatives or strategic advantages to lead the legislative body toward a particular outcome.

In contrast, the conditional agency perspective—while accepting that leaders may actively use their positions to secure certain outcomes when their followers are in agreement—proposes that leaders can be consequential in a broader range of political situations: specifically that leaders can also be consequential in shaping outcomes in Congress when followers are dissatisfied with the institutional or policy status quo but the followers' preferences regarding new alternatives are ill defined, uncertain, or even in substantial conflict. During these political situations, the potential for the agency of leaders to matter for outcomes is greatest and a risk-tolerant leader may use the strategic advantages of a leadership position to advance his or her own goals. In the contextual theories, congressional leaders matter only in the limited sense of implementing the details of what their followers already agree on or in building support at the margins for consensual goals; in the conditional agency perspective leaders can matter to a much greater degree by shaping what followers want or deciding which alternative they get when followers' preferences are unclear or not in agreement. Resolving these competing claims about congressional leadership politics requires us to leave the realm of theory and examine the actual politics of leadership in Congress.

## Evaluating Theories of Leadership

To evaluate these contrasting explanations of the politics of congressional leadership, three important cases of House leadership will be examined. The cases on which the book focuses are the speakerships of Henry Clay (1811–1814, 1815–1820, 1823–1825), Thomas Reed (1889–1891, 1895–1899), and Newt Gingrich (1995–1998). The cases of Clay, Reed, and Gingrich were selected because each provides an opportunity to examine the politics of leadership during a period when a figure reputed to be a strong congressional leader occupied the speaker's chair. In surveying the political science and historical literature on Congress, each of these figures stands out as a strong speaker of the House, one who used the prerogatives of the office of speaker aggressively to influence both the direction of public policy and the organization of the House. Investigation of these cases revealed evidence that each possessed strongly held goals beyond holding the office of speaker.

The central claim of the conditional agency framework is that leaders whose intensely held goals make them willing to take risks with their positions can be an important, independent cause of institutional and policy outcomes in Congress. Thinking in terms of evaluating this causal proposition, these three speakerships all involve cases in which the causal factor of interest (an active, risk-taking leader with goals beyond remaining speaker) is present and takes on a high value. These three speakerships are also cases in which the outcome of interest—major institutional or policy change—is present for each case. Major changes in public policy occurred during each of these speakerships as did changes in the institutional structure of the House. Speaker Clay was the first to establish the speakership as the central leadership institution in the House and influenced both foreign and domestic policy decisions over the period from 1811 through 1825. Speaker Reed was responsible for rules changes in 1890 that transformed the House into a truly majoritarian legislative body and played an important role in House decisions on economic policy and electoral reforms. Speaker Gingrich was the key figure in the creation of a new type of party government regime after Republicans won control of the House in 1994, and succeeded in orchestrating some important policy changes through the "Contract with America" and a balanced budget initiative. These three cases are examined in the chapters that follow using the qualitative methods of structured-focused comparison (George and Bennett 2005) and within-case causal process analysis (Collier, Brady, and Seawright 2004).[24]

From the perspective of the conditional agency framework, these can be considered crucial cases in the sense that they should be "easy" cases for the theory. That is, if the agency of leaders matters for explaining institutional and policy changes in Congress, clear evidence in support of that proposition should be present in these cases because leaders known to be highly assertive are present in each. For an initial test of a new theory, selecting easy cases is an appropriate strategy for establishing that the theory has merit. These are also substantively important cases that involve some very important institutional and policy developments in Congress. What cannot be conclusively established on the basis of these cases alone is how frequently the agency of leaders influences outcomes in Congress. However, as I argue in chapter 6, there is good reason to believe that the same conditions that created opportunities for the agency of leaders to influence outcomes in these cases are present quite often in congressional politics.

A separate chapter is devoted to each of the three leaders. The discussion of each leader is organized around a set of theoretically grounded questions derived from the contextual theories and the conditional agency framework. The objective in each of these chapters is, through careful analysis of a number of important policy and institutional outcomes under each speaker, to assess whether the causal process implied by each of the two competing theoretical frameworks is or is not present in the politics of the leader-follower relationships observed within these decisions.

For the contextual theories, in instances of strong or active leadership by House speakers we should find the following causal process at work: 1) homogeneous preferences are present among party followers on the institutional or policy issue to be decided; 2) the leader consults with followers to determine their preferences or acts only after some reasonably clear expression of broad agreement among followers has occurred.[25] In addition, this theory implies: 3) because leaders are concerned primarily with remaining leader and maintaining support among followers, in situations where followers' preferences are unclear or known by leaders to be heterogeneous, leaders will shun aggressive use of leadership prerogatives or active attempts to influence outcomes in the legislature prior to the emergence of consensus or near consensus among their followers.

The conditional agency framework accepts the proposition that strong leadership can occur in Congress when followers' preferences are homogeneous and leaders act aggressively to advance those preferences. The main point of difference between the two perspectives involves the question of whether this is the only political situation in which consequential leadership occurs in Congress. For the conditional agency framework, the causal process involved in strong, consequential leadership by legislative leaders may also involve: 1) a leader whose behavior clearly indicates that the leader has intensely held goals beyond holding the office of speaker; 2) followers who are discontented with the institutional or policy status quo but have preferences that are ill defined or even known to be heterogeneous on alternatives that might be adopted; 3) the leader perceives that support among followers for his or her actions is uncertain or that his actions to influence the outcome involve risks of failure; 4) the leader actively uses the prerogatives of his or her leadership position to advance the alternative he or she personally prefers in the face of that risk.

## Conclusion

Different perspectives on the importance of leaders in congressional politics in part reflect different understandings of how Congress works. These differences have also arisen in part from divergent views within political science about the types of explanations political scientists should aim to produce. Those who seek to develop broadly applicable, lawlike explanations of politics modeled on the natural sciences will inevitably be drawn toward contextual approaches because the conditions that create opportunities for the agency of leaders to matter are more episodic than are contextual causes and because incorporating variation in leaders' goals or other characteristics introduces a "wild card" that makes predicting the outcome of the game much more difficult (Hargrove 2004, 583). Those who study the political world at closer range, doubt that it exhibits the same degree of regularity as the physical world, and have a less restrictive view of science are drawn to explanations that incorporate the agency of individuals. Both approaches have contributed to our understanding of political leaders and political leadership. However, of late a greater emphasis on parsimonious theoretical explanations in political science has resulted in less attention being devoted to the study of leaders.

One goal of this book is to try to address this imbalance. To be persuasive in arguing that this imbalance is a problem, the challenge is to show that a conditional agency framework explains important aspects of congressional politics that the contextual approaches cannot. This is a matter to be settled by evidence, not theoretical disputation. We turn now to the first case, the leadership of Speaker Henry Clay, who led the House during the early decades after it came into existence as part of a new, still unsettled American constitutional order.

# CHAPTER THREE

# Henry Clay

## The Unionist as Speaker

> If any one desires to know the leading and paramount object of my
> public life, the preservation of the Union will furnish him the key.
>
> —*Henry Clay, 1844*

From his time to ours, opinions of Henry Clay have diverged widely. In 1825, his rival for the presidency, Andrew Jackson, described him as "the bases[t], meanest, scoundrel, that ever disgraced the image of his god." Twenty years later Jackson's views had not changed. "All who know Mr. Clay," the former president wrote in 1844, "know that individually he is void of good morals, and that he is politically a reckless demagogue, ambitious and regardless of truth when it comes in the way of his ambition" (both quoted in Remini 1991, 1, 252). Yet in 1858 in the first of the closely watched debates with Stephen A. Douglas, Abraham Lincoln singled out Clay as his "beau ideal of a statesman" (Johannsen 1965, 66). John C. Calhoun seemingly held both views simultaneously. "I don't like Clay," the South Carolina senator is reported to have said after the two had fallen out over slavery and other issues. "He is a bad man, an impostor, a creator of wicked schemes. I wouldn't speak to him, but by God! I love him" (quoted in Remini 1991, 578).

Although operating at greater distance than these eminent nineteenth-century partisans, historians and political scientists have also been divided over what to make of Clay's political career. One view among scholars echoes Jackson's assessment in viewing Clay as a "savagely ambitious" politician (Remini 1991, 687). In this interpretation, not long after he became speaker of the House Clay's driving ambition became focused on the presidency with the result that as speaker he was constantly calculating how best to position himself to achieve that goal—championing causes he thought would be popular and attempting to straddle some of the great political issues of the day, including slavery.[1] Some political scientists who have written on the early development of Congress also contend that Clay's driving ambition for the presidency was the principal motive behind his most consequential actions as speaker.[2] But others have argued that Clay's goals were more complex, that over a forty-year career in politics he pursued not just the presidency but also a principled and coherent set of policies he believed to be in the national interest. "Clay has been overrated as a politician and underrated as a statesman," concludes Daniel Walker Howe (1979, 124), a leading proponent of this second view.[3] Historian Peter Knupfer also advises that Clay's political career is misunderstood if viewed as a relentless quest for the presidency: "Clay's business address for over forty years was the legislature, a workplace that did much to shape his thinking and his tactics and where he spent just as much time trying to limit the presidency as he did trying to win it" (1991, 120).

This chapter addresses one part of Henry Clay's long legislative career, his service as speaker of the House between 1811 and 1825. It was during these years that Clay first achieved national visibility in American politics. Clay's speakership is also of particular interest to students of congressional politics because of the important institutional developments that occurred in the House of Representatives during these years. The House speakership emerged as the central leadership institution in the House during Clay's tenure and some of the main features of the modern institution, including the standing committee system, became well established. The first protective tariff and the first legislative compromise on the future course of slavery were enacted as well. Here again we find diverging views among scholars about Clay's influence on these developments. Some accounts have attributed primary responsibility to Clay for transforming the office of speaker and establishing the foundations of the modern standing committee system; others contend that Clay's role in these institutional developments was modest at best. Regarding policy leadership, scholars have generally agreed that Clay played an important role in leading efforts in Congress to prosecute war with Britain in 1812. But the longest period of Clay's speakership came after the War of 1812. Clay's influence on national policymaking during these years has also been a matter of controversy among scholars.

The goals of this chapter are twofold. First, it will explore evidence on Henry Clay's political goals and how his leadership as speaker may have been consequential for policy and institutional development in the House. Second, it will consider the Clay speakership in light of the competing perspectives on leadership discussed in chapters 1 and 2. Recall that contextual theory holds that active, consequential leadership occurs in Congress only when there is a high level of agreement among followers.[4] In contrast, the conditional agency framework proposes that sufficient leeway exists in the leader-follower relationship that leaders may also be active and consequential in situations when followers are uncertain of their preferences or even deeply divided, if the leader views the issue as an opportunity to advance his or her strongly held goals and is willing to take political risks to achieve those goals.

Turning to Henry Clay's service as speaker between 1811 and 1825, we find a leader who led the House during two very different periods: the first was dominated by war and the second, a period when the country was at peace. At the outset of Clay's speakership in 1811, a Jeffersonian Republican majority in the House of Representatives was mostly unified in support of prosecution of war with Britain. Consistent with the contextual theory, this political situation created an opportunity for exercising active leadership from the speaker's chair, and Clay made the most of that opportunity. But contrary to what the contextual perspective would lead us to expect, the evidence in this chapter will also show that Clay continued to use the prerogatives of the speakership actively to lead the House during the years after the War of 1812. Rather than adopting a more restrained mode of leadership after 1815, when his Republican followers became highly factionalized, Clay instead chose to continue to lead the House aggressively and to use the powers of the speakership to advance a political project focused on strengthening the union.

## War and Peace: The Political Context of the Clay Speakership

First elected speaker in November 1811 at the beginning of the Twelfth Congress (on his first day as a member of the House), Clay was reelected speaker for the Thirteenth Congress and held the position until he resigned in January 1814 to take an appointment as one of the commissioners sent to Europe by President James Madison to negotiate an end to the War of 1812. After returning from negotiations that resulted in the Treaty of Ghent, Clay again served as speaker for the Fourteenth, Fifteenth, and part of the Sixteenth Congresses (1815–1821). He resigned from the speakership in 1820 (to attend to his personal finances in the aftermath of the Panic of 1819) but remained a member in the House for the rest of the Sixteenth Congress. He remained away from the House for the Seventeenth Congress but was reelected to the House in 1822 and again served as speaker in the Eighteenth Congress (1823–1825). Accounts of congressional politics during this period coincide in describing a political context in which Clay's Jeffersonian Republican followers in the House were mostly unified on issues related to war with Britain during the Twelfth and Thirteenth Congresses (1811–1815), followed by a period of intense factionalism among Republicans over the decade that followed. The Federalist minority in

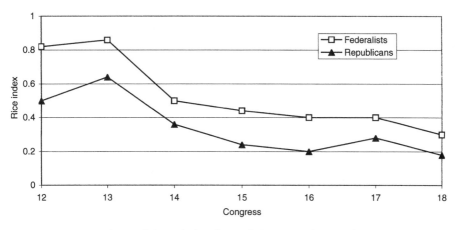

Figure 3.1. Party Cohesion (Rice Index), 12th to 18th Congresses (1811-1825).
*Source:* Calculated from ICPSR Congressional Roll Call Records (Study No. 4).

the House was initially unified in opposition during the two "war" Congresses but declined in both size and cohesiveness afterward (Nielsen 1968; Gamm and Shepsle 1989; Binder 1997, 53–55; Jenkins 1998).[5] Figure 3.1 shows the sharp decline in voting cohesion that began to occur in the Fourteenth Congress and continued for the remaining Congresses Clay served as speaker. Figure 3.2 shows the dominance of the Jeffersonian Republicans in the House and the declining strength of the Federalists after the Fourteenth Congress.

Throughout the Twelfth and Thirteenth Congresses (1811–1815), the House was occupied primarily with measures related to prosecution of the war, especially issues involving strengthening the armed forces and financing the war effort. After the conclusion of the war, the focus of congressional activity shifted primarily to economic issues, including the rechartering of a national bank, protection of domestic manufactures, and the building of internal improvements such as roads and canals. House debates on these issues focused on the constitutionality of federal action, with a clear imprint of regional economic interests on patterns of support and opposition. The slavery issue emerged briefly but intensely between 1819 and 1821, when the application of Missouri for statehood provoked a proposal in the House to restrict slavery in the new state and led to a series of compromises that again suppressed the issue for the remainder of the period Clay served as speaker. In the area of foreign policy, the most prominent issues involved economic relations with Britain and negotiations with Spain over cession of "East" Florida. The House also repeatedly debated issues related to diplomatic recognition of newly independent republics in Latin America, a course of action strongly favored by Clay but opposed

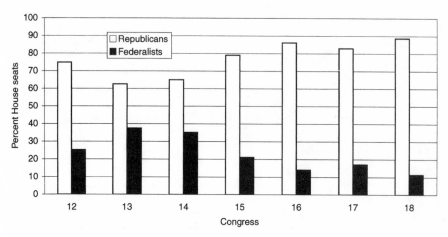

Figure 3.2. Party Strength in House, 12th to 18th Congresses (1811-1825). *Source:* Martis 1989.

by President James Monroe and his secretary of state, John Quincy Adams, who wished to postpone the issue until after resolution of the Florida negotiations.

## Clay's Leadership of the War Congresses, 1811–1814

From the First Congress on, the office of speaker was assigned a number of important powers, including the authority to rule on questions of order, appoint members of committees, and decide who had the floor when more than one member rose. In the earliest years of the operation of the House, the speaker had been expected to stand above party or faction in exercising these prerogatives, functioning more as a parliamentary officer than a political leader. Early House rules prohibited the speaker from voting except in cases where the speaker's vote would make or break a tie, and only provided for the speaker to address parliamentary matters or questions of order from the chair (*Annals of Congress,* 1st Cong., 1st sess., 103–104). This early understanding of the office followed logically from the suspicion with which most of the founding generation viewed political parties and partisanship (Peters 1997, 22–30; Risjord 1992, 629; Fuller 1909, 22–31). The first speaker, Frederick Muhlenberg of Pennsylvania, expressed his political views "out of doors" and at social functions but studiously refrained from addressing the House on the same matters (Peters 1997, 25–26). Peters also notes that during the early Congresses James Madison was passed over for serious consideration as a candidate for the speakership because he "was considered as too valuable to be lost to debate, an indication that the members did not expect the speaker to be a deliberative leader" (ibid., 25).

Clay has frequently been described as the most influential of the early House speakers, one who made a decisive break with this earlier idea of the speaker as primarily a parliamentarian or moderator. In her classic 1896 study *The Speaker of the House of Representatives,* Mary Parker Follett compared him with the powerful House leader of her day, Thomas Reed. "Clay," she claimed, "added to the previously existing body of the speaker's powers much more than has been added by any subsequent speaker, even including Mr. Reed" (1896, 79). Joseph Cooper (1970, 47) observes that the earliest speakers were never simply impartial moderators but also that Clay's speakership still represents a major shift in the role and importance of the office in the House:

> Henry Clay . . . wrought basic and permanent changes in the role of the speaker. Once he assumed the office in 1811 he transformed it from a weak and rather apolitical position into the focal point of leadership within the House. In contrast to his predecessors, he involved himself deeply and extensively in the decision-making process and employed his considerable talent and charm to assemble and maintain majority support for major policies that bore his stamp. Similarly, in the interests of his program he boldly began to exploit and even extend the various sorts of leverage the rules conferred on the speaker.[6]

Clay's reputation as the first powerful speaker of the House rests partly on his actions during the Twelfth and Thirteenth "war" Congresses, the period just before and during the War of 1812. From his election as speaker in 1811 until he left the position in January 1814 to participate in peace negotiations with the British, Clay actively wielded the speaker's authority in support of war-related measures. Although unity among his Republicans could not be taken for granted on issues related to war mobilization and strategy, during these years he had the support of a large Republican majority that was mostly unified in support of prosecuting the war. Clay shared leadership on war-related issues with a group of prowar Republicans, mostly from the West and South, who became known as the War Hawks.[7] In a letter written in 1812, Clay lamented the absence of strong leadership from President Madison, describing him as "wholly unfit for the storms of War." Now into his second year as speaker, Clay made it clear that he had received strong support from his followers in the House: "On the part of the Legislature never was there a body assembled more disposed to adopt any and every measure calculated to give effect and vigor to the operations of the War than are the Members of the 12th Congress" (Clay to Rodney, December 29, 1812, *Clay Papers,* 1: 750).[8]

Clay actively wielded the powers of the speakership during the war Congresses. First, he used the speaker's committee appointment power to ensure that key House committees would have majorities supportive of war-related measures, especially the Select Committee on Foreign Relations and the Committee on Ways and Means, which had jurisdiction over financial matters. During the Twelfth Congress Clay himself sometimes attended deliberations of the Foreign Relations panel (Hatzenbuehler 1976, 15). He also took to the House floor frequently to speak in favor of war measures and used the speaker's parliamentary authority to check efforts by opponents of the war to delay House proceedings. The ability to limit House debate had been clearly established at the outset of the Twelfth Congress by the codification of a new interpretation of the previous question motion, which now could be used to cut off debate by majority vote (Binder 1997, 43–67; Cooper 1962). Under Clay's leadership the Republican majority repeatedly availed itself of this rule to check efforts by opponents of the war to obstruct legislation (Fritz 1977, 36–37). In May 1812, after one of Clay's parliamentary rulings had cut off a long, rambling antiwar speech by Republican dissident John Randolph of Virginia, the two engaged in a public exchange on House rules in the *National Intelligencer* newspaper. Randolph charged that Clay was unfairly restricting House debate; Clay vigorously defended the use of rules that allow the majority to limit debate when a single member or minority of members were attempting to delay action (*Annals of Congress*, 12th Cong., 1st sess., 1451–1479).

Given the unity of his Republican followers during the war Congresses, Clay's active leadership during this period supports the proposition from contextual theory that strong legislative leadership will occur during periods when followers' preferences are homogeneous (Rohde and Shepsle 1987). However, looking beyond the war years to the period when the congressional agenda shifted from matters of war to issues of governing the developing nation and economy in peacetime, a puzzle emerges in light of the contextual leadership framework. Although Republican unity fractured with the war's end, Clay not only continued to be elected speaker by large majorities in the Fourteenth, Fifteenth, Sixteenth, and Eighteenth Congresses but also continued to use the prerogatives of the speakership actively to advance policy goals despite the fact that his followers were deeply divided.

### The Puzzle of House Leadership, 1815–1825

One solution to the puzzle of how House leadership politics worked during Clay's speakership was first set forth by James Sterling Young in his book *The Washington Community, 1800–1828* (1966). Young proposes that Clay's repeated success in being reelected speaker came about primarily because he turned over policy leadership to House committees. In this view, Clay was able to remain speaker in a divided chamber because he was willing to delegate control over policy to committees and because he "parceled out committee patronage so as to satisfy the largest number of individuals and blocs in the congressional community" (1966, 133). By employing this strategy, Young contends, Clay succeeded in remaining speaker in a factionalized House but "virtually foreclosed any real chance of leadership for himself" (ibid., 134).

Young's interpretation of the politics of the Clay speakership has been developed further by some proponents of contextual theory (see Rohde and Shepsle 1987). From the contextual perspective, Clay would not have been able to lead the House assertively in the postwar period if his followers were deeply divided. Scholars drawing on Young's interpretation have proposed that Clay developed "an institutional solution to leadership survival" in the new political context after 1815, orchestrating the delegation of greater authority to the standing committees and distributing important committee appointments across all of the major House factions in order to win reelection as speaker (Gamm and Shepsle 1989, 60; see also Jenkins 1998). These scholars have also argued that this strategy severely limited Clay's ability to exercise leadership on policy matters in the House. "Clay was returned to the speakership time after time by large majorities not because he led the House toward particular policy objectives (as he had in the Twelfth Congress), but rather because he 'gave away the store'" (Rohde and Shepsle 1987, 113–114). While the logic of this interpretation is ingenious, a closer look at the evidence on how Clay actually used the prerogatives of the speakership during the period he served as speaker between 1815 and 1825 shows that this explanation is inaccurate, or at best incomplete.

The remainder of the chapter focuses on the leadership politics of this second period Clay served as speaker, with the objective of determining whether the conditional agency framework provides a more satisfactory solution to the puzzle of explaining Clay's leadership of the House during these years than does contextual theory. I begin this closer examination by considering evidence from Clay's political career about his political goals and his propensity to take risks in pursuit of his goals. Specifically, what were Clay's goals as speaker, and why might he have taken it upon himself to risk actively wielding the powers of the speakership when his followers were so deeply divided?

## Henry Clay's Goals as Speaker

Henry Clay's service as speaker of the House was part of a career in American politics that spanned almost fifty years. Born and raised in Virginia, Clay moved to Kentucky as a young lawyer and had already begun to achieve prominence in legal circles when he won election to the Kentucky legislature in 1803 at the age of twenty-six. He quickly rose to become a leader of the Jeffersonian Republicans in Kentucky and served as speaker of the state House. Clay's entrance on the stage of national politics came in 1806, when he was chosen to fill the remainder of an unexpired term in the U.S. Senate. He was chosen again to serve part of a Senate term in 1810. Winning election to the U.S. House that same year, Clay was chosen as speaker and held the position for most of the period between 1811 and 1825. Clay left the House to serve as secretary of state under President John Quincy Adams from 1825 to 1828. He returned to Congress in 1831, now a senator, and served in the upper chamber from 1831 to 1842 and again from 1849 until his death in 1852. Despite his extensive service in the legislature at both the state and national levels, historians have focused on Clay's presidential ambitions for good reason. He was a candidate for the presidency three times—in 1824 as a Republican, in 1832 as a National Republican, and in 1844 as a Whig—and also sought the presidential nomination of the Whig Party unsuccessfully in 1840 and 1848.

When considering the question of whether Henry Clay was the type of leader willing to take risks in pursuit of his political goals, it is also worth considering another remarkable feature of his political career—that Clay twice dueled with pistols with political opponents.[9] The first duel, in which he received a bullet wound in the thigh, occurred in 1809 when the thirty-one-year-old Clay was leader of the Jeffersonian Republicans in the Kentucky House. Clay's opponent in the duel was Kentucky Federalist Humphrey Marshall, the cousin and brother-in-law of Chief Justice of the United States John Marshall (Van Deusen 1937, 48–55; Remini 1991, 47–56). The second duel, with the mercurial, if not unhinged, Virginia Republican John Randolph (with whom Clay had frequently clashed in the House), occurred seventeen years later, after Clay had left the House speakership, was serving as secretary of state, and thought he was in the line of succession to the presidency. Unlike the earlier duel, historians think it unlikely that either party in the Clay-Randolph affair was seriously trying to kill his opponent (Van Deusen 1937, 219–223; Remini 1991, 292–295). But the fact that Clay was willing to risk his life more than once over questions of honor and reputation is surely an interesting piece of evidence in assessing his motivations and tolerance for risk in politics.

It was not a foregone conclusion that a politician of this era would take up a challenge of a duel in response to a public insult.[10] Note, for example, how Representative John Tod of Pennsylvania, chair of the House Committee on Manufactures, responded to the challenge issued by James Hamilton of South Carolina in the course of an 1824 House debate on tariff legislation that had been written by Tod's committee. Hamilton stated that he was willing to be held responsible for what he had said "both in this House and out of this House," then launched a personal attack on Tod for "gross ignorance of the operation, bearing, and character, of this measure" (*Annals of Congress*, 18th Cong., 1st sess., 2206). Tod declined Hamilton's challenge: "It is a call to a sort of honor which I do not want. I live, and am glad of it, in a part of the country where what little respectability a man may chance to have, needs no such propping nor does the cause of domestic industry require any such support. If it does, I for one, have no ambition to be a martyr to the best tariff that ever was devised" (ibid., 2219).

In judging Clay's attitude toward risk, a second notable fact is that Clay had a reputation, formed primarily in the early part of his political career, as a frequent participant in high-stakes card games. In a letter to a friend written while he was speaker, Clay acknowledged his enjoyment of gambling, commenting: "I have always paid peculiar homage to the fickle goddess" (Clay to Rodney, December 29, 1812, *Clay Papers*, 1: 751).[11] In addition to card playing, Clay was known as well for enjoying an active social life. During his early years in Washington, as one historian put it, Clay developed something of a reputation as "the capital's premier party animal" (Knupfer 1992, 321). John Quincy Adams reported in his diary that when he and Clay were in the Netherlands in 1814 for the peace talks with the British, rising early one morning to prepare for the day's negotiations he heard a card game that had begun the night before just breaking up in Clay's room (1875, 3: 32). Clay's political opponents later made much of this reputation, along with his well-known history of dueling. In 1844, one Democrat joked that Clay should be campaigning for the presidency under a flag emblazoned with a pack of cards, a pistol, and a bottle of brandy (Van Deusen 1937, 371).

Partisan jibes aside, even some of Henry Clay's contemporaries who were not partisan opponents sometimes doubted whether he was guided by any principle in politics other than winning. As Adams (1875, 5: 59) observed in another diary entry in 1820: "In politics, as in private life, Clay is essentially a gamester, and with a vigorous intellect, an ardent spirit, a handsome elocution, though with a mind very defective in elementary knowledge, and a very undigested system of ethics, he has all the qualities which belong to that class of human character." Two years later, Adams (1875, 5: 496) added: "I esteemed the talents of Mr. Clay, and knew him to have some good qualities. But his ambition was too ardent to be very scrupulous or delicate, and he was too addicted to intrigue."[12] As we have seen, some historians and political scientists share Adams's view of Clay as a talented but calculating politician whose ambition was less than delicate, while others have contested this view. On what grounds does the case rest for viewing Clay as a politician motivated by a serious concern with good public policy as well as political ambition?

First, we should consider Clay's account of his own motives. A number of times during his political career he addressed the question of whether he had tailored his positions on policy issues to win political support. In 1832, a partisan opponent in the Senate tried to embarrass Clay by reading from an earlier speech in which Clay had argued that a national bank was unconstitutional—the opposite position from the one Clay now held. In response Clay took up the question of his consistency on the issues and the change in his position on the bank during the time he was speaker. With the expiration of the charter of the first Bank of the United States in 1811, severe problems with currency and credit developed during the War of 1812. As Clay explained the shift: "During a long public life . . . the only great question in which I have ever changed my opinion, is that of the Bank of the United States . . . In 1816, being Speaker of the House of Representatives, it was perfectly in my power to have said nothing and done nothing, and thus have concealed the change of opinion which my mind had undergone. But I did not choose to remain silent and escape responsibility. I chose publicly to avow my actual conversion. The war, and the fatal experience of its disastrous events, had changed me" (*Register of Debates,* 22nd Cong., 1st sess., 1268).[13]

Again in 1844, just after he received the Whig Party nomination for the presidency, Clay felt compelled to offer an account of his political motives after having stirred up controversy within his party by taking a public position on the controversial issue of the annexation of Texas. After stating that he was opposed to immediate annexation, Clay had been accused of pandering to northern abolitionists, who strongly opposed annexation as a measure that would extend the reach of slavery. He responded in a public letter intended to reassure southern Whigs. He could support annexation of Texas in the future, he explained, if it could be achieved without jeopardizing the stability of the union. "If any one desires to know the leading and paramount object of my public life," he wrote, "the preservation of the Union will furnish him the key" (Clay to Miller, July 1, 1844, *Clay Papers,* 10: 79).

The historical record supports both claims. Clay articulated a set of policy positions early in his national political career and with very few exceptions continued to focus on those same policy goals throughout his long involvement in public life. And the common thread running through the policy positions to which Clay devoted the greatest attention and effort was a concern with strengthening the federal union. During his two brief stints in the Senate in 1806–1807 and 1810–1811, Clay first began to develop a reputation as a strong proponent of federally funded internal improvements. He also began to advocate tariff protection to encourage domestic manufactures as early as 1810 (Van Deusen 1937, 46–48, 59–60; Peterson 1987, 16–17; Remini 1991, 59–63; Baxter 1995, 4–5). His early service in the Senate also established

Clay's reputation as an aggressive nationalist in foreign policy, a stance that was instrumental in his initial election to the speakership of the House in 1811, when tensions with the British were running high. As we have seen, Clay was a leading advocate of war with Britain to defend American honor and commercial interests, and during the first two Congresses he actively led the House to adopt war-related measures.

After the War of 1812, Clay became focused on advancing a program of federally guided economic development centered on a national bank, internal improvements, and protective tariffs.[14] By the 1820s this program had become known as the "American System" and Clay's program supplied some of the major planks in the platform of the new Whig Party in which he became a leading figure. After the war, Clay shifted from opposing to supporting the Bank of the United States, a position more consistent with his program of federally directed economic development but not widely popular in his western political base (Peterson 1987, 48; Remini 1991, 140–141; Baxter 1995, 35–37). With the exception of the bank question, however, Clay consistently pursued the same basic economic policy positions throughout his political career.

Given the importance of the slavery question during this period of American politics, Clay's position on slavery is also of interest in assessing his goals. Throughout his career he consistently stated the view that slavery was unjust and should be ended. He supported and tried to implement a policy of gradual emancipation of slaves and colonization of freed slaves to Africa. However, Clay also believed the federal government had no authority under the Constitution to interfere with slavery within existing states and openly criticized abolitionists who contended that national authority should be used for that purpose.[15] Clay is probably best known for playing a leading role in the efforts to reach compromises acceptable to slaveholding and nonslaveholding states in the 1819–1821 controversy over the admission of Missouri and again later in his career during the 1850 controversy over the status of slavery in the territory acquired after the war with Mexico.

The one major new issue Speaker Clay took up in the postwar years was to promote the cause of recognition of new South American republics fighting to establish their independence from Spain. Clay first took a public position in support of the independence of the new republics in 1813 (Remini 1991, 154). In 1816 he vigorously opposed neutrality legislation recommended by President Madison to prevent warships in support of Latin American independence movements from being outfitted in American ports. After 1816, Clay's position placed him in a direct confrontation with President James Monroe, who was seeking an agreement with Spain to acquire Florida before recognizing the new Latin American states (Hoskins 1927;

Peterson 1987, 52–55, 57–58; Remini 1991, 154–157). Historians have long debated whether Clay's motive in advancing the cause of Latin American independence was a sincere commitment to the cause of liberty abroad or resentment of Monroe for passing him over for appointment as secretary of state (the traditional stepping stone to the presidency) and a desire to embarrass John Quincy Adams, who did receive the appointment. However, Clay's earlier involvement with the issue during Madison's presidency indicates that opposition to Monroe and Adams could not have been his sole motivation. Remini's (1991, 157) judgment seems well supported by the evidence: "However much Clay hoped to wreak revenge on an administration that had passed him over, he did in fact sincerely and wholeheartedly support Latin American independence."

Returning to the economic policy questions on which he focused most of his efforts during the later period of his speakership, a closer look at his actions on these issues provides further evidence that the view of Clay as a political "gamester" casting about for policy positions to smooth his path to the White House is a serious oversimplification. While Clay was hardly the type to spend his evenings penning treatises on politics, taken together his House speeches from the period he served as speaker after the War of 1812 provide a coherent view of American constitutional and political development, and his political actions demonstrate consistent attention to policies he believed would advance "that greatest of all . . . those objects" he believed had guided the Founders, "the cementing of the Union" (*Annals of Congress*, 15th Cong., 1st sess., 1166).[16] Clay believed that the federal Constitution had created the political framework for union and the preservation of liberty in the United States but that these political ties would need reinforcement from national policy if the Constitution was to survive in the face of powerful causes for division that would come into play as the country continued to expand and develop.[17]

In speeches he delivered to the House, Clay discussed two types of political forces that should be considered in framing national policy: forces that provide cohesion and work to hold the union together and forces of separation that could eventuate in its breakup. The forces of cohesion included the Constitution itself, as well as common ideas, sentiments, and historical experiences—what we might today call a common political identity or political culture. The latter type of cause he sometimes characterized as "moral." The most important causes that tended toward separation or division he termed "physical" causes, which included the dispersion of the population across a greater and greater extent of territory and the divergence of economic interests between different regions of the country. As Clay described the condition of the country in his House speeches after 1815, the central problem of

American politics was that the forces of cohesion holding the union together were weakening, while those of separation were growing stronger.

The political ties established by the Constitution were still tenuous and vulnerable, in Clay's view, because these were not sufficiently reinforced by mutual economic interest among the regions of the country. "Now our connexion is merely political," Clay argued in a debate over tariff legislation in 1820. "There is scarcely any of that beneficial intercourse, the best basis of political connexion, which consists of the exchange of the produce of our labor" (*Annals of Congress,* 16th Cong., 1st sess., 2044). "Moral" causes could not be relied upon to sustain the union in the future. As Clay explained in a House debate on the constitutionality of federally funded internal improvements in 1818:

> Moral causes have a powerful operation; and the immigration of people from the Atlantic to the Western States will produce an affinity and consanguinity between the population of the East and of the West, which will last for a long time; but depend upon it, when society is settled down, as it will before long be, these moral causes will lose their effect . . . The man who does not look forward to another state of things, when physical causes will have their influence, is unworthy of having a place here . . . We ought, by the means within our power, to counteract the operation of these physical causes. (*Annals of Congress,* 15th Cong., 1st sess., 1173)

Clay reiterated this theme in an 1825 speech again supporting federal funding for internal improvements: "Happily, there exists among us great and powerful principles of cohesion—a common origin—common language—a common law—common liberty—common recollection of national glory." But, he added, "causes of the opposite kind" also exist, "and they call on us to look far ahead, and to prevent if possible, the disastrous evil which they threaten." Chief among the "causes which go to increase the tendencies to separation" are "the extended space over which our population and government are spread, together with the different scenes to which commercial pursuits lead the citizens of different districts of the Union" (*Annals of Congress,* 18th Cong., 2nd sess., 234). By 1825 both Clay and his House colleagues were surely aware that the division between slave and nonslave states could give rise to an even more powerful cause of separation. It is perhaps a sign of Clay's hope after the Missouri Compromise of 1820–1821 that the issue of slavery would stay out of national politics that caused him to avoid mentioning it in this context.[18]

Clay's legislative program of protective tariffs and internal improvements was therefore the means of counteracting the "physical" causes he believed could undermine the federal union if these causes were allowed to progress unchecked. The tariff would protect and stimulate the development of a domestic manufacturing sector (including hemp bagging for cotton bales and rope made in Kentucky, iron produced in the Mid-Atlantic states, and New England textiles) and help to create a larger home market for American agricultural products (especially southern cotton but also western grain), much of which was being produced for export. Regarding the tariff, Clay told the House in 1824:

> Its importance, in reference to the stability of our Union, that paramount and greatest of all our interests, cannot fail warmly to recommend it . . . Now our people present the spectacle of a vast assemblage of jealous rivals, all eagerly rushing to the sea board, jostling each other in their way, to hurry off to glutted foreign markets the perishable produce of their labor. The tendency of that policy, in conformity to which this bill is prepared, is to transform these competitors into friends and mutual customers; and, by the reciprocal exchanges of their respective productions, to place the Confederacy upon the most solid of all foundations, the basis of common interest. (*Annals of Congress*, 18th Cong., 1st. sess., 1999)

Internal improvements—a national network of roads, canals, and navigable rivers—would likewise counteract the centrifugal effects of physical causes by reducing travel times for people and goods and helping to foster greater economic exchange across regions. "And is it not the solemn duty of this House," Clay asked in his final major speech as speaker in 1825

> to strengthen, by every means in its power, the principles of cohesion which bind us together—to perpetuate the union of these states, and to weaken and diminish to the utmost of its ability, whatever has an opposite tendency? Can the imagination of man conceive a policy better calculated than that of which the present measure forms a part, to bring the opposite extremities of our country together—to bind its various parts to each other, and to multiply and strengthen the various and innumerable ties of commercial, social, and literary intercourse—in a word, to make of the various and wide-spread population of these confederated Republics one united people? (*Register of Debates*, 18th Cong., 2nd sess., 234–235)

The issues to which Clay chose to devote most of his time and effort provide strong evidence in support of his claim that the guiding motive of his political career was to preserve the union. Both the economic program he advanced during his speakership and his active efforts in resolving the three great controversies that threatened to disrupt the union during his political lifetime—the Missouri controversy of the 1820s, the nullification crisis of the 1830s (ironically, triggered by tariff legislation), and the controversy in 1850 over the status of slavery in western lands acquired after the Mexican War—provide evidence of the strength of Clay's commitment to this goal.

Finally, with regard to assessing Clay's goals, if he was seriously committed to advancing policies to strengthen and preserve the union, it is also clear that his personal ambition became focused on the White House while he was speaker and that he sought to win the presidency almost continuously over the next three decades. One history of the period concludes that Clay had begun to think seriously about gaining the office by 1814 and after 1816 "arranged every detail of his political behavior with reference to his succession to [President] Monroe" (Dangerfield 1952, 102). Certainly by the spring of 1822 Clay's correspondence shows that he was polling his political allies about his prospects for winning the presidency, including whether continued service in Congress would advance or hinder his chances (Remini 1991, 210–212; *Clay Papers,* 3: 190–198, 199–201, 210–214, 226–227, 251–252, 264–265, 273–274). As he put it in an 1822 letter to Langdon Cheves explaining his decision to run again for the House that year: "I would have preferred remaining a year or two longer in private life. But my friends every where concurred in thinking my presence there might be material in relation to another object [i.e., the presidency], and one must, though he should do it rarely, yield his opinion to theirs" (*Clay Papers,* 3: 292).

Among the considerations raised by Clay's supporters was the possibility that a crowded field of candidates in 1824 would result in no candidate receiving a majority of the electoral vote and the selection of the president being made by the House of Representatives—in which case his presence in Congress could be especially helpful for his prospects (Beatty to Clay, April 17, 1822, *Clay Papers,* 3: 193). This prediction of course proved correct, although Clay did not win enough electoral votes in 1824 to be among those from whom the choice was made by the House. His decision to support John Quincy Adams for the presidency and acceptance of the office of secretary of state in Adams's administration have been considered among Clay's biggest political miscalculations. Although the position of secretary of state had been the stepping stone to the White House for the previous four presidents, Clay left himself open to the charge from Andrew Jackson and his supporters that a "corrupt bargain" had been struck between him and Adams. This proved a damaging accusation when Clay ran unsuccessfully for the presidency against Jackson in 1832.

The evidence regarding Clay's motives during the time he was speaker is therefore conclusive on the point that his goals reached beyond holding that office. He was both seeking to position himself to win election to the presidency and seeking to advance a national program to strengthen the federal union. Howe's (1979, 124) assessment captures the complexity of Clay's goals: "There was a serious statesman in him along with the gamester-politician; behind his never ending series of plausible expedients there was a consistency of purpose." With Clay we find a leader with a history of risk-taking behavior and strongly held political goals beyond holding the office of speaker of the House. From the perspective of the conditional agency framework the type of leader likely to assert active leadership under a wide range of contextual conditions was present in this case. The question to be addressed now is how Clay responded to the changed political conditions in the House after the War of 1812—whether he continued to wield the prerogatives of the speakership actively to influence decisions that could further his goals or whether he pulled back from assertive leadership in response to the deep divisions that had emerged among his House followers on the new issues that became the focus of the congressional agenda after the war.

## Clay's Leadership of the Postwar House, 1815–1825

Answering the question of how Clay led the House during the Fourteenth, Fifteenth, Sixteenth, and Eighteenth Congresses presents a challenge. We know from records of House roll call votes that the unity that had been present among Clay's Republican followers broke down (see figure 3.1 above). How did Clay respond to this new political situation? Unfortunately, during this early period of congressional politics it is difficult to trace closely through the processes by which legislative and organizational matters were decided. In comparison to the other cases examined in the book, during this period we have much less information about how decisions were actually made. The evidence that is available on how Clay led the House in these years comes primarily from the public record of congressional action as contained in the *Annals of Congress* and *Register of Debates,* records of roll call voting, and occasional comments that appear in Clay's correspondence or that of his House colleagues. There is important evidence to be found in these sources about how Clay led the House in the postwar years, but with the limited record of the actual process of leader-follower interactions, the inferences we can draw are less certain.[19]

Two types of evidence will provide the focus in determining whether Clay continued to provide assertive leadership of the House as speaker during the period after the War of 1812. The first is evidence on whether Clay continued actively using the prerogatives of the speakership to lead the House on policy matters and whether his leadership was consequential for passage of legislation. The second involves evidence on whether Clay's leadership was consequential for the institutional development of the House in the two areas in which important changes occurred during this period: the emergence of a new, more political speakership and the increased importance of standing committees in the legislative process. Contextual theory leads to the expectation that Clay could not have exercised consequential policy leadership because of the deeply divided condition of his followers. Given that Clay was a leader with strongly held policy goals as well as strong ambition to win the presidency, the conditional agency framework implies that Clay might have been willing to risk using the powers of the office to continue to advance those goals even in the presence of heterogeneous preferences among his followers. As we have seen, a "leadership survival" explanation of Clay's leadership proposed by Young and others links these two dimensions, proposing that Clay orchestrated the emergence of a more powerful committee system, trading off influence over policy to win reelection as speaker in a highly factionalized House.

Regarding policy leadership, three forms of evidence addressed in the next section shed light on Clay's approach as speaker during the postwar years. The first is participation in floor debate. Clay frequently addressed the House on policy matters during the war years. Records of House debates show that Clay's policy advocacy through floor speeches continues unabated during the postwar Congresses. A second source of evidence on Clay's leadership as speaker during this later period is his use of the speaker's committee appointment power. Here we find evidence that Clay also continued to "stack" some key committees with members sympathetic to his legislative program. Finally, we can also look at the overall record of House passage of measures Clay advocated. Turning to Speaker Clay's influence on institutional changes in the House, the evidence here is even more limited and circumstantial. From this evidence it appears that Clay's impact on the institutional development of the House consisted primarily of enhancing the importance of the speakership as a leadership institution. The available evidence does not provide strong support for the claim that Clay was responsible for orchestrating important changes that occurred in the House committee system during these years.

## Clay's Policy Leadership

One of the main features of Clay's approach to leadership during the war Congresses had been his willingness to go before the House and speak in favor of war-related measures. Perhaps because the formal powers of the office were still relatively modest, Clay seems to have relied heavily on persuasion as a means of influencing his followers on legislative decisions. Some scholars have argued that Clay was the speaker who made a decisive break with an earlier tradition that the speaker should

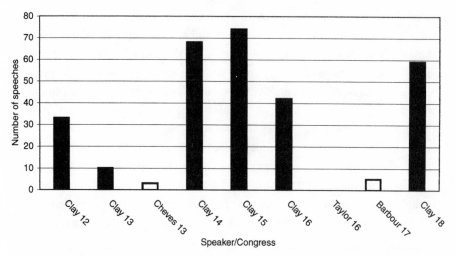

Figure 3.3. Number of Policy Speeches Delivered by Speaker, 12th to 18th Congresses (1811–1825). *Source: Annals of Congress, Register of Debates.*

refrain from active participation in House debate. Clay, writes Follett, "established the tradition that a party in putting a leader in the chair does not deprive itself of his services on the floor" (1896, 75). Swift characterizes Clay's leadership in similar terms: "He refused to give up one of his greatest assets in that age of oratory—his right to debate when the House was in the Committee of the Whole" (1998, 22). Clay was not the first speaker to address the House frequently on policy issues, but he was among the most active of the early speakers in terms of participation in House debates (Strahan, Gunning, and Vining 2006).

What is most interesting from the perspective of understanding how Clay led the House after 1815 is that we see no decline in his use of floor speeches to attempt to persuade his followers on legislation. Figure 3.3 shows the number of times Clay came before the House and delivered policy-related speeches during each Congress he served as speaker.[20] For purposes of comparison, the numbers of policy speeches are also shown for the speakers who served during the periods Clay was not in the speaker's chair between 1811 and 1825: Langdon Cheves (1814–1815), John Taylor (1820–1821), and Philip Barbour (1821–1823). When comparing the "war" Congresses (Twelfth and Thirteenth), when his followers were unified, to the postwar Congresses (Fourteenth, Fifteenth, Sixteenth, and Eighteenth), in which they were deeply divided, it is clear that Clay did not rein in his efforts at persuasion on the House floor. In fact, Speaker Clay's participation in floor debate actually *increased* during the postwar Congresses. As can be seen in figures 3.3 and 3.4, Clay's floor participation increased both in terms of the number of speeches he gave and their

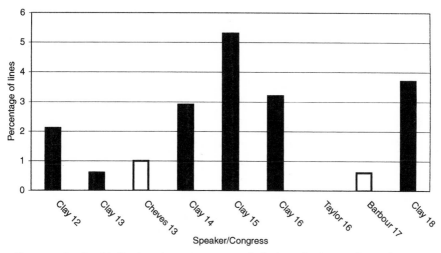

Figure 3.4. Speakers' Policy Speeches as Percentage of All Lines of Debate, 12th to 18th Congresses (1811–1825). *Source: Annals of Congress, Register of Debates.*

length as a percentage of total lines of floor debate for those Congresses. If Clay changed his mode of leading the House after 1815 or shunned policy leadership because his followers had become highly factionalized, we see no evidence of that change in his willingness to advocate legislation he favored on the House floor.

A second tool Clay had used to lead the House during the war Congresses was the use of the speaker's authority to assign members to committees to ensure that key committees would be favorably disposed to war-related measures. Thus a second place to look for evidence on whether Clay continued to use the powers of the speakership actively to lead the House on legislation is in the committee assignments he made in this second period. To what extent did he persist in using the speaker's committee assignment power to advance his policy goals? As we have seen, the "leadership survival" explanation proposes that Clay shifted his approach during the postwar period. Rather than using committee assignments to advance policy goals as he had in the earlier period, Young and others have argued that Clay now distributed committee assignments primarily with an eye toward maintaining support to remain speaker across House factions.

From the time he resumed the speakership in 1815 until he left the position in 1825, Clay was most interested and active in three policy areas: protective tariffs and internal improvements—both of crucial importance to his broader political goal of strengthening the federal union—and foreign policy matters involving support for independence movements and newly independent republics, especially in South America. The appointments Clay made to committees with jurisdiction over these policy areas therefore provide the most telling evidence on whether Clay continued to use the speaker's committee assignment power to advance his policy goals or had altered his approach to leadership in response to the breakdown in unity among his Republican followers.

To establish whether Clay continued to use committee assignments to advance his policy goals during the postwar Congresses we need to determine if he stacked these committees with supporters of his views on tariffs, internal improvements, and foreign policy. Clay's public statements, floor speeches, and floor votes provide evidence of his positions on the major measures that came before the House in these policy areas. A simple measure of House members' support for Clay's position in each issue area can be calculated using House roll call votes on each issue on which the speaker stated a public position.[21] These "Clay support scores" can also be used to measure support for Clay's policy positions by individual House members and among the four main regional groupings of members around which House politics tended to be structured during these years: New England, the Mid-Atlantic states, the West, and the South.

By comparing the makeup of committees Clay appointed with the makeup of the full House chamber during each of these Congresses, we can get some useful leverage on the question of how Clay used the speaker's committee assignment power in the postwar years. Looking both at sectional representation on committees and at levels of support for the speaker's policy views, a "stacked" committee would be one whose members were clearly more supportive of Clay than was the membership of the House as a whole or that clearly overrepresented the regions most supportive of Clay's policy views.[22]

As shown in table 3.1, support for Clay's program in the postwar period varied considerably across different issues and regions of the country. Looking at the entire membership of the House, Clay was least successful in attracting support for his positions challenging Presidents Madison and Monroe on support and recognition of newly independent republics; for example, on average only about one-fourth (28 percent or 0.28 mean support) voted in support of the speaker's position in the Fifteenth Congress. Mean support of all members for Clay's positions on all foreign policy votes during the postwar Congresses was only 0.40. On the other two issues in which Clay was most interested, protective tariffs and internal improvements, the House was usually narrowly divided between supporters and opponents of the speaker's positions. Mean chamber support for the speaker's positions on all postwar tariff votes was 0.50, and for all internal improvement votes, 0.53. The closest approximation to homogeneous preferences we find among House members was actually in opposition to Clay's foreign policy positions; on average 60 percent of

TABLE 3.1
*Clay Support Scores by Issue Area for House Chamber and Region*

| | Chamber | New England | Mid-Atlantic | West | South |
|---|---|---|---|---|---|
| **14th Congress** | | | | | |
| Tariff | 0.52 | 0.50 | 0.80 | 0.76 | 0.23 |
| Internal Improvements | 0.51 | 0.13 | 0.80 | 0.64 | 0.46 |
| Foreign Policy | 0.39 | 0.08 | 0.52 | 0.90 | 0.32 |
| **15th Congress** | | | | | |
| Internal Improvements | 0.50 | 0.23 | 0.80 | 0.62 | 0.37 |
| Foreign Policy | 0.28 | 0.14 | 0.32 | 0.67 | 0.19 |
| **16th Congress** | | | | | |
| Tariff | 0.51 | 0.42 | 0.91 | 0.61 | 0.17 |
| Foreign Policy | 0.52 | 0.33 | 0.66 | 0.76 | 0.37 |
| **18th Congress** | | | | | |
| Tariff | 0.47 | 0.37 | 0.69 | 0.80 | 0.11 |
| Internal Improvements | 0.56 | 0.40 | 0.58 | 0.94 | 0.41 |
| Internal Improvements, 18th Congress, New York State only | | | 0.27 | | |
| Internal Improvements, 18th Congress, other Mid-Atlantic States | | | 0.87 | | |

NOTE: Values are means. New England includes CT, ME, MA, NH, RI, VT; Mid-Atlantic, DE, NJ, NY, PA; West, IL, IN, OH, KY, MO, TN; South, AL, GA, LA, MD, MS, NC, SC, VA.

the House voted against the speaker on these issues during the postwar Congresses. In terms of support across different regions, support for Clay's domestic program (tariffs and internal improvements) was strongest in the West and Mid-Atlantic regions and weakest in the South and New England. His foreign policy views won strong, consistent support from his own western region, attracted very little support in New England, and found mixed but limited support in other regions.

Turning to the committee appointments Clay made, consider first regional representation on committees. Historian Ronald Formisano (1981, 37) observes: "The political coalitions which formed in the early national period . . . had a pronounced sectional basis." With the decline of the Federalist Party and fragmentation of Republicans in Congress after 1815, regional and sectional interests took on greater importance in House politics. Many of the issues on the congressional agenda during the 1815–1825 period—taxation, tariffs, banking and currency questions, internal improvements, the expansion of slavery, foreign policy matters—evoked distinctive regional interests. Also, during a period in which turnover of the membership of the House reached 40 percent or higher with every election, a speaker seeking to influence the policy views of committees might not have been familiar with every member's political views but probably could have done fairly well in anticipating policy preferences on many issues simply by noting the member's home region.[23]

Table 3.2 shows regional representation in the full House, together with regional representation on the committees with jurisdiction over tariffs, internal improvements, and foreign affairs during the Congresses Clay served as speaker after the War of 1812. The most striking evidence of committee stacking is in the makeup of committees with jurisdiction over tariff legislation. During the Fourteenth Congress tariffs fell within the jurisdiction of the southern-dominated Ways and Means Committee. However, when southern members shifted toward intense opposition to protective tariffs after 1816 (see Stanwood 1903, 161; Taussig 1892, 73; Peterson 1987, 72–76; Vipperman 1989, 119–143, 204–232), Clay steered tariff jurisdiction from the Ways and Means Committee to a new Committee on Manufactures. The new committee, which assembled the major tariff bills passed by the House in the Sixteenth and Eighteenth Congresses (1820 and 1824), was dominated by members from the two regions most supportive of Clay's tariff views—the Mid-Atlantic (0.82) and the West (0.80).[24] Members from these two regions constituted 71.5 percent of the panel's membership in the Sixteenth Congress and 85.7 percent of its membership in the Eighteenth Congress (Clay did not serve as speaker in the intervening Seventeenth Congress). By contrast, the regions least supportive of Clay's tariff views— New England (0.43) and the South (0.18)—were consistently underrepresented in the speaker's appointments to the Committee on Manufactures.

Internal improvements measures were handled by select (temporary) committees throughout Clay's speakership. Here again, Clay's appointments produced panels that were consistently dominated by members from the regions most supportive of the speaker's policy views, the Mid-Atlantic (0.71) and the West (0.78).[25] Members from those two regions constituted majorities of all five select committees that exercised jurisdiction over internal improvement measures on which Clay took a position from the Fifteenth through the Eighteenth Congresses.[26] On the other hand, representatives from New England, who mostly opposed the speaker's positions on internal improvements (0.25 support), were underrepresented on four of the five committees, and in three of the five, completely shut out of appointments.

When we turn to Clay's appointments to the committees responsible for foreign policy issues, however, the patterns in appointments to these committees look quite different. Foreign policy matters fell within the jurisdiction of a select committee until the Seventeenth Congress, at which point a standing committee on Foreign Affairs was created. During the postwar years the only region whose representatives showed strong support for Clay's foreign policy views was the West (0.78). On average, members from the Mid-Atlantic region were evenly divided (0.50). Little

TABLE 3.2
*House and Committee Regional Representation in Postwar Congresses Clay Served as Speaker (%)*

| 14th Congress | | | | |
|---|---|---|---|---|
| Region | Chamber | Ways & Means[a] | Bonus[b] | Foreign Affairs[c] |
| New England | 20.4 | 14.3 | 00.0 | 14.3 |
| Mid-Atlantic | 32.0 | 28.6 | 40.0 | 42.9 |
| West | 12.6 | 00.0 | 20.0 | 00.0 |
| South | 35.0 | 57.1 | 40.0 | 42.9 |
| 15th Congress | | | Internal | |
| Region | Chamber | Ways & Means[a] | Improvements[b] | Foreign Affairs[c] |
| New England | 21.7 | 14.3 | 14.3 | 28.6 |
| Mid-Atlantic | 31.3 | 14.3 | 42.9 | 14.3 |
| West | 12.1 | 14.3 | 14.3 | 00.0 |
| South | 34.8 | 57.1 | 28.6 | 57.1 |
| 16th Congress | | | | |
| Region | Chamber | Manufactures[a] | | Foreign Affairs[c] |
| New England | 22.8 | 14.3 | | 14.3 |
| Mid-Atlantic | 30.7 | 42.9 | | 14.3 |
| West | 12.9 | 28.6 | | 00.0 |
| South | 33.7 | 14.3 | | 71.4 |
| 18th Congress | | | Roads | |
| Region | Chamber | Manufactures[a] | and Canals[b] | Foreign Affairs[c] |
| New England | 18.0 | 00.0 | 00.0 | 00.0 |
| Mid-Atlantic | 32.0 | 71.4 | 57.1 | 42.9 |
| West | 18.5 | 14.3 | 14.3 | 14.3 |
| South | 31.5 | 14.3 | 28.6 | 42.9 |

NOTE: Values are means. New England includes CT, ME, MA, NH, RI, VT; Mid-Atlantic, DE, NJ, NY, PA; West, IL, IN, OH, KY, MO, TN; South, AL, GA, LA, MD, MS, NC, SC, VA.

[a] Committee of jurisdiction for tariff isues.
[b] Main committee of jurisdiction for internal improvements issues.
[c] Committee of jurisdiction for foreign affairs.

support existed for Clay's foreign policy views among southerners (0.29), and even less among New Englanders (0.17).

In contrast to what we find with the other committees in which Clay was most interested, majorities on the foreign affairs committees during this period were usually appointed from the regions *least supportive* of the speaker's policy views—New England and the South. This pattern in appointments occurred in three of the four Congresses. Also, no members at all from the West (the region most supportive of Clay's foreign policy views) were even assigned to the foreign affairs panels in three of the four Congresses. Recall that average support for Clay's foreign policy positions in all of the postwar Congresses was only 0.40, meaning that on average 60 percent of the House voted against the speaker's position. Unlike the committees appointed to review tariff and internal improvements measures—issues over which the House was closely divided—Clay seems to have been careful in his appointments related to foreign policy issues to ensure that the large majority of the House opposed to his views would control these committees.

Comparing support for the speaker's policy positions among individual members appointed to committees with support for these positions in the full House provides additional evidence for the conclusion that Clay continued stacking key committees in an effort to advance his legislative goals—again with the exception of the foreign affairs committees. As shown in table 3.3, with only one exception (the Ways and Means Committee in the Fourteenth Congress), the members of committees with jurisdiction over tariffs and internal improvements always displayed substantially higher support for the speaker's policy positions than did the House chamber as a whole.[27] Given the variety of factors that may have come into play in making committee assignments, no single committee-chamber comparison can be considered conclusive evidence that Clay was stacking committees. But consistent patterns in appointments favoring Clay's positions on committees responsible for tariffs and internal improvements legislation seem very unlikely to have occurred as the result of the chance convergence of other factors.

What we find, then, is that on issues over which the House was very closely divided during these years—tariffs and internal improvements—Speaker Clay continued to use the powers of the speakership actively to advance the policies he favored, including appointment of committees that would be supportive of those policies. Henry Baldwin of Pennsylvania, who chaired the Committee on Manufactures, said of Clay's role in tariff legislation during this period: "He discharged the triple duties of a rank-and-file man, captain, and general-in chief" (Colton 1846, 2: 146). Still, in leading a divided House, Clay does appear to have been sensitive to the limits of leadership in this context.

In the one issue area where the factional balance in the chamber consistently produced large majorities opposed to the speaker's own views—foreign policy—Clay appears to have taken a different approach and appointed committees decidedly unsympathetic to his own views. And in contrast to the favorable treatment usually accorded Clay's preferred policies during the postwar years by committees responsible for tariffs and internal improvements, the foreign affairs panels regularly recommended foreign policy measures the speaker opposed, or, together with the full House, failed to support those he favored (Remini 1991, 154–157, 160–161; Peterson 1987, 52–57).[28] The two members Clay appointed to chair the foreign affairs committee during the postwar years, John Forsyth of Georgia and William Lowndes of South Carolina, both were outspoken critics of the speaker's foreign policy views (Duckett 1962, 20–21, 37; Vipperman 1989, 160–163). In other words, Clay seems to have been politically astute enough to realize that it was necessary to give away part,

TABLE 3.3
*Mean Support for Speaker Clay by Issue Area, Committees and Full House*

| 14th Congress | Chamber | Ways & Means | Foreign Affairs | Bonus |
|---|---|---|---|---|
| Tariff | 0.52 | 0.30 | | |
| Internal Improvements | 0.51 | | | 1.00 |
| Foreign Policy | 0.39 | | 0.00 | |

| 15th Congress | Chamber | | Foreign Affairs | Internal Improvements |
|---|---|---|---|---|
| Internal Improvements | 0.50 | | | 0.63 |
| Foreign Policy | 0.28 | | 0.60 | |

| 16th Congress | Chamber | Manufactures | Foreign Affairs |
|---|---|---|---|
| Tariff | 0.51 | 0.91 | |
| Foreign Policy | 0.52 | | 0.20 |

| 18th Congress | Chamber | Manufactures | Roads & Canals | Cumberland Road | Navigation of Ohio & Mississippi |
|---|---|---|---|---|---|
| Tariff | 0.47 | 0.69 | | | |
| Internal Improvements | 0.56 | | 0.71 | 0.95 | 0.83 |

NOTE: Values are means. Internal improvements issues were assigned to multiple committees in the 18th Congress.

but only part, of the policy "store" to committees in order to retain support to win reelection to the speakership. He did not use his power as speaker to try to impose his policy views on the House when a sizable majority of his followers consistently opposed them. But on the other issues, on which the chamber was very closely divided, he continued to use the prerogatives of the speakership actively to pursue his own program of protective tariffs and federally funded internal improvements.

In assessing Clay's ability to influence legislative outcomes during this period, it is important to note that appointing sympathetic committee majorities did not by any means guarantee passage of the policies he favored. Neither the speaker nor committees could exercise very strict control over the agenda of the House during this early period. Committees gained authority over the legislative process during these years, but they did not have the gate-keeping and jurisdictional authority of their modern counterparts (Cooper 1970; Cooper and Young 1989, 69–71; Jenkins and Stewart 1998). Still, committees did provide institutional capacity for gathering information and developing supportive coalitions in advance of floor action. In a political context where the old Federalist-Republican partisan cleavage no longer structured House politics, and much of the membership was inexperienced, these were not inconsiderable advantages.

On the importance of committees for advancing the speaker's policy goals, note Clay's response when amendments began to be offered to a tariff bill he was seeking to get enacted in 1820. As reported in the *Annals of Congress* (16th Cong., 1st sess., 1946) Speaker Clay,

> rose to say, that it became the friends of the manufacturing system [protective tariffs] not to lend themselves with too much facility to alterations proposed in the system which has been reported by the Committee on Manufactures. That committee had, with a patience and industry never surpassed in this House, prepared and reported a general system. Its provisions were no doubt the result of much calculation; and if the friends of the general features of it listened to every application which should be made to change this or that particular item, the effect would be, that they would lose the whole.

Opponents of Clay's protectionist views certainly saw control of the Manufactures Committee by protariff legislators as a significant disadvantage. In the debate on the 1824 tariff, Robert Selden Garnett of Virginia complained to the House that agricultural interests had not been sufficiently represented in the development of tariff legislation, while "the manufacturers were provided with a committee to prepare, organize and concentrate the means of attack" (*Annals of Congress,* 18th Cong., 1st sess., 1686). A supportive committee majority did not ensure enactment of legislation favored by the speaker but did confer real advantages in assembling political and substantive information, drafting legislation and establishing the starting point for floor debates.

Finally, additional evidence supporting the view that Clay continued to use the powers of the speakership actively to advance legislation is found in his record of legislative success in the postwar Congresses. In *The Washington Community,* Young contends that earlier scholars such as Mary Parker Follett (1896)—who viewed Clay as the most powerful of the early House speakers—had confused Clay's popularity with his effectiveness in getting bills passed by the House. Young claims that Clay had a very limited record of legislative success (1966, 131). A sweep of the major Clay biographies, historical narratives of the period, and the record of House debates turns up twenty-four issues during the period he served as speaker between 1815 and 1825 on which Clay took a public role advocating passage and which came before the House in the form of bills or resolutions. Of those twenty-four measures, the House voted in support of Clay's position on final passage on sixteen, a success rate of exactly two-thirds (see appendix).

While passage of all of these measures cannot be attributed to Clay's leadership (much of Clay's program in the Fourteenth Congress, for example, was also supported by President Madison), it is clear that Clay not only continued to exercise active leadership from the speaker's chair during the postwar Congresses but also that he achieved a significant measure of legislative success. These successes included major tariff measures in 1816 and 1824.[29] Clay's postwar record on internal improvements and other economic measures was mixed but hardly one that suggests his leadership was inconsequential. After President Madison's veto of a major internal improvements bill on constitutional grounds in 1817, Speaker Clay had to settle for a much more limited program of internal improvements than he would have preferred. Still, he continued to advance his agenda in this area during his final Congress as speaker, winning approval in the Eighteenth Congress for funds to conduct a survey of future road and canal projects, to improve navigation on western rivers, and to continue construction of the Cumberland Road (Baxter 1995, 46–54; Minicucci 1998, chap. 2; Larson 2001, chaps. 2, 4). An interesting political irony is that the postwar House consistently rejected Clay's leadership in the area of foreign policy. Clay may have led the House forcefully on matters related to war with England during the Twelfth and Thirteenth Congresses, but he found very limited support for his legislative efforts after the war to advance early recognition of the newly independent states in Latin America. Even during a period not known for powerful executives, the politics of internal improvements and recognition of new Latin American states clearly demonstrated the power of the presidency to limit the scope of policy leadership by the speaker.

## *Clay's Leadership and the Institutional Development of the House*

If the evidence shows that Speaker Clay continued to advance his policy goals actively in the postwar Congresses and remained consequential as a legislative leader, there remains the question of Clay's influence on the institutional development of the House. Some scholars have attributed to Clay an important role in the development of the system of standing committees in the House; others have argued that he transformed the office of the speakership into a more important leadership position. Unlike his policy views, which were laid out in detail in his House speeches, Clay never explicitly set forth his views on the organization of the House. He offered no blueprint for institutional reform or account of his views on how the House should be arranged to conduct its business effectively. Clay's influence on the institution arose from how he actually conducted the office of speaker, the precedents he set, and the organizational changes he may have advanced in the course of doing business as speaker over the six Congresses in which he served in the chair.

Standing committees were already important bodies in the House prior to Clay's election as speaker in 1811, but three interrelated developments that occurred during Clay's speakership resulted in a more central role for standing committees in the legislative process. First, the total number of standing committees increased from nine in the Twelfth Congress (1811–1813, Clay's first as speaker) to twenty-four in the Eighteenth (1823–1825, Clay's last) (Stewart et al. 1995, table 1).[30] Second, the practice of referring subjects likely to lead to legislation primarily to standing committees was firmly established during this period.[31] Third, in contrast to earlier practice in which committees had required prior authorization from chamber majorities to recommend specific pieces of legislation, committees were also granted broader discretion to introduce bills (Harlow 1917, 219–226; Cooper and Young 1989, 69–71). As Cooper and Young (1989, 71) have shown in their careful study of early legislative procedures: "By the early 1820s, a new system of legislating had emerged in the House in which both major and minor subjects were typically referred to standing committees and standing committees possessed power to report by bill at their own discretion."

Turning to the evidence of Clay's involvement in the development of the standing committee system between 1811 and 1825, there is strong circumstantial evidence that Clay orchestrated the creation of one new standing committee, the Committee of Manufactures, during the Sixteenth Congress. This new committee was created in 1819 after a period of jurisdictional conflict over tariff measures between the Committee on Commerce and Manufactures and the Committee of Ways and Means, neither of which was particularly supportive of Clay's preferred tariff policies. Shortly after the opening of the Sixteenth Congress, the existing Commerce and Manufactures Committee was renamed the Committee of Commerce and a new Committee of Manufactures established (*Annals of Congress*, 16th Cong., 1st sess., 708–710). The new committee immediately began to receive referrals of tariff measures (Kennon and Rogers 1989, 86–88, 452). Clay appointed a committed protectionist, Henry Baldwin of Pennsylvania, as chair, and as we have seen, a majority of its membership from the protariff Mid-Atlantic and western states.

A letter written by Clay some years later to a longtime political ally, former representative Peter B. Porter of New York, suggests how the creation of this new committee fit into the speaker's political strategy on passing tariff legislation. During the first session of the Eighteenth Congress, Clay wrote: "We entertain high hopes of passage of the Tariff. The South as usual is against it, but we trust that the coincidence of opinion which happily exists between the West and the middle states will ensure passage of that salutary measure" (*Clay Papers,* 3: 629). The new standing committee on manufactures provided the vehicle for Speaker Clay to ensure by means of his committee appointment power that the "coincidence of opinion" in favor of the tariff in the West and Mid-Atlantic regions would prevail within the House committee of jurisdiction in the Sixteenth and later Congresses. This is an important case, given that it involved jurisdiction over one of the most prominent national issues of the day, but only one piece of a much larger puzzle. And beyond this single case, there is simply no clear evidence that other developments in the standing committee system during these years were due primarily to Clay's leadership (see Stewart 2004, 27–35).

The significance of Clay's leadership for the early institutional development of the House probably lies more in his influence on the development of the office of speaker. Only once, during a speech to the House in 1823—after he had been reelected speaker for the sixth time—did Clay ever comment directly on how the office should be conducted. In this speech, he enumerated a series of "principles which should regulate the execution of the duties of the incumbent of the Chair," but these represented mostly a nod to the older view of the speaker as an impartial moderator rather than a description of how Clay had actually been running the House or what he intended to do in the Eighteenth Congress just getting under way.[32] A more revealing comment on his view of the office is an observation he offered six weeks later (January 1824) while addressing the broader question of the responsibilities that come with holding a position of political power: "Of all the trusts which are created by human agency, that is the highest, most solemn, and most responsible, which involves the exercise of political power. Exerted when it has not been intrusted, the public functionary is guilty of usurpation. *And his infidelity to the public good is not, perhaps, less culpable when he neglects or refuses to exercise a power which has been fairly conveyed, to promote the public prosperity*" (*Annals of Congress,* 18th Cong, 1st sess., 1023, emphasis mine). The subject of this speech was the constitutionality of congressional power to enact legislation on internal improvements, and in that context Clay is making a case for the obligation of public officeholders not only to avoid abusing power but also to use power actively to promote the public good. This is as close a statement as we have of Clay's view of political leadership during the time he was speaker; it is certainly consistent with his activist approach to the office.

A number of the speakers who preceded Clay had already begun to break with the older idea of the speaker as a moderator or parliamentary official who would stand above House politics. With Clay's successful use of the office as a position of active partisan and policy leadership over a period that represented almost one-third of the time the House had been in existence, the break with the earlier conception of the speakership was decisive. Clay's personal qualities seem to have been important for sustaining this activist mode of leadership beyond the initial years in which the Republican majority was mostly unified on prosecuting the War of 1812. Among those qualities were intensely held goals that involved shaping national policy and developing a national reputation that could carry him to the White House. Clay's strong personal appeal and moderation on the slavery issue no doubt also worked in his favor. Also as Follett (1896, 80) noted in one of the first scholarly works to call attention to the importance of Clay's leadership for the development of Congress: "Few Speakers have known so well as Henry Clay how to measure their power so as to obtain the utmost possible and yet not go beyond that unwritten standard of 'fairness' which exists in every House of Representatives." In this balance between an inclination to exercise power within the legislature and respect for its limits is found an important quality that made Clay such an important congressional leader during this critical early period in the development of the House.

The case for viewing Clay as responsible for transforming the speakership into a more important leadership institution does not rest on his having been the first to assert the prerogatives and advantages of the office. Earlier speakers had also used the committee assignment power to advance partisan or policy goals (Risjord 1992; Stewart 2004), and contrary to some accounts that claim Clay was the first speaker to participate actively in House debates, other speakers—including the Federalist speaker, Jonathan Dayton, who served over a decade earlier—had done this as well (Strahan, Gunning, and Vining 2006). Rather than being the first to exercise leadership using the tools available to the early speakers, Clay's main contribution to the development of the office seems to have been using *all* of the leadership tools available to the speaker during this period effectively and thereby demonstrating to his House colleagues the benefits of having the speaker function as the central leadership institution for the chamber. As Adam Sheingate (2003, 190) has noted, political entrepreneurs often produce important innovations through "creative re-combinations of known elements" of existing practices and institutions.

Two types of evidence support the conclusion that Clay brought about a transformation in the role and political significance of the speakership over the period from 1811 to 1825. The first is a shift that occurred in the politics of speakership elections during his tenure. As Stewart notes, the period from 1789 to 1811 (prior to Clay's service as speaker) was characterized by "a sense within the House that the speaker was a minor prize." In the years that followed, "Clay's speakership demon-

TABLE 3.4
*Vote on Resolution of Thanks to the Speaker, 1st–18th Congresses (%)*

| Congress | Speaker | Voting No | Seats Held by Opposition Party |
|---|---|---|---|
| 1st | Muhlenberg | 0 | — |
| 2nd | Trumbull | 0 | — |
| 3rd | Muhlenberg | 0 | — |
| 4th | Dayton | 0 | 57 |
| 5th | Dayton | 35 | 49 |
| 6th | Sedgwick | 47 | 46 |
| 7th | Macon | 0 | 36 |
| 8th | Macon | 0 | 28 |
| 9th | Macon | 0 | 20 |
| 10th | Varnum | 12 | 28 |
| 11th | Varnum | [a] | 35 |
| 12th | Clay | 0 | 25 |
| 13th | Clay | 6 | 37 |
| | Cheves | 0 | 37 |
| 14th | Clay | 0 | 35 |
| 15th | Clay | 0 | 21 |
| 16th | Clay | 0 | 14 |
| | Taylor | [b] | 14 |
| 17th | Barbour | 0 | 17 |
| 18th | Clay | [a] | — |

SOURCE: *Annals of Congress* and *Register of Debates.* Opposition party strength from Martis 1989 and party of speaker from Peters 1997, 299–300.

[a] Not recorded.
[b] "One negative voice only"

strated the strategic value of the speakership, and thus contests for the office became more heated" (2000, 5).

The second type of evidence supportive of the proposition that Clay's leadership transformed the office involves patterns in support recorded for the customary resolution introduced at the end of each Congress thanking the speaker for his service to the House. Unlike the treatment received by some of his predecessors who had been most active in exercising leadership from the speaker's chair—Federalist speakers Dayton and Theodore Sedgwick—the House repeatedly voted overwhelming support for resolutions thanking Clay. As shown in table 3.4, a third or more of the House opposed the resolution of thanks to Speakers Dayton and Sedgwick when each left the chair.[33] Clay, on the other hand, received either unanimous or near unanimous support from the House in each of the five Congresses in which he served as speaker for which the vote on the resolution was recorded. It is particularly noteworthy that the resolution thanking Clay won unanimous support in the Twelfth Congress—during which Clay actively led and Federalists actively opposed the move to prosecute war with Britain—even though Federalists still held 25 percent of the seats in the House. Partly as a result of Clay's skill as a legislative leader, something important had changed in the politics of the House and the nature of the speakership by the time of his departure from the chamber in 1825. The older view of the office of speaker as a moderator or a parliamentary official who was of minor importance or who would remain above politics was now a thing of the past.

## Conclusion

The evidence in this chapter on the politics of leadership during the Clay speakership demonstrates that Henry Clay actively wielded the prerogatives of the office throughout the period he served as speaker, including the years after the War of 1812, when his followers were often deeply divided on policy issues. The evidence suggests that Clay also remained a consequential leader on legislative decisions during both periods of his speakership and that his leadership of the House was important for establishing the legitimacy of the speaker functioning as the central leadership institution for the House. The sparse evidence we have on the processes through which decisions on legislation and organizational matters were made during these years means that these conclusions about Clay's influence in policy and organizational outcomes cannot be stated with certainty.

The conditional agency framework gains some initial support from this case. While Clay's active leadership during the war Congresses is consistent with contextual theories that predict strong legislative leadership will emerge when followers are unified, the continuation of an activist mode of legislative leadership by Clay during the period when his followers' preferences clearly were not homogeneous presents a puzzle for that perspective. In the causal process implied by contextual theory a leader should shun active policy leadership on issues over which followers are deeply divided. In light of the fact that Clay held strong policy goals and political ambitions reaching beyond the House, the conditional agency perspective offers insight into why Clay would have been willing to risk actively leading deeply divided followers; he cared deeply about advancing a program to strengthen the union and he wanted badly to be president. From Clay's perspective both goals could be advanced by continuing to use the office of speaker to establish a record of legislative accomplishment on issues such as tariffs and internal improvements.

From what evidence we have of early House politics, Clay's leadership seems to have involved mainly persuasion, along with use of what limited powers early speakers had over the agenda. Clay was an accomplished political orator in an age of oratory. On the measures he wanted to see passed, he made frequent and sometimes lengthy appeals to the House for support. As speaker, Clay sometimes used the rules or the parliamentary authority of the office to limit debate or check moves by dissidents such as John Randolph (see Follett 1896, 37–74), but his main efforts toward controlling the agenda involved appointing sympathetic committees to draft legislation that served as the starting point for House deliberations. Clay may also have used committee appointments as rewards to supportive members, but we have no direct evidence that this was the case.

In his history of the speakership, Peters observes: "Perhaps the most striking aspect of the House during this era was its fluidity" (1997, 35). In this early period the rules and institutional forms of the House were still being defined. Clay's ability as an orator and widely acknowledged personal charm seem to have equipped him well to lead in an institutional context in which the speaker had limited institutional resources under his control (ibid., 35–39). The limited institutionalization of the House also limited the resources available to members who wanted to oppose Clay's leadership on policy issues.

Finally, after considering the politics of Clay's leadership as speaker of the House, there remains the very long running debate about what finally motivated Henry Clay as a political leader. Was he a calculating politician driven, or sometimes even blinded, by ambition for the White House? Or was he a principled statesman who sought to complete the work of the Founders by strengthening the bonds of the federal union? What seems not to have been sufficiently appreciated in assessments of Clay's political leadership is that the relentless personal ambition he displayed for the presidency and his consistent pursuit of policies he thought to be in the national interest may have been more complementary than contradictory political goals.

Just as Clay was returning to the House for his final term as speaker and focusing on strategy for his first run at the presidency, one of his contemporaries, Supreme Court Justice Joseph Story, reflected on the path of Clay's career. In an 1823 letter to a fellow judge, Story wrote: "Clay has argued before us [the Supreme Court] with a good deal of ability; and if he were not a candidate for higher offices, I should think he might attain great eminence at this Bar. But he prefers the fame of popular talents to the steady fame of the Bar" (quoted in Van Deusen 1937, 29). Story's assessment of Clay's choice to pursue politics over law recalls the discussion in chapter 2 of the importance of historical reputation or "fame" as a motive for political leaders. In the political science of the Founding era and before, political ambition was understood to have a broader dimension than simply satisfying a personal need or desire to hold power. For leaders motivated by fame, power is desirable as the means to secure a lasting place in history. However, a lasting historical reputation as a great statesman is achieved not simply by holding power but by using a powerful office to advance the national interest in some great undertaking. We have no direct evidence that what Henry Clay sought most in politics was fame, but the apparent tension between a restless and driving personal ambition and principled pursuit of policy measures that has caused his motivations to be debated from his day to ours may be resolved if we consider Clay's career in light of this older understanding of political ambition. For Clay, both holding a position of political power—preferably the presidency, the first office in the republic—*and* gaining recognition for championing policies that completed the task of establishing the union during this critical period in American political development may have been thought necessary to establish his place in history.

The subject of the next chapter, Speaker Thomas Reed, wrote of Clay in 1896: "While other men were struggling with their own inertia and mistaking it for the Constitution, Clay saw not only the utility but the absolute necessity of straining every power to bind the union together" (1896, 12). That we are still studying Clay's leadership over a century after Reed wrote these lines suggests that Clay may have realized his ultimate political goal even though he never occupied the White House.

# CHAPTER FOUR

# Thomas Reed

## The Responsible Partisan as Speaker

> The best system is to have one party govern and the other party watch;
> and on general principles I think it would be better for us to govern
> and for the Democrats to watch.
>
> —*Thomas Reed, 1880*

In January 1890, Thomas Brackett Reed made an unexpected and controversial ruling from the speaker's chair with the objective of clearing the way for the House of Representatives to adopt pathbreaking rules changes. A parliamentary battle over Reed's move raged on the House floor for two days, became front-page news all over the country, and made "Czar" Reed a national political figure. The new rules adopted under Reed's leadership both enhanced the powers of the speakership and transformed the House from a legislative body in which minorities of legislators could obstruct action to one in which a majority could pass legislation.

The reforms orchestrated by Speaker Reed were a turning point in the history of Congress. "Adoption of the Reed rules in 1890," writes Eric Schickler (2001, 32), "is without question one of the most significant events in the institutional development of the Congress. No single change did more to secure majority rule." Adds Douglas Dion (1997, 125): "Reed's single-minded determination to quash the ability of members of the minority party to obstruct legislation has left an institutional legacy that the House still operates under today." Gary Cox and Mathew McCubbins describe the rules changes orchestrated by Speaker Reed as "the central watershed in House procedural history" (2005, 222).[1]

As speaker from 1889 to 1891 and again from 1895 to 1899, Reed also played an important role in shaping legislation on some of the most important issues of his day, including the question of whether the country should maintain the gold standard in the face of a growing movement in the South and West demanding change in the nation's currency policies and measures to secure voting rights for southern African Americans that would prove to be the last such efforts for over half a century. However, even with the enhanced powers conferred on the office of speaker by the new rules, Reed still encountered the limits of leadership in the House. He proved powerless to stem the groundswell of support among his Republican followers for war with Spain and acquisition of new territories in the Caribbean and the Pacific—policies with which he vehemently disagreed and which ultimately led to his resignation from the speakership. Nevertheless, because of the important institutional changes Reed led the House to adopt in 1890, and also because he played a key role in a number of major national policy decisions during an important period in American political development, the Reed speakership is an unusually important case for exploring the politics of leadership in Congress.

Thomas Reed was also an unusual politician. Political historian Morton Keller has written: "The most distinctive feature of late nineteenth century American politics was its domination by highly organized parties and professional politicians" (1977, 522). In some respects, Reed fits this description; he was a professional politician who held public office for almost thirty years. First elected as a Maine state legislator in 1869, he served in both houses of the Maine legislature and also as attorney general of that state before serving in the House of Representatives continuously from 1877 until 1899. Reed was also a candidate for the Republican presidential nomination in 1896.

Most professional politicians during these years rose in politics through loyal service to their party organizations and focused as much on controlling patronage jobs for their party's supporters as on debates over public policy. But Reed was never close to the leaders of the Republican Party organization in his home state of Maine, disliked patronage politics and political dealmaking, and displayed a serious intellectual bent. Serving in a Congress full of horse-trading machine politicians, Reed wrote essays on governance and public policy for the *North American Review* and other journals, published a book on parliamentary procedure, and took up the study of the French language as he was rising into the leadership of the House. After he became a national political figure, when interviewed for a profile in a national magazine Reed was as likely to hold forth on the novels of Balzac as the rules of the House or the partisan debates raging over the tariff or the currency (see Porter 1893).

His longtime Republican colleague (and later speaker), Joseph Cannon of Illinois, expressed admiration for Reed's intellect and his courage yet observed, "Reed was never a politician, nor could he enter into their minds" (Busbey 1927, 168). But

Cannon—who was a politician's politician—also said of Reed: "I have known no other man in public life who had his power of sarcasm or sardonic wit, who in half-a-dozen words could annihilate an opponent or, what was worse, make him appear ridiculous" (ibid., 167–168). To cite only one example, when one of Reed's least favorite House colleagues, Democrat William Springer of Illinois, used a line attributed to Henry Clay—"I would rather be right than be President"—in a speech Reed responded: "The gentleman need not worry. He will never be either" (Robinson 1930, 390). After Springer served a stint as chair of the House Ways and Means Committee—and by virtue of that committee's jurisdiction over tax and tariff measures became a leader for his party on economic issues—Reed commented: "The [Democratic] party can contemplate [Springer's] work of this session with the calm certainty that there is no intellect so subtle, no mind so broad, no sympathy so delicate, as to detect therein the slightest trace of a principle of economic science or a system of revenue" (1892, 229).

The Reed speakership brings into sharp focus the central questions about congressional leadership addressed in this book. Reed's use of the speakership to secure major changes in House rules at the beginning of the Fifty-first Congress offers one of the most important cases in the history of Congress within which to explore the conditions under which the agency of a leader can influence outcomes in the legislature. Some previous studies have concluded that Reed's activism as speaker represents a case of strong leadership emerging in the context of a high degree of unity among party followers (see Cooper and Brady 1981; Rohde and Shepsle 1987). High levels of party unity and party conflict in House roll call voting during the Reed speakership, as well as a greater tendency of Republicans to represent more industrialized or economically developed areas, have both been cited as evidence that Reed's Republican followers were unified on the major policy questions before Congress during these years (Cooper and Brady 1981, 414–415; Forgette 1997, 385–388).

The evidence presented in this chapter will show that the politics of leadership during Reed's speakership were more complex—and more interesting—than these accounts suggest. On institutional reforms in the Fifty-first Congress as well as some major legislative initiatives during that Congress, Reed aggressively led his party followers in the face of uncertainty about their preferences or even clear knowledge of serious divisions among them. Only two months after he became Speaker, Reed pushed rules changes well beyond those on which House Republicans were in agreement and was uncertain about whether he would succeed. With respect to Reed's leadership on legislative matters, as Schickler (2001, 33) has observed, "there is good reason to doubt whether Republicans actually enjoyed the near-consensus on major policy objectives that recent scholarship has attributed to them." In fact, despite the unity they normally displayed in roll call voting, Reed's followers were sharply divided on some of these issues.

Speaker Reed's actions in pushing his divided followers to adopt more fundamental reforms to secure the capacity of the House majority to legislate, and to pass legislation to maintain the gold standard and to protect voting rights for southern blacks in the early 1890s, are puzzling in light of the leadership politics we should expect to find according to contextual theory. So is Reed's refusal later in his speakership to take an active role in advancing measures in support of acquiring new territories during and after the Spanish-American War, policies on which his followers did have homogeneous preferences. The conditional agency perspective, by focusing attention on the individual leader's goals and tolerance for risk and leaders' ability to shape followers' preferences again may help illuminate this important case.

The examination of the politics of the Reed speakership will begin with an overview of the political context during the period Reed held the office of speaker. Next the chapter will consider Reed's goals as leader. Unlike Henry Clay, who was elected speaker on his first day as a member of the House, Reed had served for twelve years before being elevated to the speaker's chair. His actions during these years provide important evidence about the goals that motivated him once he became speaker and why these goals may have encouraged a willingness to take risks with his leadership position. Then the chapter will examine three areas central to understanding the politics of the Reed speakership: the adoption of the Reed Rules in 1890; legislative initiatives in the areas of the tariff, the currency, and electoral reform during the Fifty-first Congress; and finally Reed's failed efforts to influence his Republican followers on the question of annexation of new territories during and after the Spanish-American War and his subsequent resignation in 1899.

With each of these issues we will be attentive to evidence of the causal processes in leadership politics implied by the contextual leadership theories and the conditional agency framework. Specifically, as speaker did Reed focus primarily on maintaining his hold on the office and using the prerogatives of the speakership to advance goals on which he knew—or had good reason to believe—his Republican followers' views were homogeneous? Or is there evidence that the leader possessed strongly held personal goals and was willing to take risks with his position to advance those goals, even in situations in which he knew his followers had not yet reached agreement on the question to be decided or were seriously divided? Before taking up these questions directly, it will be helpful first to consider briefly the most important features of the political context within which Reed led the House.

## The Political Context of the Reed Speakership

Thomas Reed first occupied the speaker's chair during the Fifty-first Congress (1889–1891) and occupied it again during the Fifty-fourth and Fifty-fifth Congresses (1895–1899). Four features of the political context are of greatest importance for understanding House leadership politics during these years. First, the electoral politics of this period featured strong political party organizations and highly competitive national elections. Second, developments in House rules that occurred before and during the Reed speakership had resulted in a remarkable concentration of institutional powers in the office of speaker. Third, the issues on the congressional agenda were primarily economic. Although both parties experienced some factional splits on these issues, this was generally a period of high levels of party conflict and party unity in the House. And fourth, presidential-congressional relations during this period were marked by growing but still modest presidential influence in Congress.

Ronald M. Peters (1997, 51) describes the period from 1861 to 1910 as the "partisan speakership," an era "in which the speakership of the House became an artifact and architect of party government in the United States." As Peters rightly emphasizes, this was an era in American politics marked by strong partisan attachments in the electorate, strong, patronage-based party organizations, and high levels of party voting in Congress (Keller 1977; Silbey 1991; Cooper and Brady 1981; Brady, Cooper, and Hurley 1979). At the time Reed became speaker, many members of Congress were politicians who had won nomination by state or local party "machines" as a reward for service to the party. In general these were legislators who sought tangible rewards from politics: "office for the office-seeker, patronage for the party, and local benefits for local constituents" (Swenson 1982, 21). Capturing the tone of American politics during this era, one wit defined a lighthouse as "a tall building on the seashore in which the government maintains a lamp and the friend of a politician" (quoted in Morgan 1969, 27). Legislators were accustomed to a style of politics in which advancement came by demonstrating loyalty to party and honing the bargaining skills required to ensure that one's constituents and supporters shared in the benefits (especially jobs) distributed by government. For most politicians during these years, party loyalty was both the path to political advancement and an end in itself that required little justification.

Until the late 1890s, when Republicans established dominance in national electoral politics, this was also a period of intense partisan competition for control of national institutions. As shown in table 4.1, of the eleven Congresses in which Reed served (1877–1899), Democrats controlled the House for seven and Republicans four. Reed had only had two years' experience serving in the majority before becoming speaker, and his speakership was interrupted after one term by four years of Democratic control before resuming for another four years. Republicans had greater success in maintaining control of the Senate (eight of eleven Congresses) and the presidency (four of six elections). But in a pattern that looks remarkably similar to the late twentieth century, divided party government in which at least one national institution—House, Senate, or presidency—was under the control of a different party was present for fourteen of the twenty-two years from 1877 to 1899. When Republicans took control of the House, the Senate, and the presidency at the outset of Reed's speakership in 1889, it was the first time they had effective control of all three institutions in over a decade.[2] Also familiar a century later, such a highly competitive electoral environment found the two parties seeking every possible advantage in the attempt to win or hold congressional majorities, including frequent and aggressive gerrymandering of House districts by state legislatures.[3] Denial of voting rights to blacks by states and localities in the South also had significant national consequences—favoring Democrats—when the national balance of power between the parties was so close.[4] Selective admission of new western states also took place as the parties sometimes weighed judgments of partisan advantage in the newly admitted state above more objective criteria (Argersinger 2001; McCarty, Poole, and Rosenthal 2002).

A second important feature of the context within which Reed led the House was the rules of the chamber. Partly as a result of Reed's own efforts, House rules conferred much greater institutional power on late nineteenth-century speakers than was the case when the office was first emerging as an important leadership institution during the Clay years. Assignments to House committees had been made by the speaker since 1790, and as we have seen with Speaker Clay this power had long provided speakers with a means of advancing favored legislation as well as a store of rewards that could be conferred or withheld. During the 1870s and 1880s two additional developments added to the speaker's prerogatives: increased discretion over recognition of members on the floor and assumption of the chairmanship of a standing Rules Committee with authority to expedite consideration of individual bills.

House rules adopted for the First Congress gave the speaker authority to decide who would be recognized to speak if more than one member sought the floor. But this power was initially understood primarily as a simple parliamentary function of deciding who had risen first. The power of recognition took on greater political significance as the House grew larger and the press of business intensified. Precedents established in the post–Civil War decades extended the speaker's power in this area. During the speakership of Republican James G. Blaine (1869–1875) the principle

TABLE 4.1
*Speakers of the House and Party Control of the House, Senate and Presidency, 1877–1899*

| Speaker | Congress | Party Division in House | Party Control | |
|---|---|---|---|---|
| | | | Senate | Presidency |
| Samuel J. Randall (D-PA) | 45th (1877–79) | 156D/137R | R | R (Hayes) |
| | 46th (1879–81) | 150D/128R/14[a] | D | R |
| J. Warren Keifer (R-OH) | 47th (1881–83) | 152R/130D/11[a] | R[b] | (Garfield-Arthur) |
| John G. Carlisle (D-KY) | 48th (1883–85) | 200D/119R/6[a] | R | R |
| | 49th (1885–87) | 182D/140R/2[a] | R | D (Cleveland) |
| | 50th (1887–89) | 170D/151R/4[a] | R | D |
| Thomas B. Reed (R-ME) | 51st (1889–91) | 173R/156D/1[a] | R | R (Harrison) |
| Charles F. Crisp (D-GA) | 52nd (1891–93) | 231D/88R/14[a] | R | R |
| | 53rd (1893–95) | 220D/126R/10[a] | D | D (Cleveland) |
| Thomas B. Reed (R-ME) | 54th (1895–97) | 246R/104D/7[a] | D | D |
| | 55th (1897–99) | 206R/134D/16[a] | R | R (McKinley) |

SOURCE: Ornstein, Mann, and Malbin 1998, 41, table 1.19.

[a] Other parties.
[b] Party strength in the Senate was a perfect 37–37 tie with two additional members (a Readjuster and an independent), one of whom caucused with each party. Republicans organized the Senate on the strength of the vote of the Republican vice president Arthur but lacked a reliable majority.

was established that the speaker would award recognition based on his judgment of the relative importance of the motions being offered (Hinds 1907, 875, 918). An even broader interpretation of the speaker's power of recognition was established in 1881, when Democrat Samuel J. Randall (speaker from 1876 to 1881) ruled: "There is no power in the House itself to appeal from the recognition of the chair. The right of recognition is just as absolute in the chair as the judgment of the Supreme Court is absolute in the interpretation of the law" (House 1935, 838–839). As one historian of the House has pointed out, the consolidation of the speaker's power over recognition during the 1880s "put members desiring recognition for measures not privileged wholly at the mercy of the chair" (Alexander 1916, 60). Speakers before Reed had used the power of recognition to reward or block individual members who were seeking to advance constituency measures, as well as to advance or block movement of legislation for party or even personal reasons (ibid., 58–61; Follett 1896, 253–266).

Prior to 1880, the House Rules Committee had functioned primarily as a select committee convened at the beginning of each Congress to review and make recommendations on House rules. The speaker was first named chair of the committee in 1858. The potential influence of the panel expanded when the Rules Committee received standing committee status under new rules adopted in 1880. Rulings by Speaker Randall that same year established that all proposed rules changes would be referred to the committee and that it could report on matters related to the rules of the House at any time (Committee on Rules 1983, 55–61; Alexander 1916, 194–196; House 1935, 839–841). During the 1880s resolutions drafted by the Rules Committee (known as "special orders" or simply "rules") and adopted by a simple majority vote began to be used as a means of expediting action on legislation that otherwise might have failed to survive the complex and congested order of business in the House. By the mid-1880s, the Rules Committee, chaired by the speaker, "began to fill the public eye. Like Pandora's box it seemed to conceal surprising possibilities" (Alexander 1916, 204).

Possessing wide discretion to recognize members on the House floor, chairing the increasingly important Rules Committee, and continuing to wield power over members' standing committee assignments, the House speaker exercised formidable influence over both organizational and legislative matters by the time Reed won the office. Still, until the reforms of the Fifty-first Congress, the ability of the majority party to legislate under the speaker's leadership was far from assured. In the period just prior to Reed's election as speaker, the business of the House had repeatedly been brought to a standstill as various minorities took advantage of opportunities for obstruction allowed by House rules. The order of business required by the rules often made it difficult to bring legislation before the chamber for a vote unless at least two-thirds of the membership supported doing so. And if a measure finally did come up for a vote opponents could still delay action by offering motions to adjourn or recess the House or employing the tactic known as the "disappearing quorum." With party majorities often very narrow during this period, the minority—especially when supported by a few dissidents from the majority party—could bring the business of the House to a standstill by simply refusing to vote and thereby denying the House the quorum needed under the Constitution to conduct business (a majority of the membership). Unless the majority could muster a quorum entirely of its own members, House rules provided no means of checking this practice, even when more than enough members to make up a quorum were physically present in the chamber.

In 1890 at the very beginning of his speakership, Reed orchestrated reforms that ended the disappearing quorum and other forms of minority obstructionism and streamlined the order of business in the House. The politics of the adoption of these reforms are discussed in more detail later in the chapter. The main point to be noted here is that Reed not only led the effort to enact these reforms but afterward was also a beneficiary of the new rules as leader of the majority party in the House. As Cooper and Brady (1981, 412) have pointed out, the rules in place after 1890 "gave the Speaker great power to control outcomes in the House." The speaker could influence legislation at the committee stage through controlling committee assignments and also influence which measures reached the floor for a vote through his position on the Rules Committee and the power to recognize (or not recognize) members seeking to make motions on the House floor. At the same time the rules provided the speaker and the majority party with a wide array of rewards and sanctions that could be brought to bear on individual members. The reach of party influence was extended even further through the practice of appointing top party lieutenants as chairs of the two most important money committees—Ways and Means and Appropriations—and to the majority positions on the Rules Committee. As George Rothwell Brown describes the resulting situation for members of the House during the Reed years:

> Under this system the Speaker's two lieutenants, supported by the other leading men of the organization, controlled every avenue to preferment through the federal purse, every dollar a Member might hope to see expended for an improvement in his district, a new post-office, a customs house, a river or harbor development, the dredging of a creek or the construction of a bridge, and every duty he might desire to see levied in a tariff bill for the support of encouragement of an industry in which his constituents were interested, and upon the securing of which his very political life might depend. (1922, 87)

The speakers of this era were thus in a very strong position to influence House outcomes by means of two of the causal mechanisms that can be employed by legislative leaders: the use of selective rewards and benefits to build majorities; and controlling the agenda or framing issues in ways that favor certain outcomes over others. From 1890 until the heavy-handed leadership of Speaker Joseph Cannon provoked a new wave of decentralizing reforms in 1910–1911 (see Jones 1968), the rules of the House placed the widest array of institutional resources in the hands of the speaker of any period in congressional history before or since, with the fewest institutional checks or controls.

A third important aspect of the political context was the congressional agenda and the effects of the different issues on the agenda on the unity of parties in Congress. At the time Reed was elected speaker in 1889, older issues tied to post–Civil War Reconstruction had been mostly eclipsed by economic issues and newer regional conflicts arising from the costs and benefits of advancing industrialization. These conflicts were heightened by downward movement in prices and severe economic

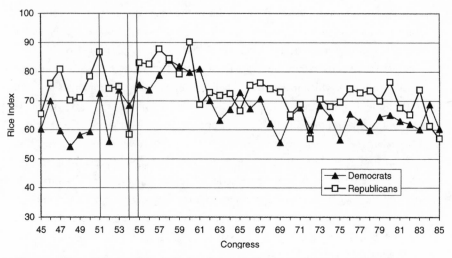

Figure 4.1. Party Cohesion (Rice Index), 45th to 85th Congresses (1877–1959). *Source:* Cooper 2006.

downturns in 1882–1885 and 1893–1897. One of the last measures tied to Reconstruction, a federal elections bill intended primarily to protect access to the ballot for southern blacks, was taken up during Reed's first Congress as speaker. Tariffs to protect American manufacturers from foreign competition, and currency policies that would either continue to tie the value of the currency to gold or incorporate silver as a basis for American money, were the main issues in the economic sphere. Tariff controversies became intertwined with debates about the economic effects of the persistent budgetary surpluses that accumulated during these years. Congress also maintained and repeatedly expanded a generous system of pensions for Union veterans and their dependents, which provided the major outlet for spending the federal revenues generated by the tariff and broadened the base of political support for the Republican high tariff policy (McMurry 1922; Skocpol 1992, 102–151; Bensel 2000, 457–509). After a long period in which domestic concerns dominated congressional politics, foreign policy issues reemerged at the end of the century with the outbreak of the Spanish-American War in 1898 and debates over annexation of Hawaii and territories ceded by Spain in the Caribbean and Pacific.

Figures 4.1 and 4.2 show two different measures of party unity for the period between 1877 and 1959 (Rice cohesion index and mean party unity scores). Congresses during which Reed served as speaker are indicated by vertical lines. Both measures show comparatively high party unity in House voting during the late nineteenth century—especially for Republicans—followed by a long decline in unity in party

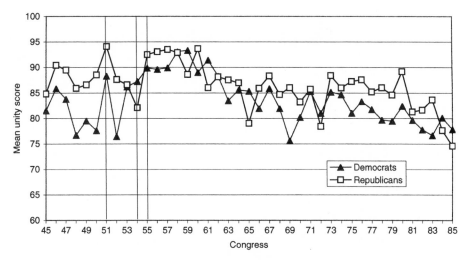

Figure 4.2. Mean Party Unity Scores, 45th to 85th Congresses (1877–1959). *Source:* Cooper 2006.

voting that begins after the turn of the century. Figure 4.3 shows that the period Reed served as speaker was also a period of comparatively high levels of ideological polarization between the parties (as measured by the distance between the parties' median first-dimension DW-NOMINATE scores). However, as we shall see, party unity displayed in votes on the House floor during this period cannot always be interpreted as evidence of underlying unity or homogeneity of policy views within parties. Given strong norms of party loyalty and the powerful array of sanctions controlled by the majority party leaders, high levels of unity in roll call voting sometimes masked serious divisions over policy.

Until the mid-1890s, both congressional parties experienced major divisions over economic issues, mostly along regional lines. The tariff and currency issues created major challenges for party leaders because of divergent economic and regional interests represented within each party's electoral coalition. Most Democrats were supportive of the inflationary prosilver currency policies and lower tariffs popular in their southern base, but Democratic leaders still had to contend with protectionist and hard-money wings. Congressional Republicans were more unified in support of protective tariffs but experienced sharp divisions on currency issues because of differing economic interests of eastern and western constituencies (Morgan 1969, 43–51, 165–170; Brady 1988, 53–55, 77; Bensel 2000, 19–100, 355–509). Recent research by Jenkins, Schickler, and Carson (2004) has shown that the divergence in the types of economic interests represented by House Republicans and Democrats was actu-

Figure 4.3. Ideological Polarization: Distance between Parties' Median NOMINATE Scores, 45th to 85th Congresses (1877–1959). *Source:* First-dimension DW-NOMINATE party medians, Poole 2006.

ally fairly modest when Reed first became speaker (1889–1891) and did not increase significantly until the mid-1890s—that is until after the Reed Rules had been adopted (see also Schickler 2001, 33–34, and Bensel 2000, 360–366).[5] Worth noting as well from a party government perspective is that partisan attachments for some voters during this period were rooted in local conflicts and ethnic-cultural loyalties and resentments as well as national issues (Silbey 1991; Kleppner 1979). Prior to the realigning elections of 1894–1896, both parties' coalitions were also threatened in some areas by the rise of agrarian discontent, with Republicans standing to lose support in the Midwest and West, and Democrats in the South.

A final important feature of the political context was the state of presidential-congressional relations. With only a few exceptions, congressional leaders neither received nor accepted much in the way of direction from the executive in acting on the issues that rose to the national agenda during these years. Leonard D. White (1958, 17–18) observes that "the curve of presidential power was upward" during the presidential administrations from Grant to McKinley, but two mutually reinforcing features of late nineteenth-century American politics limited the upper range of presidential influence. First, the constitutional system was generally understood to proscribe active presidential leadership of Congress, particularly of the type that seeks to mobilize public opinion in support of executive policy initiatives. Although the last three nineteenth-century presidents—Grover Cleveland, Benjamin Harrison, and William McKinley—on occasion spoke out publicly on policy matters before Congress, efforts by presidents to mobilize public pressure on Congress were still deemed to be of questionable legitimacy (Tulis 1987, 84–87). The main instruments available to the president to influence Congress during this period were patronage appointments and the veto.

Second, Lincoln's extraordinary conduct of the presidency notwithstanding, Republican Party doctrine reflected its Whig antecedents on the question of relations between president and Congress. As Ohio Republican senator John Sherman reaffirmed this doctrine in a letter he sent to newly elected President Benjamin Harrison in 1888: "The President should have no policy distinct from that of his party and that is better represented in Congress than in the executive" (quoted in Binkley 1962, 222; see also White 1958, 20–28). Grover Cleveland, the one Democrat to occupy the White House during this period, faced divided government six of the eight years he held office. Though he actively confronted Congress over private pension bills (in the process exercising a record 301 vetoes in his first term) and pushed Congress to act on tariff and currency measures, he declared early in his administration: "I did not come here to legislate" (Morgan 1969, 270). Only with the return of unified party control after 1896 and the reemergence of foreign policy issues on the national agenda did the presidency under William McKinley regularly work cooperatively with Congress in passing legislation. For the most part late nineteenth-century presidents reacted to congressional leaders rather than vice versa.

To conclude, Reed served as speaker of the House in a political context defined primarily by strong parties and weak presidents. Partisan competition for control of national institutions was intense. Both parties had to deal with serious factional divisions on the economic policy issues that dominated the agenda during this period, although the 1894–1896 elections created greater homogeneity in the congressional parties and began a period of Republican hegemony in national politics. Looking specifically at the House of Representatives, the office of speaker reached the peak of its institutional authority with the rules changes adopted in 1890 and increased in visibility as one of the top positions of party leadership in national politics.

Within this political setting, Reed rose quickly to a position of prominence in the House Republican Party because of his skill as a floor debater and parliamentarian. His Republican colleagues no doubt also soon came to enjoy his skill in skewering Democrats who tangled with him on the House floor. An 1884 *New York Times* profile identified Reed as one of the rising stars in the Republican Party, noting both his parliamentary acumen and that he "delights in sticking pins in windbags" ("The Ablest Republicans," February 9, 1884). "Reed's wit is enjoyable," observed Representative (and future president) William McKinley of Ohio, "especially if you do not happen to be the person to whom it is directed" (Robinson 1930, 390). During the years before he became speaker, Reed also demonstrated strong views on a number of public policy issues and took a serious interest in the rules and governance of the House. As with his predecessor in the speaker's chair, Henry Clay, at some point Reed's ambition also became focused on the White House. We now turn to Reed's goals and the question of whether these may help explain his actions as speaker.

## Thomas Reed's Goals as Speaker

Thomas Reed was first elected to the House in 1876, as the representative of the First District of Maine, which included his home city of Portland. Prior to entering Congress he had attended Bowdoin College, taught school, done a stint in the Union Navy, practiced law, and served in both houses of the state legislature and as attorney general of Maine.[6] Although Reed received his initial nomination for a congressional seat because of a conflict between the incumbent and the Maine Republican organization run by James G. Blaine and Senator Hannibal Hamlin, after he won election to the House he was never very closely allied with the Republican Party leaders in his home state.

Because of a surge in support in Maine in the late 1870s for an expansion of the currency, Reed experienced close races with "Greenback" candidates in 1878 and 1880. Throughout his national political career Reed was an opponent of schemes to expand the currency and a strong supporter of maintaining the gold standard. He risked reelection by his outspoken defense of that policy in these early campaigns. He also passed up an opportunity to be considered for a Senate seat in 1880 because of concerns that the Republican Party might lose his seat if he relinquished it. Looking ahead to the 1882 election, he wrote a friend, "I have a gauntlet to run at the polls . . . I have twice gone home with my scalp loose, and shall do so again." Reed expressed satisfaction with his service in the House—"I am getting to like the business"—but made clear he did not look forward to campaigning. "I hate to address my fellow citizens; but I shall never let them know short of political extinction" (TBR to Gifford, March 3, 1882).[7] As it turned out, despite his lack of enthusiasm for the campaign Reed won reelection comfortably in 1882, and he never again encountered a serious electoral challenge.[8] In a speech delivered to his constituents at the end of his political career, Reed expressed his gratitude for the support he had received at home over the years and for the wide leeway his constituents had allowed him to pursue his interests in Washington: "Other men have had to look after their districts, but my district has always looked after me . . . Office as a ribbon to stick in your coat is worth nobody's consideration. Office as opportunity is worth all consideration. That opportunity you have given me, untrammeled, in the fullest and amplest manner" (quoted in Robinson 1930, 380).

That Reed indeed devoted limited effort to looking after his district, or at least was less than enthusiastic about the local patronage politics that were the stock in trade of most of his fellow politicians during these years, is illustrated by his response to a request from a professor at Bowdoin College, who wrote asking his assistance in the appointment of a local Maine postmaster:

> Between you and me I have such a dread of these post office fights that I feel every time I hear of one in the air that I ought to call on every good friend for his sympathy and good wishes that I may be happily and safely delivered thereof. The man who gets appointed knows that it is owing to his own virtues and the man who don't, and his friends, are sure to doubt me being a statesman even if they acquit me of corrupt motives. But then I suppose even Professors have their troubles. In the shoes of all mankind there is sand and also unboiled peas. (TBR to Chapman, February 8, 1884)

When asked on another occasion by some constituents for help in obtaining some retired cannon for a soldiers' monument, he responded dismissively: "I am not in the old junk business" (Robinson 1930, 100). Reed's correspondence and diary entries from the years he served in the House show that he did look after local interests and weigh in on patronage appointments, but his evident lack of enthusiasm in dealing with these matters strongly suggests that these aspects of political life were of minimal interest.[9]

Where Reed did display real aptitude and enthusiasm was in forcefully articulating and defending party positions and dealing with parliamentary matters inside the House. During his first term he ably defended Republican interests as a member of a special committee charged with investigating voting fraud in the 1876 Hayes-Tilden presidential contest. By his second term he had established a reputation as a skilled parliamentarian and as one of the best debaters in his party. Reed spoke against proposals to weaken the gold standard, contributed to debates on a major revision in House rules in 1880, and clashed with Democratic speaker Samuel J. Randall over the use of the congressional appropriations process to enact substantive legislation. When Republicans gained control of the House at the beginning his third term (the Forty-seventh Congress, 1881–1883), Reed's name was placed in nomination for speaker. He received only eleven votes, but the eventual winner, Speaker J. Warren Keifer of Ohio, appointed him chair of the Judiciary Committee and later named him to fill an opening on the Rules Committee, which, as we have seen, was rising in importance in the House.

Five years into his House career, Reed privately expressed doubts that he would ever become speaker, partly because he was not on close terms with the influential Republican leader and former speaker from his home state, James G. Blaine, but also because he did not consider himself skilled at the dealmaking involved in winning speakership contests. "You are good to hope for the Speakership for me," he wrote to a friend in November 1881, "but I have no such expectations. I am too badly situated. Maine is hardly big enough for Blaine alone and his fortunes will be better subserved by somebody else. Then also the place is subject of much truck and dicker [i.e., wheeling and dealing] wherein I am not expert" (TBR to Gifford, November 7, 1881).

However, after Keifer proved to be an ineffective speaker, Reed became the leading figure in the House Republican minority over the next three Democrat-controlled Congresses (Forty-eighth to Fiftieth, 1883–1889), serving as a member of both the Rules and Ways and Means Committees. Over these years he further burnished his reputation as a parliamentary strategist and proponent of the main tenets of Republican Party orthodoxy. In May of 1888 Reed delivered a speech in opposition to Democratic efforts to reduce tariff duties that was considered one of the most effective statements to date of the Republican position on that issue and gained wide circulation in the election campaign of that year (McCall 1914, 161; Robinson 1930, 178–181). On the day after Reed's speech, the *Chicago Daily Tribune* reported, "No man has so fully aroused the enthusiasm of his party followers" ("End of the Tariff Talk," May 20, 1888). De Alva S. Alexander, who served in the House with Reed, summed up his style in House debate as follows: "His power as a floor leader was in his directness, his contentiousness, his ability to help men make up their minds, and to justify them in following him. He never scattered. His arguments bore directly on the issue before the House at the moment . . . No one yawned while he was on his feet" (1916, 131).

Reed's views on governance of the House evolved as he gained experience in the body. During his second term, when the reform on which Reed would later stake his speakership—elimination of the disappearing quorum—was proposed in the course of the 1880 debate on revision of House rules, Reed took the conventional position that the minority had the right to refuse to vote even if the result was to bring the action of the chamber to a halt for want of a quorum (*Congressional Record*, 46th Cong., 2nd sess., 578–579). In 1880 there was so little support for altering House rules to check this practice that the proposal was withdrawn without a vote.

But when the House took up an election reform measure later in the same session, Reed delivered a strong statement on the importance of party government and party responsibility as the only means for effective democratic governance. Typically for Reed, a principled argument for party government was joined to a sharp attack on the Democrats, whom Reed characterized as a party whose appeal was to less intelligent voters and whose main organizing principle was unthinking resistance to progress. "The best system," Reed pronounced as a second-term House member, "is to have one party govern and the other party watch; and on general principles I think it would be better for us to govern and for the Democrats to watch" (*Congressional Record,* 46th Cong., 2nd sess., 2661). And from his third term on, Reed became engaged in a concerted effort to establish a system of rules through which the majority party could control the business of the House and be held responsible by the voters for legislation it enacted or failed to enact.

Reed first began to act on his views on House party government in the early 1880s, when Republicans held a majority in the House (Forty-seventh Congress). From Reed's perspective a fundamental problem with the existing House rules was that legislation not "privileged" under the rules (a category reserved primarily for money bills) could be very difficult to bring before the chamber for debate and a vote, even when a majority favored doing so. Often, either a two-thirds vote to suspend the rules or unanimous consent would be required, leaving an effective veto in the hands of one-third of the chamber or even a single member. In March of 1882, Reed introduced a proposal from the Rules Committee to amend House rules to allow any bill to be brought up for debate with a simple majority vote at the request of the committee reporting the bill. Although Reed's party was in the majority, the Republicans exceeded a House quorum by only four, and it proved impossible to maintain a quorum to decide on the proposal (Robinson 1930, 85). Some years later Reed's irony was at work when he commented on the failure of his proposal: "We could never get a quorum here except for those non-partisan judicial performances which are called [contested] election cases" (*Congressional Record,* 48th Cong., 1st sess., 869). Reed again took up the cause of restricting minority obstruction of the business of the House two months later, this time while the House was actually considering a contested election case.

Reed's new initiative was an effort to rein in motions frequently used by the minority for purposes of delay. These were "privileged" motions under House rules so the speaker could not refuse to entertain them. If members of the majority were away from the House floor, motions offered by the minority to adjourn or recess could pass and bring the business of the House to a halt. Or even if the majority had sufficient strength present to defeat these motions, each would require a time-consuming roll call vote. In May 1882, after members of the Democratic minority had blocked action for seven days on a contested election case, Reed brought before the House another report from the Rules Committee, this time establishing strict limitations on motions to adjourn or recess during the consideration of election cases. When Democrat Samuel J. Randall (himself a former speaker) offered yet another motion to adjourn as the House debated the report from the Rules Committee, Reed upped the ante by raising a point of order that motions made for purposes of delay should also be restricted during consideration of changes in House rules. Speaker Keifer's favorable ruling on Reed's point of order was sustained by the Republican majority with the result that House rules now restricted these dilatory motions both when the body was considering contested election cases and when it was deciding on proposed rules changes (Robinson 1930, 85–90; Alexander 1916, 196–202).

Reed took the lead in supporting the speaker's ruling. "Whenever it is imposed upon Congress to accomplish a certain work," Reed argued, "it is the duty of the speaker, who represents the House . . . to carry out that rule of law or of the Constitution. It then becomes his duty to see that no factious opposition prevents the House from doing its duty. He must brush away all unlawful combinations to misuse the rules and must hold the House strictly to its work" (*Congressional Record,* 47th Cong., 1st sess., 4306). Some in the Democratic minority began to recognize the broader design that lay behind Reed's parliamentary moves. Stated Joseph Blackburn of Kentucky: "It is proposed to turn the American Congress, or this branch of it, without any limitation, without any restraint, over to be guided by a partisan majority" (*Congressional Record,* 47th Cong., 1st sess., 4313).

More evidence that Reed's goal was indeed to change the rules to allow the majority party to govern came at the end of the same Forty-seventh Congress. On February 24, 1883, Reed "startled the House" by introducing another Rules Committee report, which proposed to alter the rules temporarily to allow the House to send a tariff bill to a conference with the Senate by a simple majority vote (Alexander 1916, 202). Normally, a vote of two-thirds would have been required, but there was no prospect of getting such a vote because the Democratic minority (knowing they would be in the majority in the next session of Congress) was determined to block action by the Republicans on the tariff.

Reed's newest parliamentary innovation was heatedly denounced by the Democratic minority but also appears to have come close to the limits of what the Republican majority was prepared to support. A Republican caucus meeting two days earlier endorsed the goal of seeking changes in the Senate-passed tariff that was before the House but had broken up in disagreement when a proposal was offered to amend House rules temporarily to allow the fate of the measure to be decided by majority vote ("A Caucus on the Tariff," *New York Times,* February 23, 1883). On the day before Reed introduced just such a resolution in the House, the *New York Times* reported continued division and uncertainty within Republican ranks about the tariff bill as well as claims by Democratic leaders that the bill was dead ("The Tariff in the House," February 24, 1883).

When Reed did bring a report from the Rules Committee before the House to allow the decision on the tariff bill to be made by a simple majority vote, the resolution initially failed for lack of a quorum, with thirty-two members of his own Republican majority joining most of the Democrats in refusing to vote. The move succeeded the following day only when a group of third-party members "suddenly seized with a desire to go on record in opposition, swelled the vote to a quorum," allowing the measure to pass (Alexander 1916, 204; see also Robinson 1930, 91–96; "A Struggle in Congress," *New York Times,* February 27, 1883). After a conference with the Senate in which the bill was modified to address concerns of House Republicans, the compromise tariff measure passed both chambers and was signed into law. Reed's biographer William A. Robinson (1930, 96) observed that "as a matter of party strategy and parliamentary tactics its passage was one of the most daring maneuvers of Reed's entire career." Reed took a similar view. "I venture to say," he recorded in his diary, "that the Tariff Bill was passed by as brilliant a parliamentary manoeuvre as was ever made" (TBR Diary, 1883).[10]

Reed was back in the minority for the three Congresses that followed (Forty-eighth to Fiftieth). Under the leadership of speaker John G. Carlisle of Kentucky, the Democratic majority continued to experiment with using resolutions from the Rules Committee to expedite consideration of legislation (Roberts and Smith 2003) but dropped the rules changes restricting dilatory motions. While in the minority Reed continued his efforts to advance rules changes to allow the majority party to control the legislative process. In February 1884 at the beginning of the Forty-eighth Congress, he again offered his proposal to amend House rules to allow committees to secure consideration of legislation by a simple majority vote. When the House took no action, Reed offered the same proposal again in 1885 (Robinson 1930, 106–112, 120–121).[11] In January of 1889 he introduced yet another resolution to rein in minority obstructionism (in this case limiting the use of a "call" of the states and territories to block consideration of other legislation). "The rules of this House are not for the purpose of protecting the rights of the minority," he argued, "but to promote the orderly conduct of the business of the House. They can have no other object" (quoted in ibid., 188).

Reed's efforts to secure rules changes to clear the way for majority control even when his own party was in the minority are of particular significance for two reasons. First, these efforts demonstrate that his goal in seeking reforms in the rules was not simply short-term partisan advantage or advancing policies he or his party favored but to establish party government. Even Reed's most determined parliamentary adversary on the Democratic side, Samuel J. Randall, conceded as much.[12] Second, in explaining why he was willing to confer power on a Democratic as well as a Republican House majority, Reed offered his clearest statement of the principle of responsible party government that motivated his efforts:

> I know what [the proposed rules change] will result in; it will result in the consideration and passage of a great many bills I do not believe in. But the question is not what I believe in but what a majority of this House, elected by the people, may believe in. If you gentlemen on the other side [Democrats] are willing do any wrong things, I am willing to risk your punishment by your superiors, the people. And if my side was in the majority and was willing to do wrong, I should be willing to risk my punishment by my superiors. (*Congressional Record,* 48th Cong., 1st sess., 868)

The Democratic majority was unmoved and took no action on Reed's proposals. Partly as a consequence, the business of the House repeatedly came to a halt because of obstruction by the Republican minority as well as factions within Democratic ranks. Reed sometimes joined in these tactics and did not pass up opportunities during these years to taunt the members of the majority when the business of the House ground to a halt. "We offered you complete control of the House and you did not dare take it," he pointed out on one occasion (quoted in McCall 1914, 122). By the Fiftieth Congress (1887–1889) the result was unprecedented congestion in the legislative business of the House. Peters (1997, 62) notes that these years "were among the most frustrating ever experienced in the post–Civil War House." Accounts critical of the parliamentary stalemate during the late 1880s proliferated in the national press, including stories entitled "Slowly Doing Nothing" and "Legislative Lunacy" (Robinson 1930, 182–189). Especially among Republicans, "resentment was mounting over the manner in which existing rules and procedures obstructed majority will and limited the role of the federal government in national development" (Cooper and Young 1989, 93).

Looking back over Thomas Reed's House career up to the time he was elected speaker in 1889, a number of conclusions about Reed's personal interests and goals seem justified. First, Reed had established a consistent record as a strong supporter of certain policy positions—in particular the protective tariff and maintaining gold as the basis for the currency. Second, Reed had developed strong personal views on governance of the House. Over the better part of a decade he had attempted to advance a project of restructuring House rules to allow the majority party to govern, and had done so whether in the majority or the minority, and whether his own party was united in support of his proposals or not. As Dion (1997, 137) has commented, "Reed's dedication to eliminating obstruction went well beyond anything that would be required by practical politics."

If there was any question about Reed's intention to continue to advance that project, he published two essays in national magazines just before the speakership election in 1889, both of which called for reform of House rules. "Our government," he wrote in the first essay (1889a, 794–795), "is founded on the doctrine that if 100 citizens think one way and 101 think the other, the 101 are right. It is the old doctrine that the majority must govern . . . The rules, then, ought to be arranged so as to facilitate the action of the majority." In the second essay, Reed (1889b, 427–428) predicted: "Undoubtedly some effort will be made [when Congress reassembles] to change the rules so that business can be done and the scandals of the last Congress avoided . . . There will be an effort to establish new rules which will facilitate the public business—rules unlike those of the present House, which only delay and frustrate action."

Along with his policy views and longstanding interests in the rules and governance of the House, a third goal of Reed's also merits attention, which is his ambition to be president. Reed made a serious bid for the 1896 Republican presidential nomination and was bitterly disappointed when he lost decisively to his former House colleague, William McKinley of Ohio. Unlike Henry Clay, whose ambition for the presidency emerged early in his speakership and whose political moves were sometimes transparently influenced by that ambition (his decision to return to Congress and resume the speakership just before the 1824 presidential election, for example), it is harder to judge when Reed's ambition for higher office emerged and how it may have influenced his conduct as speaker.

In 1885, when he first received the nomination of the House Republican minority for the speakership, Reed was asked by a reporter about running for the presidency. He responded with a satirical account in which contempt for the presidential politics of his day seems very thinly veiled. Reed joked that he would buy off his main rival, promise pensions to every man, woman, and child who claimed to be entitled to one, espouse vague platitudes on the main issues, and "if I have omitted to declare my position on any interest representing a considerable number of votes, it shall be my earnest endeavor to amend or enlarge my platform accordingly" (McCall 1914, 142).

After meeting success in the highly publicized 1890 fight over reforming House rules, Reed became a very well-known national figure and was frequently mentioned in national political circles and the press as a likely presidential candidate. Reed quipped with reporters about his prospects in 1892 but sought the nomination in earnest in 1896. As the contest for the Republican nomination developed, Reed was seriously outmatched by his former House colleague William McKinley (and McKinley's talented and aggressive campaign manager, Marcus Hanna). For his part, Reed (now speaker) remained minimally accommodating to requests for local pork from members of the House, refused large campaign donations, brusquely turned away those who suggested their support would be conditioned on consideration for appointments, refused to reach out to key Republican senators or state party leaders he did not respect or who did not share his views on policy issues—and lost to McKinley at the Republican convention in St. Louis by a vote of 661½ to 84½ on the first ballot (Robinson 1930, 321–350; Dunn 1922, 162–165).

Writing to a friend just before the convention vote—when McKinley's nomination had become a foregone conclusion—Reed claimed that he had taken the same approach to the pursuit of both the speakership and the presidency:

> It does seem as if the Office of President was too powerful for any man to hold for himself alone, for his idea of justice and right. The Speakership has seemed the same and yet I have had the great good fortune to hold it without mortgage or even a shadow on the title. Was it not too much to expect the Presidency on the same terms? Nevertheless it was more than known that on no other terms would I have it . . . I do not dare to look into the future. I only know that there will never be any place worth my while wherein I shall not be free to do justice as the Higher Powers give me light. Office without opportunity is not worth consideration. (TBR to Gifford, June 14, 1896)

Reed actively supported McKinley's successful 1896 presidential campaign but was stung so hard by his failure to win the nomination that he seriously considered leaving politics (McCall 1914, 226; Robinson 1930, 348). Along with his determination to establish party government in the House and his strong views on the tariff and currency issues, this evidently strong ambition for the presidency has to be included among the goals that motivated Reed (at least up through 1896). But if Reed's ambition reached beyond the speakership, that ambition seems to have had limited effects on his behavior because of the strong view he held against making concessions on principle to hold office. As we have seen, some political theorists have viewed "fame"—a desire to secure a place in history—as an important motive for political leaders, especially those drawn to an office such as the presidency. If what ultimately motivated Reed was fame, he seems to have been determined to pursue it on his own terms.[13] We turn now to how these goals may have influenced Reed's leadership as speaker.

## The Politics of the Reed Speakership

Reed had received the nomination for speaker from the Republican minority in both the Forty-ninth (1885–1887) and Fiftieth (1887–1889) Congresses but still encountered a serious contest for the office after Republicans won a narrow House majority in the elections of 1888. The position of House Speaker was of even greater political importance than usual to Republicans because they had won the presidency and maintained control of the Senate and would finally be in a position to enact a legislative program after an extended period of divided government. Reed enlisted the help of close political allies—including Henry Cabot Lodge of Massachusetts and a rising New York politician named Theodore Roosevelt—to line up support among House Republicans but refused to engage in the practice of exchanging commitments on legislation or committee assignments for support (Robinson 1930, 187; Dunn 1922, 20–22).[14] Reed's ability as a parliamentary leader was widely acknowledged in his party, but his sharp tongue and sometimes aloof manner meant that other leading Republicans—especially William McKinley of Ohio—were better liked among the members. Reed's views in support of the gold standard and high tariffs were also well known and were more popular among eastern than western Republicans. When the House Republican caucus met on November 30, 1889, no candidate won a majority on the first ballot, but Reed received one more than a majority on the second, besting his chief rivals, McKinley and Joseph Cannon of Illinois.[15]

Reed's first Congress as speaker, the Fifty-first, convened in December of 1889. The most prominent issue dividing the parties in the preceding election had been the tariff. The new Republican president, Benjamin Harrison, had campaigned on his party's pledge to maintain tariff protection as well as a renewed commitment to prevent electoral fraud and secure voting rights, the latter position referring primarily to the suppression of the black vote in the South. The question of whether to use gold or some combination of gold and silver as the basis of the currency had not been a major campaign issue in the national election and continued to divide both parties along regional lines. Still, addressing this issue became unavoidable for Republicans in the Fifty-first Congress because of the depressed economic conditions and strong support for prosilver legislation in the West (Socolofsky and Spetter 1987, 10, 49–64; Williams 1978, 10–13).

Turning to Reed's leadership of the House as speaker, three cases provide the focus for the analysis. The first case, and because of its importance to the institutional development of Congress the one that will be examined most closely, is the adoption in 1890 of the Reed Rules, which finally secured the ability of a majority to control the business of the House. The second part of the analysis will consider Reed's leadership on the most important legislative measures that came before the House during the Fifty-first Congress (1889–1891)—the McKinley tariff, the Sherman Silver Purchase bill, and a federal elections act (the "Force" bill) intended to secure voting rights for southern blacks. Finally, the chapter will consider Reed's leadership on issues of foreign policy and acquisition of new territories during the second period he served as speaker (the Fifty-fourth and Fifty-fifth Congresses, 1895–1899) and how the politics of these issues influenced his decision in 1899 to leave the speakership and resign from Congress.

## The Reed Rules, 1890

The Fifty-first House convened in December 1889 with a very narrow Republican majority present, only three more than the quorum at the time of 165. Everyone knew that a major parliamentary battle over the House rules was coming early in the session. "This question of restoring movement to the House of Representatives is that which will confront the Fifty-first Congress at the threshold of its existence," Republican Henry Cabot Lodge of Massachusetts had written in September (1889, 294). Reed had also stated publicly that the Republican majority would enact new rules to allow the majority to govern. Now in control of both houses of Congress and the presidency, Republicans seemed likely to back their speaker in order to establish more efficient House procedures and clear the way for enactment of party measures, especially tariff legislation, which had been the main focus of the previous campaign (Peters 1997, 62; Forgette 1997, 385–388).

If Reed and his Republican allies viewed the new Congress as an opportunity to establish a record for their party and rein in the minority obstructionism that had recently made the House ungovernable, Democrats saw a raw partisan power grab in the offing. As Congress was convening, an article by Democrat Roger Q. Mills of Texas appeared in print charging that the true motivation behind Republican plans to limit the parliamentary rights of the minority was to make sure they could prevail in the seventeen contested House seats to be decided at the beginning of the session. "These vacated and added to the Republican side," Mills explained, "would give them a working majority large enough to place beyond the domain of doubt the passage of such laws as will materially aid in preserving and perpetuating their party ascendancy."[16] Mills left little doubt about how the Democrats would respond: "The great difficulty in the way is the quorum the Constitution requires to do business. *This rule cannot be changed,* and with a [Republican] margin of three over the constitutional requirement it will be very difficult, in so large a body, to keep in their seats the indispensable number" (1889, 669, emphasis mine). If Republicans changed the rules to restrict the parliamentary rights of the minority and then attempted to unseat Democrats in contested election cases, Mills predicted, Democrats would refuse to vote and deprive the House of a quorum.

In February 1890, just over two months after the Fifty-first Congress convened, the House adopted the reforms that became known as the Reed Rules. Approval of the new rules represented a dramatic completion to earlier developments that had begun to strengthen the hand of the speaker and the majority over the business of the House. Majority control was enhanced by changes in House rules in four areas: 1) parliamentary motions offered for purposes of delay would no longer be entertained by the speaker; 2) nonvoting members would be counted as present for purposes of establishing a quorum; 3) procedures for debating and amending bills in the Committee of the Whole were streamlined and the quorum for that procedure reduced to 100 members; and 4) changes were made in the order of business, including granting the speaker power to refer measures to committee without debate and formal recognition of the practice of using special rules from the Rules Committee to expedite consideration of bills when approved by a majority vote (see Alexander 1916, 206, 220–222; Robinson 1930, 223–231; Cooper and Young 1989, 94–96). Of these procedural reforms, the most controversial and most revolutionary was the change in the quorum rule, which involved overturning precedents that reached back to the 1830s.

The Reed Rules were adopted on February 14, 1890, by a vote of 161–144, with Republicans displaying perfect unanimity in voting to approve the new rules. In fact, all of the roll call votes taken on questions related to the House rules in the early weeks of the Fifty-first Congress witnessed the same high level of Republican unity (Schickler 2001, 281). But understanding of the politics of leadership in this and the other cases during the Reed speakership requires looking beyond roll call votes to trace closely the processes by which these decisions were made. Closer analysis of this case reveals followers who were initially divided over what reforms to enact and a leader not only determined to persuade them to go further but willing to risk his position to advance the more fundamental reforms he favored.

After the House met in December 1889, the initial weeks of the session were occupied mostly with routine matters and minor legislation. Committee assignments were announced, with McKinley of Ohio named chair of Ways and Means and Cannon of Illinois, chair of Appropriations. Together with Speaker Reed, these two would also constitute the majority of the House Rules Committee to which the existing rules of the House were referred for review. Speaker Reed announced that until the committee reported back a set of revised rules for approval, the House would operate under general parliamentary law. This arrangement gave the speaker wide discretion to control business on the House floor so long as his rulings were backed up by a majority of the House.[17]

As the wait for the introduction of new rules stretched into January 1890, there was considerable uncertainty about just how far Reed and the Republican majority might go in restructuring the rules—some reports in the press suggested only minor changes would be forthcoming, while others included speculation that a change in the quorum rule was under consideration. In early January the *Washington Post* reported that it was "rumored" that an initial draft of the new rules "gave the Speaker the power to declare a quorum in existence" but noted also that "Mr. Cannon is said to have expressed himself strongly against such arbitrary power" ("Reed Will Count Them," January 6, 1890; see also "The Republican Plan," *New York Times,* January 7, 1890). Another story hinted at dissension in the top ranks of the Republican leadership on this question, as the third Republican member of the Rules Committee, William McKinley, had refused to be interviewed on whether a new rule on establishing a quorum might be needed ("Changes in the Rules," *Washington Post,* December 20, 1889). During the last week in January, both parties caucused to discuss strategy for the impending clash over the rules. Journalists' reports of these caucuses provide key evidence about Reed's strategy in advancing reform of the House rules and about the amount of support that was actually present for reforms among his followers.[18]

The Democrats met first, on January 24. Former Democratic speaker John G. Carlisle of Kentucky, one of the two minority members on the Rules Committee, gave his Democratic colleagues a detailed explanation of the new rules that he said would be proposed when the Rules Committee finally reported back to the House. The changes discussed by Carlisle included limitations on the use of some specific motions and important alterations in the order of business in the House, but no mention was made of any proposed change in the rule for establishing a quorum. Discussion then turned to the strategy Republicans were now expected to employ: taking up the contested election cases before proposing new rules. "It was generally agreed," said the *Washington Post,* "that the intention of the Republicans was to unseat as many Democrats and seat as many Republicans as will give them a fair working majority and ensure a quorum in order to force through the rules." The Democratic strategy would be to fight the adoption of the "obnoxious sections" of the rules whenever these were presented and in the meantime to prevent resolution of any contested election cases before new rules were debated. Democrats would refuse to vote in the contested election cases, denying the House a quorum until the

Republicans agreed to take up the new rules first ("Democrats Up in Arms," January 25, 1890). What was not discussed in the Democrats' strategy session was the possibility there might be a change in the rule for establishing a quorum. Democrats had no idea that such a move was being seriously considered.[19]

Remarkably, Reed's Republican followers were in the same boat. All of the evidence we have leads to the conclusion that Reed neither sought his followers' approval for overturning the existing rule nor signaled to them beforehand the strategy he intended to pursue—using his power as presiding officer under "general parliamentary law" to assert a new interpretation of the rule while the two parties were locked in combat over a contested election case. House Republicans finally caucused on January 27, 1890, to discuss the new rules. Reed announced that the report containing the revised rules was not yet ready for submission to the House but still spent an hour going over with the Republican members the substance of what would be proposed. "The greatest harmony characterized the proceedings," according to the *Washington Post*. However the changes Reed discussed with his Republican colleagues appear to have been the same ones Carlisle had discussed with the Democrats two days earlier; there is no mention of any discussion in the Republican caucus of changing the rule for establishing a quorum ("New Code Is in Sight," January 28, 1890).

As the Democrats had anticipated, the Republican caucus agreed to take up the election cases first, then introduce the new rules for approval. After some of the contested seats were filled with Republicans, the discussion went, a more comfortable Republican majority would be in place to vote in new rules. But the argument reported to have been made in the Republican caucus in support of this strategy is remarkable given what was to follow. "It was felt by some of these members [who supported taking up the election cases first] that after a safe working majority had been secured under the operations of general parliamentary law, the rigidity of the new code might be relaxed with benefit, and the Republicans might thus be relieved of enacting a code which in time might, perhaps, be felt by themselves in its full severity" (ibid.). That is, after adding to their majority Republicans would be able to maintain control of the House with a *less* far-reaching reform of the rules than Speaker Reed had just discussed with the caucus.

The January 27 Republican caucus concluded with a long discussion of whether it would be possible to keep a quorum of their own members on the House floor in the event of the expected refusal of Democrats to vote on the election cases. The result was agreement that a "bare" quorum of 165 Republicans could be present to take up the first election case.[20] The *Washington Post* commented that the extended discussion of keeping a quorum of Republican members on the House floor "is regarded as an indication that the Speaker hardly contemplates adopting the radical course of counting as present members not voting to secure a quorum" (ibid.).

In keeping with the Republican plan, two days later on January 29, 1890, the first of the contested election cases, *Smith v. Jackson* from West Virginia, was called up for consideration by the House. The Democrats wasted no time in setting their own plan in motion. Charles Crisp of Georgia demanded a roll call vote on the motion to take up the case. The result was a vote of 162–3 with 163 members not voting (all but three Democrats refused to answer, those three voting no).[21] Two Democrats then withdrew their votes, leaving the total two votes short of the number required for a quorum (165). Under existing House precedents the only way to establish the presence of a quorum was to conduct another roll call. Ignoring calls from Democrats of "no quorum" Reed enraged the minority and surprised the other leaders and the rank and file of his own party by coolly reciting in alphabetical order the names of Democrats who had not voted and instructing the clerk to record them as present.[22]

As Reed continued methodically calling out names, bedlam broke out on the House floor. An exchange that ensued with Democrat James McCreary of Kentucky made it clear that Reed's sarcastic wit remained in good working order even as the House teetered on the brink of chaos. The exchange also demonstrated how untenable the position of the minority was if the question of the presence of a quorum was posed as one of common sense rather than House precedents:

> *The Speaker* (continuing). Mr. Holman, Mr. Lawler, Mr. Lee, Mr. McAdoo, Mr. Mc-
> Creary.
>
> *Mr. McCreary.* I deny your right, Mr. Speaker to count me as present, and I desire to
> read from the parliamentary law on that subject.
>
> *The Speaker.* The Chair is making a statement of fact that the gentleman from Ken-
> tucky is present. Does he deny it? [Laughter and applause on the Republican side.]
> (*Congressional Record*, 51st Cong., 1st sess., 949)

Over boisterous Democratic objections Speaker Reed continued until he had supplied the clerk with forty names. Then he rose and addressed the House. First, he noted the increased seriousness of the interference with House business that had been caused by the refusal of the minority to vote in recent years. Next he cited precedents from the New York and Tennessee legislatures in which Democratic presiding officers had ruled that all members present in the chamber whether voting or not could be counted to establish a quorum.[23] Then Reed addressed head-on the Democrats' claim that the existing rule was required by the Constitution. He observed that the Constitution provided that the House could compel the attendance of its members and that this provision would be "entirely nugatory" if members could be compelled to attend but then prevent the House from conducting business by refusing to vote. "The Chair thereupon rules that there is a quorum present within the meaning of the Constitution" (*Congressional Record,* 51st Cong., 1st sess., 951).

One of the most dramatic and raucous debates in the history of Congress followed. Reed remained improbably calm as insults rained down on him from the Democratic side of the House. The first two days were taken up with debate on the Democrats' appeal of the quorum ruling. Early in the debate Joe Cannon, who was known to have reservations about such a move, took to the floor to speak in support of the speaker's ruling. Although conceding that "under a supposed partisan necessity" he had also refused to vote in contested election cases when the Democrats were in the majority, Cannon offered a strong defense of Reed's new interpretation of the rule (*Congressional Record,* 51st Cong., 1st sess., 956–958). Reed must have breathed a sigh of relief when Cannon publicly fell into line. Potential Republican dissidents were now on notice that they would be running afoul not only of the speaker but of the hard-nosed chair of the Appropriations Committee if they failed to do the same. At the end of the second day it was clear that the first step in Reed's strategy had succeeded; Republicans voted unanimously to table the appeal and uphold the speaker's new interpretation of the quorum rule. On the following day, when Democrat William Springer of Illinois offered a motion to adjourn, Reed handed down another pathbreaking ruling establishing wide authority in the hands of the speaker to rule out of order motions made for purposes of delay. Republicans again voted unanimously to table the Democrats' appeal. The Republican majority was now firmly in control, and the House spent the next three days on the contested election case that had occasioned the clash over the quorum. On February 3, 1890, the contested West Virginia seat was awarded to Republican Charles B. Smith by a vote of 166–0, 162 not voting.

Reed's rulings had eliminated the most potent means of minority obstruction, but three months into the Fifty-first Congress the House was still operating without a formal set of rules. In a Republican caucus that met on February 5 and lasted six hours, Reed finally made the case to his followers for a much broader revision of House rules than the one that had been presented to the caucus only eight days earlier. Now the proposed rules package would codify both precedents he had just established through his floor rulings: the speaker could count nonvoting members present for establishing a quorum and would have broad authority to rule motions out of order if offered for purposes of delay. We lack any account of how Reed approached the task of persuading his followers to support the more extensive rules changes, but given the consistency of his public statements on the importance of party government and the need to enable the House to govern more effectively, these arguments were surely among the appeals he made. Reed or others who spoke must also have called attention to the Democrats' stated intention to obstruct legislation in areas such as the tariff that Republicans had pledged to enact in their recent electoral victory. Absent the more extensive rules changes, delivering on those pledges would be more difficult. In Schickler's (2001, 38) view, Reed's success in winning over his party reflected the multiple interests of Republicans to which he appealed: "Reed played a crucial role in fusing concerns about congressional capacity with the GOP's partisan interests, rallying Republicans around the idea . . . that the party's reputation would be enhanced by reforming House institutions."

Although Reed won the support of the caucus to proceed with the introduction of the new rules, the report we have of this discussion offers a striking contrast to the unanimity Republicans had displayed when backing the speaker's rulings in the heat of the contested election fight. "The Republicans of the House caucused for six hours yesterday, and there was a lengthy debate, which at times was exceedingly stormy," reported the *Washington Post.* "The fact is known that the debate became very exciting about 5 o'clock over the proposition regarding how a quorum should be established on the Journal." Still, Reed "carried the points on which he insisted" ("The Speaker's Victory," February 6, 1890) and after four days of debate Republicans voted unanimously in support of adopting the new rules on February 14, 1890.

Having traced through the actual process by which the Reed Rules were adopted, it is clear that Speaker Reed was not acting on behalf of a consensus among his followers on the most far-reaching reforms. As Arthur Wallace Dunn (1922, 23), a Washington journalist who was personally close to Reed, described what happened: "He kept the secret so closely guarded that no one knew of his intention to count a quorum until he actually did so. Had he taken the proposal before a Republican caucus, several members of his own party would have refused to follow him in such a radical step and he would have lacked the majority necessary to success, but he sprang his new system at a time when party feeling ran high over a contested elections case and the fierce denunciations of the Democrats solidified his own party."

Absent Reed's determination to establish control of the business of the House for the majority party, his strategic skill, and his willingness to risk repudiation by his followers to see his longstanding goal of responsible party government in the House realized, it is hard to imagine that the House rules would have undergone such a sweeping revision in 1890. Consider the most plausible counterfactual: that either of Reed's two main Republican rivals for the speakership in 1889, William

McKinley or Joseph Cannon, had been elected speaker. Neither had supported radical changes in House rules before Reed made his ruling on the quorum. Cannon himself later observed that McKinley "was too amiable, too sweet-tempered, too reluctant to encourage innovation. I am quite sure I was not. It required Reed to count a quorum" (Busbey 1927, 166–167). Another leading Republican of the Fifty-first Congress, Henry Cabot Lodge of Massachusetts (1911, 614), offered a similar assessment: "It was [Reed] who did it, he alone, and I know of no other man then in public life who could have done it."

While there appears to have been broad support among House Republicans for some limitations on the parliamentary rights of the minority and for rules changes to streamline the order of business in the House, Reed's strategy of delaying an up-or-down vote on new rules until after he had actually handed down rulings on the more radical changes during the intensely partisan battle over the contested seat was probably crucial to the enactment of the more sweeping rules reform. And it was not accidental that Reed forced these questions during a contested election case.

Reed once observed of contested election cases, "The House never divides on strictly partisan lines except when it is acting judicially" (Luce 1924, 203). Recall that in the early 1880s, when Republicans were last in the majority, Reed had sought an up-or-down vote on amendments to the rules that would have placed some modest limits on minority obstructionism. A quorum could never be assembled to vote on the proposal. However, a second effort by Reed to restrict obstruction by the minority during the Forty-seventh Congress—this time during consideration of a contested election case—succeeded. As in the Forty-seventh Congress, when the Republican majority in the Fifty-first was presented with the alternatives of altering House rules or losing control of the process for deciding whether they or the Democrats gained a seat in the House, Republicans chose the former. Also, Reed's strategy was probably even more effective in the Fifty-first Congress because the quorum ruling immediately drew intense interest and attention of the press throughout the country (Schickler 2001, 40). As a result, the decision for the Republicans in 1890 was not only about control of contested House seats in a narrowly divided House but also about their willingness to deliver a highly visible rebuke to the leader of their own party when the time came to vote on the Democrats' appeal of Reed's ruling the next day and when the vote on the final rules package occurred two weeks later. Reed's move is a classic example of a risk-tolerant leader getting out ahead of his followers and assembling a supportive majority after the fact.

Institutional innovations involving suppression of the parliamentary rights of minorities are more likely to get enacted when the majority party needs more help from the rules to maintain control over legislation (Binder 1997). Some scholars who have studied institutional changes in Congress have found that rules changes such as those involved in the Reed Rules are more likely to occur at times when narrow party majorities are present (Dion 1997; Gamm and Smith 2006; Smith and Gamm 2005). The vanishingly small Republican majority at the beginning of the Fifty-first Congress was clearly an important factor in the success of Reed's strategy. Had Republicans been able to muster a reliable quorum at the beginning of the session there would have been no occasion for Reed's ruling on that question and no justification for such an extensive reworking of the rules. But if the narrow margin of control by the majority party may have been a necessary condition for Reed's strategy to work, the testimony of other Republican leaders that no one else would have attempted the more far-reaching reforms even with such a slim majority shows that the narrow margin was not a *sufficient* condition for the rules changes to be adopted (see Dion 1997, 137). The more likely counterfactual without Reed in the chair is that there would have been a more incremental change in the rules of the House, possibly involving a negotiated settlement with some moderate members of the Democratic minority, who could have insisted on more limited rules changes as a condition of contributing to a quorum.[24]

Finally, in assessing the politics of the adoption of the rules reforms in 1890 we have Reed's own account of what happened, from an interview published three years later. When asked about the controversy over the rules, he replied:

> Oh, you mean what were my feelings when the uproar about the rules of the Fifty-first Congress was going on and while the question was in doubt? Well, I had no feeling except that of entire serenity, and the reason was simple. I knew just what I was going to do if the House did not sustain me . . . I should simply have left the Chair, resigning the Speakership, and left the House, resigning my seat in Congress. There were things that could be done, you know, outside of political life, and I had made up my mind that if political life consisted in sitting helplessly in the Speaker's chair, and seeing the majority powerless to pass legislation, I had had enough of it and was ready to step down and out. (Porter 1893, 375)

That Reed was uncertain of success, and that his claim of being willing to resign was not bluster, are confirmed by his biographer Samuel McCall (1914, 167), who verified that Reed had made arrangements in advance of the quorum ruling to resign and take a position with a New York law firm if the ruling was not supported by his party. In reforming the rules, Reed was advancing an objective he believed was right in principle and would be beneficial to his party, but he was *not* acting to advance an objective about which his followers were in agreement or responding to their homogeneous preferences. Through leadership in the form of persuasion and skillful use of the speaker's powers to control how the reforms were framed and decided, he succeeded in shaping his followers' preferences on changing the rules.

Partly as a consequence of the new rules the legislative productivity of the House increased dramatically during the first session of the Fifty-first Congress, with new tariff, currency, and electoral measures being among the most important bills passed by the Republican majority. But for their efforts the newly productive Republican majority was rewarded with a massive defeat at the polls in 1890 (more on this below). Democrats regained control of the House for the Fifty-second and Fifty-third Congresses (1891–1895) and elected one of the most vocal critics of the Reed Rules, Charles F. Crisp of Georgia, to the speakership. Crisp oversaw adoption of a modified version of the rules of the Democratic Fiftieth Congress, which dropped the new restrictions on dilatory motions and the new quorum rule. From the very beginning of the period of Democratic control, Reed made it clear that he would press the majority to reinstate the rules of the Fifty-first Congress. "We are willing to be governed by the same rules we adopted for their government," he explained as the Democrat-controlled Fifty-second Congress convened in 1891. "If they try to shirk responsibility for it they must answer" ("The Rules Committee," *Washington Post*, December 17, 1891).

Reed proved true to his word and while in the minority continued to press for the adoption of rules to give the majority control and responsibility for the business of the House. In August of 1893 as the Fifty-third Congress met in a special session, Reed and Crisp clashed on the House floor during one of the many encounters that ensued over the rules. Reed tweaked the Democrats for contradicting themselves by adopting some of the new rules from the Fifty-first Congress but refusing to give the majority full control. Crisp took offense at Reed's speech and took the unusual step of leaving the speaker's chair to respond before the House. Referring dismissively to his predecessor's concern with the rules as "a hobby with him," Speaker Crisp countered that Reed's ruling on the quorum was unconstitutional, "high-handed," and had been repudiated by the country when Republicans were voted out of power in 1890 (*Congressional Record*, 53rd Cong., 1st sess., 1034–1035). Reed was hardly chastened, responding, "Perhaps I am unreasonable to expect the Democratic party to catch up with us entirely within four years" and predicting that "as their education progresses" Democrats would eventually embrace all of the rules of the Fifty-first Congress. Regarding Crisp's reference to his personal concern with the rules of the House, Reed offered a spirited defense of the project in which he had been engaged for over a decade: "It is true, it is my hobby; and I had it long before the 51st Congress. Many a time and oft have I addressed this House upon that subject. And is this hobby unworthy? The method of doing business on the part of the greatest legislative body on the face of the earth—is that an unworthy thing for any man to be interested in?" (*Congressional Record*, 53rd Cong., 1st sess., 1036).

With Reed as leader, the Republican minority turned the tables on the Democrats and repeatedly brought the business of the House to a halt by refusing to vote when the ranks of the majority were thin or offering motions requiring roll call after roll call. Joseph Cannon recalled: "We filibustered without shame, Reed leading us" (Busbey 1927, 183). With a narrower majority during the Fifty-third Congress, Speaker Crisp and the Democrats were forced by Reed's tactics to choose between losing control of the floor or reintroducing rules to check minority obstructionism. Finally, in April 1894 the Democratic majority chose to enact its own quorum-counting rule. Reed led his party in voting with the Democrats again to establish majority control of the House (Binder 1997, 129–131; Schickler 2001, 46–50; Robinson 1930, 294–304). Four years after Reed had initiated it, the battle over establishing majority party control of the House was over.

Following the fight over the Reed Rules to its conclusion has taken us into the interlude of Democratic control of the House between the first (1889–1891) and second (1895–1899) periods of Reed's speakership. Now we return to an examination of Reed's leadership on the most important issues that came before Congress during his first Congress as speaker and then to the issues that ultimately led to his resignation after he returned to the chair in 1895.

## Legislative Success, Electoral Disaster: Reed's Leadership of the Fifty-first Congress

After the Reed Rules were adopted in February 1890, the Republican majority in the House of Representatives was in a strong position to legislate. The GOP had won not only the House but the presidency and a Senate majority. Republicans would have their first real opportunity to govern in years and many in the party felt it could consolidate and strengthen its majority status by enacting timely legislation on the tariff, election reform, and other issues (Williams 1978, 1–14). But in reality, "the Republicans enjoyed less than a clear mandate to govern" (Peters 1997, 62).[25] President Benjamin Harrison had actually won fewer popular votes than the defeated Democrat Grover Cleveland, and Republican majorities in both the House and Senate were extremely narrow. Nonetheless, Reed was strongly committed personally to the issues on which Republicans had campaigned, and he aggressively wielded the newly enhanced powers of the speakership to ensure that House Republicans delivered on the issues of the tariff and federal election legislation and also to contain an insurgency on the currency issue that threatened to undermine the gold standard that he and most, but not all, Republicans favored.

Reed's approach to leadership on major legislation involved three main elements. First, after the legislation was drafted by a committee he would convene the Republican members in a party caucus and attempt to forge agreement on a party position. On some issues persuading the caucus to follow his lead was a significant challenge because of divisions in the party. Next, a special order or "rule" for debating the bill would be written by the Republican members of the Rules Committee—himself, Joe Cannon, and William McKinley. As one of the Democrats who served on the Rules Committee during the Fifty-first Congress, Benton McMillin of Tennessee recalled, the three Republicans would meet first, then Reed would send for the Democrats, give them a copy of the rule and announce: "Well, Mac, Joe and McKinley and I have decided to perpetrate the following outrage, of which we all desire you to have due notice" (quoted in Robinson 1930, 238). Once approved by a majority vote of the House, the rule set the terms for debating and voting on the bill, which Reed rigorously enforced from the chair. Finally, unlike Henry Clay, Reed rarely addressed the House on policy matters. But he remained an important influence in the legislative process by actively wielding the speaker's parliamentary authority to keep legislation on track when its passage was threatened either by the minority or by dissidents in his own party.

*The McKinley Tariff.* Of the three major legislative issues on which Speaker Reed took the lead in the Fifty-first Congress, Republicans were most unified on the tariff. As Richard Bensel's (2000) masterful analysis of late nineteenth-century American political and economic development has shown, the tariff was of central importance to the Republican Party during these years because tariff protection benefited manufacturing interests in the party's northeastern base, attracted some support in western states (after it had been extended to products produced in the West such as raw wool), and provided the revenue needed to fund a massive program of pensions for Union war veterans, who were a significant proportion of voters in the North and West. Party lines on the issue had been sharpened by Democratic president Cleveland's call for tariff reduction in 1888 and the national campaign just ended had been fought primarily on this issue.[26] Still, securing passage of a tariff bill in a House with such a narrow majority presented a significant challenge because of the large number of competing economic interests that had to be reconciled in deciding where to set tariff levels and because support for the legislation among Republicans from western states—which received fewer benefits from tariff protection—was uncertain (Schickler 2001, 35–36).

When House Republicans met in caucus on May 5, 1890, Reed pushed for giving the tariff bill top priority over other matters vying for action by the House, and for limiting time for debate by setting an early date for a final vote. The new rules, Reed told the caucus, would prevent Democrats from "doing a wholesale obstruction business, but they still managed to keep up a steady retail obstruction trade" ("Debate on M'Kinley's Tariff Bill," *Chicago Daily Tribune*, May 6, 1890). Chairman William McKinley and other members of the Ways and Means Committee who had drafted the bill argued for more time for debate than the single week Reed had proposed. Agreement was reached to allow twelve days for debate and set May 21 as the date for a final vote ("Adjournment in Sight," *Washington Post*, May 6, 1890). The main opposition to the plan came from western Republicans, who offered a motion to take up legislation to fund river and harbor projects first. The 90–19 vote to reject that motion showed, as the *Chicago Tribune* reported, that "the weight of sentiment was decidedly in favor of pushing the tariff measure" ("Debate on M'Kinley's Tariff Bill").

In keeping with the plan voted by the Republican caucus, the McKinley tariff bill passed the House on May 21. Passage of the bill never seems to have been in doubt, but Reed and the Republican leadership were challenged repeatedly by a coalition of western Republicans and Democrats seeking lower tariffs on specific products. For example, when it appeared that one of these amendments might pass (to lower duties on glass lamp chimneys, an essential item in rural households where there was no gaslight), allies of the Republican leadership had to go "scouting for loyal Republicans to crush the revolt" ("The Committee Scared," *Washington Post*, May 17, 1890). Even with Reed making an appearance on the House floor to shore up party discipline, the Republican leadership won by only four votes. On a number of other amendments to lower duties, the leadership lost ("Only a Pair of Bolters," *Washington Post*, May 22, 1890).

When the appointed time came to end debate and take a final vote, there was much complaining among Democrats but also among Republicans who still had amendments to offer. Republican Benjamin Butterworth of Ohio objected: "We have not had time to secure a consensus of opinion even on this side of the House to enable us to legislate intelligently for the country" ("Afraid to Vote Their Honest Sentiments," *Chicago Daily Tribune*, May 22, 1890). But the majority had previously approved the rule to cut off debate on May 21 and Reed kept to that schedule, even though the House had managed to debate only about one-third of the actual text of the bill and hundreds of amendments were pending (see comments by Democrat Benton McMillin [TN], *Congressional Record*, 51st Cong., 1st sess., 5095). The bill passed 164–142, with all but two Republicans voting yes. In the Senate, the tariff bill became entangled with the two issues on which the House would legislate next, the currency and federal election law. A final version of the tariff finally came back before the House in late September 1890, passing 151–81, again with only two Republicans breaking party ranks. Reed had delivered on the top Republican legislative priority.

*The Sherman Silver Purchase Act.* The divide between eastern and western Republicans that had been evident on the tariff bill presented a greater challenge to Speaker Reed's leadership on the currency legislation that became known as the Sherman Silver Purchase Act. Along with Reed, most Republicans from the wealthier and more industrialized northeast favored maintaining the gold standard. Having gold as the primary basis of the currency imparted stability to the value of the dollar, which was important to financial interests centered in the East and considered essential by many Republicans for encouraging investment and maintaining confidence in the American economy. Representatives from the less wealthy and developed areas in the West and South favored greater use of silver as a monetary standard to cause inflation of the currency and ease burdens of debtors and hard-pressed farmers. Increased use of silver would also provide a boost to silver-mining interests in the West (Bensel 2000, 355–456). By the Fifty-first Congress recent admissions of new states in the West had created a Senate majority of western Republicans and Democrats who favored the increased use of silver as a monetary standard. Many Democrats and a sizable faction of the Republicans in the House favored increased use of silver as well.

Republican leaders in Congress recognized that some action would have to be taken to satisfy demands from the western members of their party for relief for distressed farmers and mining interests in their region. Western Republican senators had made it clear that they were willing to hold up the tariff and other party measures until this occurred (Wellborn 1928, 471–472). Legislation was introduced in both the Senate and the House that would provide for the Treasury to purchase most of the silver production of the country but still would not fundamentally alter the gold standard. When House Republicans caucused on June 4, 1890, prosilver members led by Lewis Payson of Illinois attacked the proposal for falling short of the changes they were seeking in the currency. William McKinley proposed further changes in the bill to make it more palatable to the western members, while "Reed spoke earnestly against further concessions to the silver advocates" (Robinson 1930, 243). Reed's position prevailed and only minor modifications in the legislation were agreed to by the caucus. But a resolution binding Republicans to support the bill on the House floor failed to win a majority, and the caucus broke up leaving Republicans uncertain about whether they were bound to support the bill as a party measure ("Caucusing on Silver," *Washington Post,* June 5, 1890).

"The Speaker," the *Chicago Daily Tribune* reported, "believing that a majority of Republican members agree with him as to what kind of bill should be passed and that it should be passed without delay, took the chances of being supported by the full party vote and called a meeting of the Committee on Rules for the next morning and threw the bill into the House at once" ("The Silver Bill Passed," August 8, 1890). The rule introduced by the Rules Committee provided that the House take up the bill immediately and allowed no amendments other than those approved by the chair of the Coinage, Weights and Measures Committee, an ally of the speaker. Ten Republicans voted against the motion to adopt the rule, which passed by only a single vote.[27] Despite repeated calls during the debate for party unity, fifteen Republican dissidents voted in favor of a Democratic motion to recommit the bill to committee and add a provision for the free coinage of silver—a motion that would have carried had thirteen progold Democrats not voted to reject the motion. The bill passed the House on June 7 on a 135–119 vote, which reportedly would have been much closer except for the fact that Republican members who opposed the bill decided to vote with their party in the expectation that a measure more favorable to silver would emerge from the Senate ("They Fell into Line," *Washington Post,* June 8, 1890).

That expectation proved correct when the Senate voted on June 17 for an amendment to the silver purchase legislation to mandate the free coinage of silver, then sent the bill back to the House. Not confident of winning an up-or-down vote to reject the free coinage amendment, Reed kept the amended bill from being considered by the full House by quietly referring it to the Coinage Committee. Democrats strongly objected to the speaker's move, and on June 19 a coalition of Democrats and dissident Republicans won a series of procedural votes that signaled disapproval of the speaker's action. Reed now came very close to losing control of the legislation. As the speaker and others in the Republican leadership issued appeals for party discipline and scrambled to get loyal Republicans to the chamber, the next day was consumed with a protracted parliamentary fight over a motion to bring the free coinage measure before the House for an up-or-down vote. On July 21 Reed finally made a formal ruling that the measure would remain in committee, adding the wry observation that "gentlemen may have noticed within the last few days that parliamentary law does not seem to be an exact science" (Robinson 1930, 24). By a 144–117 vote, Reed's ruling was sustained, but eleven Republicans still voted to overturn it.

When the House finally held a direct vote on whether to agree to a free coinage amendment on June 25, the Senate measure was rejected, 134–152. But no fewer than twenty-three Republicans broke with the speaker to vote yes. Once again, Reed and the Republican leadership were able to maintain control of the process and advance a bill without the free coinage of silver because an equal number of Democrats crossed over and voted against the measure. The bill was sent to conference with the Senate, and under the leadership of Senator John Sherman of Ohio a compromise measure dropping the free coinage provision but adding some others attractive to the western members was assembled and approved by both houses in July 1890.

Although the silver purchase legislation favored by Speaker Reed had failed to win the endorsement of a majority of House Republicans when they met in caucus, enough Republicans supported the speaker on each critical vote that he succeeded in his objective of enacting a currency measure that would conciliate western Republicans but not fundamentally alter the gold standard. But note that Reed took the lead on the currency issue in the face of a significant factional split in the party and uncertainty about how much support he actually had among his followers. He blocked further compromise with prosilver interests in the Republican caucus, proposed a restrictive rule for debating the bill, and wielded the parliamentary authority of the speakership to prevent a vote on the free coinage amendment adopted in the Senate until he was confident he could defeat it. Here again we find the speaker actively using his position to influence the outcome on an issue on which his followers' preferences were not homogeneous. Ironically, given Reed's emphasis on party government, his efforts in leading the House to this outcome might well have failed had there not been a group of House Democrats who favored the same outcome as he did on the currency question.

*The "Force" Bill.* The third major legislative issue that came before the House in the first session of the Fifty-first Congress, a new federal election law, also evoked serious divisions among Reed's followers. President Benjamin Harrison had called for new legislation to protect the voting rights of southern blacks during the campaign and also in his first message to Congress. The issue had strong advocates among congressional Republicans, especially Senator George Frisbie Hoar and Representative Henry Cabot Lodge, both of Massachusetts.[28] New election legislation was introduced in both the House and Senate in 1890. These bills provided for federal election supervisors to be appointed by federal courts at the request of local citizens and for creation of new federal boards to review contested election cases. The federal supervisors would have broad powers to oversee federal elections and the boards would be empowered to decide contested elections for the House of Representatives subject to review by federal courts. Seeking to evoke memories of the use of federal forces to enforce reconstruction measures, opponents of the legislation termed it a "force" bill and the name stuck.

Given the strong attachment of most black voters to the Republican Party in the post–Civil War years, it was well understood that the practical effect of the legislation would be to increase the numbers of Republican House members elected from the South. Democrats denounced the legislation and declared their determination to block it at all costs. Even though their party's prospects for maintaining control of the House would presumably be furthered by the election of more representatives from the South, Republicans were far from unified in support of the legislation. Westerners wanted action on currency legislation to take precedence over protection of voting rights for southern blacks. Some northern businessmen, including some closely allied with Republicans, had also come out in opposition to the legislation, considering it likely to destabilize the South and threaten their trade and investment in the region. Others argued that Republicans had succeeded in winning unified control of government by focusing on economic issues and should avoid divisive issues of race and section (Hirshson 1962, 216–226; Welch 1965, 524–525; Upchurch 2004, 1–13, 167–185).

Before becoming speaker, Reed had not been among the leading proponents of legislation to protect the political rights of southern blacks. But in a speech given in Pittsburgh in April 1890 and two articles written for the *North American Review* that same year he came out strongly in favor of new legislation to protect voting rights in federal elections in the South and assign initial responsibility for settling contested election cases to the federal courts (Hirshson 1962, 210–211; Robinson 1930, 236–237; Reed 1890b, 1890c). Reed's justification for the new measures combined principle and party interest. Voting rights in federal elections, he argued, were a matter "of simple justice" to which all citizens were entitled (Reed 1890b, 671). In addition, he argued that voting fraud in the South had become so extensive that it threatened to undermine party government by unfairly tipping the balance in national elections toward the Democratic Party:

> The object of assembling the Congress together is to declare the will of the people of the United States. How can that will be declared if there be more than twenty men returned to the House [in fraudulent southern elections] who never were elected . . . ? Still less will the will of the people be declared if those twenty men shift the control of the House from one party to the other. All free countries are governed by parties. There can never be government any other way. If then, fraud changes the very principles on which a country be governed, how can it be justified? (ibid., 673)[29]

Reed dismissed southern objections about federal interference in local affairs as irrelevant: "All we ask is that in national matters the majority of the voters in this country shall rule" (ibid., 680).

In the early summer of 1890 Republicans held a series of three caucus meetings to discuss the federal election legislation, which had been drafted by a committee chaired by Representative Lodge. At the third caucus meeting on June 16 "a heated discussion" resulted when the final version of the legislation was presented ("Denounced in Caucus," *Washington Post,* June 17, 1890). The opponents of the bill included one of Reed's top lieutenants; Joe Cannon "led the attack on the bill" (McCall 1914, 176). The strongest objections came from Representative Hamilton Ewart of western North Carolina, who denounced the measure as a force bill that would provoke violence in the South and cause renewed sectional conflict, harming rather than advancing Republican prospects in future elections. When a resolution was offered to make the bill a caucus measure Republicans would be bound to support on the House floor, the resolution passed, "though many Northern Republicans joined their Southern brethren in voting against it" ("Denounced in Caucus"). We have no record of the actual caucus vote, but Reed's biographer Samuel McCall (1914, 175) reports that the caucus resolution "was finally adopted by a majority of one." When given an opportunity to register their preferences on making the election bill a party measure, if McCall's account is accurate, Reed's followers were split almost exactly down the middle. In any case, the evidence suggests House Republicans' preferences were far from homogeneous in support of this measure.

Reed again proceeded to orchestrate swift action by the House. The week after the caucus vote a rule from the Rules Committee was reported that limited debate to five days and set July 2 as the date for a final vote. Cannon again acted the part of the good party soldier, falling back into line after the caucus vote and introducing the resolution from the Rules Committee. An extremely contentious debate on the resolution followed in which Democrats decried the elections bill and vehemently objected to the restrictions the majority had proposed on time for debating and amending the bill. Accusations of voting fraud were exchanged between members of the two parties and the debate became so heated that a brawl threatened to break out on the House floor. As the *Chicago Daily Tribune* reported the scene, "Mr. Cannon of Illinois and Mr. O'Neal of Indiana [a Democrat] engaged in a colloquy somewhat personal in its nature, and this added so much to the already existing disorder that the Sergeant-at-Arms came forward with his mace of office and restored order" ("Disorder in the House," June 26, 1890). Then, in striking contrast to the divisive caucus meeting a week earlier in which only the barest majority had reportedly endorsed the legislation, Republicans closed ranks and only one Republican member was found voting against the rule ("Defeats Free Coinage: Row over Federal Elections," *Washington Post,* June 26, 1890).

The bill was taken up immediately, and as debate proceeded Republican unity held.[30] Republican absences resulted in a close vote on a hostile amendment to mandate federal supervision of elections in every congressional district, but again only a single Republican broke ranks and voted against the leadership. The day before the final vote, the bill's floor manager, Henry Cabot Lodge, expressed confidence in the outcome: "Even those in our party who disagreed with us have come to our support, and if the absentees return tomorrow morning as we have directed them to do, there will be no trouble" ("Lodge Confident," *Washington Post*, July 2, 1890). Democrats managed to delay the final vote by eight hours by offering motion after motion and demanding that the entire bill be read aloud, but Lodge's prediction proved correct when the bill was adopted on July 2 by a 155–149 margin. Only two Republicans voted nay. As it turned out, all the efforts of Reed and Lodge to get the federal elections bill through the House went for naught, as the bill ultimately died in the Senate as a result of the intense hostility of Democrats and the indifference, if not outright opposition, of western and some northern Republicans (Wellborn 1928; Hirshson 1962, 226–235; Welch 1965; Mayer 1964, 229–230; Valelly 2007; Upchurch 2004, 124–166).[31]

The morning after the election bill passed the House, the *Washington Post* ran an editorial titled "Tom Reed as Leader" (July 3, 1890). While observing that some of the legislation Reed had advanced could be criticized, the *Post* gave Reed a strong review for his performance as speaker: "On the organization of the House, on the tariff bill, on the silver legislation, and in the federal election contest, he has gone to the front when the chances for defeat seemed more than equal, and each instance he has witnessed Republican success on the floor." The voters in the country, however, when given a chance to pass on the work of the Fifty-first Congress in the fall of 1890 delivered a resounding negative. Democrats would control over 70 percent of the seats in the Fifty-second Congress, while Republicans would have their numbers reduced from 179 to 86. Reed would later comment that the Republicans in the Fifty-second Congress "behaved with gentleness and modesty, partly because they were very good men and partly because there were very few of them" (Robinson 1930, 273).

The expectations of Reed and others in his party that a strong legislative record would secure Republican success at the polls therefore proved far from correct. Most accounts at the time, including Reed's (1895) own, attributed the loss primarily to the McKinley tariff, which became law just before the 1890 election and resulted in higher costs for many items. Others have argued that the increased spending approved by the Republicans (the Fifty-first became known as the "billion dollar Congress"), the adoption of the Reed Rules and the House action on the force bill contributed to an image of Republicans as the party of centralization and big government, to which the country reacted negatively (Williams 1978, 46–47).

## *Dissuading a Cyclone: War and Territorial Expansion*

Four years later, with Democrats discredited by a deepening economic crisis, Reed returned to the speaker's chair after Republicans were swept back into control of the House by a 254–93 margin in the 1894 elections. Democratic President Grover Cleveland was in the White House and Democrats controlled the Senate, so with divided party control little major legislation was enacted over the next two years (the Fifty-fourth Congress, 1895–1897). Instead, foreign policy issues, especially the question of intervention in the Cuban fight for independence from Spain, began to occupy the attention of the country. Reed was now a national political figure and competed unsuccessfully with his former House colleague William McKinley for the Republican presidential nomination in 1896. After McKinley's decisive defeat of William Jennings Bryan in the 1896 election, a Republican victory in the Senate, and the reelection of a Republican majority in the House, unified party government returned in 1897. During the Fifty-fifth Congress (1897–1899), Reed's final period as speaker, he steered another major tariff bill to quick passage in an early special session but spent the remainder of the Congress occupied primarily with foreign policy issues (Robinson 1930, 351–354).

As the Fifty-fifth Congress progressed, Reed's views on foreign policy found him increasingly at odds with his own party. Partly as a result of sensationalist coverage in the American press of the harsh Spanish response to the Cuban insurrection, sentiment had been building in the country for American intervention. Reed was strongly opposed to intervention and kept resolutions supportive of American involvement in the conflict off the House floor during the early months of the Fifty-fifth Congress (Robinson 1930, 356–357). President McKinley initially opposed American intervention, although his position would change. Even before McKinley bowed to public support for war with Spain, Reed was already at odds with the Republican president and others in his party over the question of annexing the Hawaiian Islands as a means of extending American influence in the Pacific. There were many adherents within the Republican Party to the view that gaining control over new territories in the Pacific and the Caribbean would advance American economic and security interests. But Reed thought it unwise and unnecessary. Although he avoided publicly opposing McKinley, the title of an essay he published in April 1897 made Reed's position clear: "Empire Can Wait" (1897).

The public reaction to the explosion in February 1898 of the American battleship *Maine* in Havana harbor and the 260 American deaths that resulted altered the political balance on both issues and made Reed's position in the House extremely difficult. At the request of President McKinley, in March 1898 Republican Appropriations Committee chair Joseph Cannon introduced a $50 million bill to fund preparations for war with Spain. Knowing of Reed's opposition to American intervention, Cannon took charge of the measure and did not consult with the speaker before introducing the bill on the House floor (Busbey 1927, 186–192). The appropriation passed on March 9, 1898, by a vote of 313–0. In April, Speaker Reed had little choice but to acquiesce to overwhelming Republican support for resolutions authorizing use of military force, and taking the country to war against Spain. The joint resolution authorizing war passed by a vote of 311-6 on April 19, with Republicans voting in support by a margin of 176–5. After the vote Reed told one of the few Republicans who had voted in opposition, "I envy you the luxury of your vote. I was where I could not do it" (McCall 1914, 234). The United States went to war with Spain in May, and by August American forces had not only defeated the Spanish in Cuba but also in the Pacific and had occupied the Spanish-controlled Philippine Islands.

While the war was underway, a resolution for the annexation of Hawaii was introduced in both houses of Congress, now couched as a measure in support of the war in the Pacific. For almost a month Reed blocked action on the matter in the Rules Committee. The *Washington Post* reports that Reed's refusal to allow the resolution to come to a vote was causing "a tremendous amount of dissatisfaction" among Republicans ("To Let Hawaii Alone," May 26, 1898). Republican supporters of annexation circulated a petition calling for the caucus to meet and take a vote to bring the measure to the floor. Reed finally relented in June and announced the resolution to annex Hawaii would be taken up. On June 15 the resolution passed by a 209–91 vote, with Reed's Republican followers supporting annexation 177–3 (Robinson 1930, 364–365). Reed was ill the day of the vote but had it announced to the House he would have voted no had he had been present (*Congressional Record,* 55th Cong., 2nd sess., 6019).

The final major foreign policy issue decided by the Fifty-fifth Congress involved funding to implement the Treaty of Paris, which ended the Spanish-American War. Under the terms of the treaty, Puerto Rico and Guam were ceded to the United States, and the United States would take control of the Philippines for a payment of $20 million to Spain. On February 20, 1899, the House voted 218–33 to approve the $20 million appropriation to acquire the Philippines, with Republicans voting 143–0 in support. Reed's opposition to the move was well known, but he neither spoke out against the measure nor attempted to organize opposition to it in the House. The last session of the Fifty-fifth Congress ended in March 1899. Reed had been reelected in the fall of 1898, and Republicans would again control the House in the next Congress.

Before the new Congress assembled, Reed announced in April 1899 that he was resigning from the House and would join a New York law firm. He never offered a public explanation for his resignation. Reed had never accumulated much personal wealth, and the most widely credited explanation at the time was, as the *Washington Post* put it: "Mr. Reed has left public life because he wants to make some money" ("Speaker Reed Retires," April 2, 1899). Reed's biographers, on the other hand, characterize the decision as one driven more by opposition to the expansionist foreign policy that had been embraced by his party (McCall 1914, 237–238; Robinson 1930, 378–379). While Reed may well have been concerned about the state of his personal finances, a letter written to a friend a few months after he resigned supports the conclusion that his resignation involved a decision that he could not continue to lead a party bent on pursuing policies with which he disagreed.

"You are quite right in thinking that the money was not the cause of the change," Reed wrote, "though that same is quite soothing in small families." Instead, he explained,

> The position became quite unendurable . . . I was in a doubly impossible place. If I was again chosen Speaker, and nobody could have prevented that, my position would have been a representative's one and would not represent me. If I went on the floor I knew all too well how few followers I could muster until the people changed their minds. Hence it seemed to me that the best good of the cause would be subserved by doing what no man had yet done, resign a great place and people would then ask why and find out not by my direct outpourings but by their inferences. When a man finds a thing out for himself he's prouder of it than if it were told him by Shakespeare. Had I stayed I must have been as Speaker always in a false position aiding and organizing things in which I did not believe or using power against those who gave it to me . . . It was a hard thing to change the whole course of life. Yet I have not thus far felt any repentance. (TBR to Gifford, October 18, 1899)

Reed's determination to hold office on his own terms, and his strong belief in party government, came into irreconcilable conflict when his party embraced policies with which he strongly disagreed. He claims to have thought his resignation might give rise to a renewed debate on the wisdom of taking on an empire, but this seems a half-hearted hope. Reed had been in politics long enough to understand the intensity of the new political forces that were driving his party in the opposite direction. After being urged by a fellow antiexpansionist Republican to try to persuade House Republicans against supporting war with Spain, Reed had responded: "He might as well ask me to stand out in the middle of a Kansas waste and dissuade a cyclone" (quoted in Binkley 1962, 232).

# Conclusion

A closer look at the leadership politics of the Reed speakership makes clear that there is more to the story than a leader using his position to carry out the views of a homogeneous group of party followers. First, at the time Reed made the crucial parliamentary rulings that cleared the way for the major revision in House rules in 1890, his Republican followers were in agreement that some rules changes were needed to allow the majority greater control over the legislative process. But the evidence is clear that they were not in agreement regarding the most far-reaching changes that Reed ultimately persuaded them to adopt. Second, when we trace through the actual politics of the three major legislative measures adopted by the House during the initial Congress Reed served as speaker (the Fifty-first) we find—the high levels of party unity in floor votes notwithstanding—that House Republicans' policy views involved serious divisions on two of them (the currency and election reform measures).

Thus, on closer inspection neither Reed's success in reforming House rules in 1890 nor his activist legislative leadership during the Fifty-first Congress resemble the causal process implied for cases of strong or assertive legislative leadership by the contextual leadership theories. However, Reed's willingness to assert the powers of the speakership—even risk his position as leader—to advance his strongly held goal of establishing responsible party government in the House even though his followers were not in agreement in support of such sweeping institutional reforms is consistent with the conditional agency framework. The same is true of his willingness to use the powers of the office to advance legislative initiatives on issues he thought were important and in the interests of the Republican Party, even when his followers were deeply split on those measures.

Reed's minimal influence in foreign policy issues during the second period he served as speaker serves as clear evidence of the limits of leadership in the House. Even with the enhanced authority conferred on the speakership by the new rules, with the exception of delaying action by the House for a short time, Reed had almost no influence in the congressional decisions to go to war with Spain, to annex Hawaii, or to acquire the Philippines. On these issues Reed's followers clearly did have homogeneous preferences. But Reed's strong policy views in opposition to these decisions made him unwilling to act as the agent of his homogeneous followers. Faced with the prospect of remaining leader and having to advance policies with which he disagreed on principle, he resigned.

The foreign policy issues provide support for contextual theory in demonstrating the limits congressional institutions place on all leaders. That a leader as skilled and strong willed as Reed, operating under rules that conferred tremendous advantages on the speaker, would have so little ability to influence these outcomes offers a clear and powerful demonstration of the constraints congressional leaders face when their followers' preferences are fixed and homogeneous, as House Republicans' views on foreign policy issues had become by the spring of 1898. Reed's leadership became almost totally inconsequential for the outcomes on these issues. But as was the case with Reed's behavior in the Fifty-first Congress on issues on which his followers were divided, we gain little insight into his behavior and ultimate resignation if we try to explain it in terms of the goal said to motivate leaders in the contextual theories—office-holding ambition. If that was Reed's motivation he would have made the same calculation his former House colleague, President William McKinley, did and led his party in the direction it now wanted to go. Instead he resigned. The conditional agency framework helps explain why Reed led the House assertively during the Fifty-first Congress, even when his followers were divided, and why he refused to do so in the Fifty-fifth Congress, when they were unified: leaders' goals vary and leaders' goals matter for how leaders behave.

In assessing Reed as a congressional leader, his place in history is secure because of the importance of the Reed Rules in finally establishing majority control of the House of Representatives. However, Reed's leadership is open to criticism for his inattentiveness to deliberation and representation in the legislature. Legislative leadership involves ensuring that representation and deliberation occur, as well as orchestrating action. What Peters (1997, 68) has written of Reed's view of House rules, is applicable to his approach to legislation as well: "Speaker Reed seems to have been more concerned with efficient government than with deliberative government." The Republican electoral disaster in 1890 suggests that Reed's pursuit of party government sometimes came at the cost of representing the full range of interests present within the majority party, to say nothing of the minority. As Schickler (2001, 43) has argued: "Given Republicans' internal divisions, they may have been better off with a less ambitious legislative agenda and with more modest rules reforms that still allowed minorities within the party to block highly controversial bills." As it turns out, the Republican electoral debacle of 1890 proved to be only a temporary setback. With Grover Cleveland's election to the presidency two years later Democrats came to power just as one of the worst economic crises in American history was breaking, and shortly thereafter Republicans would establish dominance of American politics that would continue for decades.

Whatever Reed's limitations as a deliberative leader, he established and passed on to his successors a new set of rules that conferred a tremendous amount of power on the speaker of the House. Ironically, it was the individual who judged Reed not to be a politician, Joseph Cannon (speaker from 1903 to 1911), whose heavy-handed leadership provoked a revolt against those rules, with the result that assertive leadership from the speaker's chair would be more difficult in the future. Not until the twentieth century was coming to a close would another speaker be compared to Reed and Cannon.

# CHAPTER FIVE

# Newt Gingrich

## The Transformative Leader as Speaker

There were enormous differences between the role of the previous Democratic Speakers and my role. They had been essentially legislative leaders ... I, on the other hand was essentially a political leader ... seeking to do nothing less than reshape the federal government along with the political culture of the nation.

—*Newt Gingrich, 1998*

"On Capitol Hill, like it or not, the 1990s was Newt Gingrich's decade" (Mayhew 2000, ix). David Mayhew's assessment of the extraordinary character of the Gingrich speakership is shared by many observers of Congress. "With his assumption of the Speaker's chair in January 1995," Steven Smith and Gerald Gamm (2005, 196) write, "Newt Gingrich quickly, and deservedly, became known as the most assertive Speaker since Cannon." Richard F. Fenno, Jr. (1997, 34) describes the organizational changes Gingrich orchestrated on becoming speaker as "the largest concentration of majority party power in a century." As C. Lawrence Evans and Walter J. Oleszek (1997, 117) assess the consequences of this concentration of power: "Newt Gingrich [played] a pivotal policymaking role in the mid-1990s House. Indeed the scope and impact of his Speakership have been without precedent in recent congressional history."

While most observers agree that the House of Representatives witnessed some important changes during the Gingrich speakership, not all agree that Newt Gingrich's leadership was a significant factor in these developments or that Gingrich's leadership resulted in significant longer-term changes in public policy. For example, one leading proponent of the contextual perspective on leadership, Barbara Sinclair, contends that Gingrich's assertive leadership was primarily a reflection of the high level of unity among his Republican followers and thus "can be explained by changes in context that altered members' expectations" (1999, 432). From this perspective Gingrich is best understood as a "faithful agent" of his Republican followers who acted to advance their shared goals, rather than a leader whose actions were consequential for shaping those goals or whose own goals and actions had an independent impact on organizational and policy outcomes in Congress. In this view Gingrich and his fellow Republican leaders may have been influential in shaping outcomes, "but they did so as agents of a cohesive majority party" (ibid., 437). Regarding the impact of the Gingrich speakership on public policy, some have also contended that it produced more sound and fury than real policy change. Longtime Congress-watchers Thomas E. Mann and Norman J. Ornstein (2006, 103), for example, conclude: "Bicameralism and separation of powers rendered the parliamentary style leadership of Gingrich and followership of House Republicans ineffectual, at least with respect to writing new law."

This chapter examines leadership politics in the House during the tumultuous four years Gingrich served as speaker, from 1995 through 1998. As in the previous chapters on Speakers Clay and Reed, this chapter will look closely at the politics of the leader-follower relationship in a series of organizational and policy decisions during the Gingrich speakership. These decisions are examined with the objective of determining whether Gingrich provided assertive leadership only in political situations where he knew his followers were mostly in agreement on the course of action to be taken—the causal process posited by the contextual leadership theories—or whether Gingrich also used the powers of his leadership position assertively to advance his own strongly held goals in political situations where his followers' preferences were ill defined, uncertain, or seriously divided—as proposed by the conditional agency perspective.

Before taking up the politics of the Gingrich speakership, the chapter will first provide a brief overview of developments in House leadership politics over the period from the era of Thomas Reed and the strong speakers of the late nineteenth and early twentieth centuries through the speakers who preceded Gingrich in the chair. Next, the political context surrounding the Republican takeover of the House in 1994 and the two Congresses (104th and 105th) during which Gingrich served as speaker will be discussed. The third section of the chapter will consider Gingrich's goals as speaker, focusing on his extraordinarily ambitious goal of using the House speakership as a position from which to effect a major transformation of American politics. Gingrich's efforts before he became speaker to organize Republicans to win the House majority and to define an agenda for a new Republican majority are also examined. Then, a series of major institutional and policy initiatives during the Gingrich speakership will be considered with the objective of tracing through the politics of these issues to explore whether the causal processes we find in leadership politics in these cases are more consistent with contextual theory or the conditional agency framework. The decisions on which this section of the chapter focuses are: organizational changes that increased the control of the party leadership over the standing committees in the House; action on the "Contract with America" program during the 104th Congress, including passage of major welfare reform legislation and tax cuts; and the initiative begun during the 104th Congress to balance the federal budget within seven years. The chapter will conclude with an examination of the causes of Gingrich's departure from the speakership in 1998.

In some of these cases, we will see that Gingrich's leadership fits the pattern of leadership politics emphasized by the contextual theories. Speaker Gingrich indeed wielded the powers of the speakership aggressively to advance legislation on which his Republican followers were in agreement. We will also see, however, that Gingrich was engaged in a self-conscious effort to shape his followers' preferences on how the House should be organized under the new Republican majority as well as their preferences about the policy goals that should be advanced within that structure. Gingrich's goals also inclined him to take risks and lead aggressively on some important issues on which his followers' preferences were uncertain or seriously divided. As with all congressional leaders, Gingrich encountered limits to leadership and ultimately was forced out by his Republican followers after only four years in the speaker's chair. The evidence in the chapter will show, however, that even in the short span of four years, Gingrich's leadership was consequential both for the institutional development of the House and for the direction of national policy.

During the 104th Congress (1995–1996), Newt Gingrich was often compared to the powerful speakers of the late nineteenth and early twentieth centuries. Although there were a number of influential speakers in the intervening years, until the Gingrich speakership none had succeeded in establishing this level of centralized authority in the House. Thus to understand the significance of the Gingrich speakership, it will be helpful first to review the main lines of development of the speakership from the era of strong speakers that began in the late nineteenth century up through the period immediately preceding the Republican takeover of the House in the mid-1990s.

## From Reed to Gingrich: The Decline and Resurgence of the Speakership

The rules changes secured by Thomas Reed in the 1890s established majority control over the business of the House and continue to provide the majoritarian procedural framework for House politics to this day (Cox and McCubbins 2005, chap. 4).

But the highly centralized party government regime Reed established during that same decade, involving the fusion of a powerful speakership and the agenda control power that had been developed by the House Rules Committee, survived barely a decade after Reed's departure from the House in 1899. After a brief period of caucus government, standing committees began to emerge as independent power centers in the House. Over the next two decades a pattern often characterized as "committee government" developed in which speakers shared power with committee chairs, who held their positions by virtue of seniority. This "textbook Congress" persisted through the 1970s, when a new wave of institutional reforms originating primarily within the House Democratic Party again transformed the institutional structure of the House. During the 1970s reform era, changes were adopted that simultaneously reduced the autonomy of standing committees and strengthened the prerogatives of parties and party leaders. As the parties in the House became more ideologically unified in the years that followed, Democratic speakers began to take greater advantage of the new rules to assert active leadership in both organizational and policy matters. Thus when Republicans recaptured the House majority in the mid-1990s, the power exercised by the House speaker had been on an ascending arc.

The centralized party government regime Speaker Thomas Reed consolidated in the 1890s came apart within just over a decade because of "excessive leadership" by Republican speaker Joseph Cannon (Jones 1968, 619). Cannon (speaker from 1903 to 1911) was a "regular" Republican whose interpretation of party government did not include accommodating the views of the growing number of reform-oriented Republicans who were being elected to the House from the Midwest and West. Through his power over committee appointments, recognition of members on the floor, and chairmanship of the Rules Committee, Cannon actively enforced his understanding of party regularity in both organizational and legislative decisions.[1] While Cannon's highly centralized leadership initially won support for advancing Republican Party goals and reasserting the influence of the House in national policymaking (Schickler 2001, 68–71), his sometimes heavy-handed treatment of both insurgent Republicans and the Democratic minority, and resistance to reform legislation, ultimately produced a 1910 revolt in which a coalition of Democrats and insurgent Republicans adopted rules changes that included removal of the speaker from the Rules Committee and taking away his power to appoint its other members (Binder 1997, 133–140; Jones 1968; Swenson 1982; Schickler 2001, 71–83). The dismantling of the institutional foundations of speaker-led party government was completed in 1911, when a new Democratic majority stripped the speakership of the power to appoint members of standing committees.

Over the decades that followed, these rules changes interacted with party divisions to produce a more decentralized House and a new type of speakership. Described by Ronald M. Peters (1997, 92–145) as the "feudal speakership," its defining feature was a flatter institutional hierarchy in which the speaker and majority party leaders shared power with standing committee chairs who held their positions based on seniority and were thus more independent of party leaders' control. Within the institutional context that had begun to emerge by the 1920s, speakers began to act "less as the commanders of a stable party majority and more as brokers trying to assemble particular majorities behind particular bills" and "less as directors of the organizational units [in the House] and more as bargainers for their support" (Cooper and Brady 1981, 417).

Still, two speakers during these years stand out as highly influential leaders—Republican Nicholas Longworth (1925–1931) and Democrat Sam Rayburn (1940–1947, 1949–1953, 1955–1961). Longworth was the strongest speaker of the transitional period that followed the era of strong party government. He reestablished more centralized control over legislation, in part by forging cooperative relationships with leaders of the Democratic minority (Bacon 1998; Peters 1997, 103–106; Schickler 2001, 122–126). But his authority was still circumscribed by the fact that "he had to accommodate the entrenched seniority system" (Schickler 2001, 122).[2] Sam Rayburn of Texas was the longest-serving and most influential speaker of the era of strong standing committees that was firmly in place by the late 1930s. Rayburn held the office from 1940 to 1961, with the exception of the two brief periods of Republican control in the late 1940s (Eightieth Congress) and mid-1950s (Eighty-third Congress). Rayburn developed an effective style of leadership for a political context that was defined by a persistent split between southern and northern factions within his Democratic majority, strong seniority-based committees (often chaired by southern conservatives), and the frequent appearance of a conservative majority coalition of southern Democrats and Republicans (Polsby 2004, 7–20). As Cooper and Brady (1981, 420) describe this mode of leadership, its main features were "personal friendship and loyalty, permissiveness, restrained partisanship and conflict resolution, informality, and risk avoidance."

While Rayburn was influential in establishing an effective mode of leadership for the era of committee government (Peters 1997, 140–142), his approach to the office—and his longevity in holding it—reflect a different orientation from that of Gingrich and the other leaders who provide the focus of this study. In particular, Rayburn was normally a risk-averse leader who preferred working within the existing institutional order in the House rather than challenging it. As Cooper and Brady (1981, 420) explain: "Rayburn was cautious. His inclination was to avoid battles when the outcome was uncertain. To be sure, in instances when a Democratic president and/or large numbers of his fellow partisans pressed him, he would usually wage some sort of fight. But . . . his clear and decided preference was to refuse battle, to wait until prospects for victory were favorable . . . Similarly, he shied away from challenging any of the key facets of decentralized power in the House, despite their restrictive impact. His inclination was to work with what existed and endure, rather than seek basic change."[3]

The first sign of new political forces that would bring basic change to leadership politics in the House came toward the end of the Rayburn speakership, when the 1958 election tipped the factional balance in the House Democratic majority toward northern liberals. As their strength within the majority caucus grew, Democratic liberals began to seek institutional reforms to shift power in the House away from standing committees toward the party organization in which they could exercise greater influence. As one of his final acts as speaker, Rayburn reluctantly—but successfully—secured reforms in 1961 to reduce the autonomy of the House Rules Committee and clear the way for enactment of legislation favored by the liberal wing of the party (Peters 1997, 137–138; Polsby 2004, 20–35).

Support for reform continued to build over the next decade, with the 1970s becoming one of the most intensive periods of institutional change in congressional history. Congressional reforms adopted in the 1970s were multifaceted.[4] Some (for example, reforms in the congressional budget process) were intended to reassert congressional authority vis-à-vis the executive. Others were addressed to demands for greater openness in the legislative process and more opportunities for junior members of both parties to participate in legislative decisionmaking. Still others were driven by policy goals of liberal Democrats who viewed strengthening party leaders and weakening committee chairs as means of advancing those goals. The most important of these policy-oriented reforms in the House included: transferring the committee assignment power to a new party committee (called the Steering and Policy Committee) whose membership included the speaker, top party leaders, and a substantial contingent of members appointed by the speaker; giving the speaker the power to appoint the chair and members of the Rules Committee (subject to approval by the Democratic caucus); and giving the speaker greater control over referral of legislation to committees and authority to set time limits for committee action. House Democrats also enacted rules changes to ensure responsibility of committee chairs to the party majority, and although seniority remained the normal path to committee leadership positions, the Democratic caucus proved willing to override seniority in selecting chairs in a number of cases where senior members were deemed unresponsive.

Initially, the reforms that decentralized power and opened up the legislative process to broader participation had the greatest impact, causing some to conclude that reforms had fragmented authority to the point where Congress had become overly responsive to narrow interests and lacked capacity to enact coherent legislation (Davidson 1981; Sheppard 1985). However, with the development of greater unity in the House Democratic majority and sharp competition with conservative Republican president Ronald Reagan for control of policymaking, the effects of reforms strengthening the majority party leadership became more visible during the 1980s (Rohde 1991; Sinclair 1995). Speaker Thomas P. "Tip" O'Neill (1977–1987) at times wielded the enhanced powers of the speakership to advance Democratic legislative objectives but still remained hesitant to challenge the authority of senior committee chairs or to assert his authority over organizational matters such as committee assignments (Rohde 1991, 71–81).

With the elevation of a leader willing to wield the new powers of the speakership aggressively, Jim Wright of Texas, the full potential for stronger leadership under the new rules was revealed. "While the scope of the party leadership's activities had been expanding under Speaker O'Neill, the aggressive use of these powers was sharply increased when James Wright succeeded to the position" (ibid., 168). During the 100th Congress, Wright (speaker 1987–1989) became actively involved in committee assignment decisions, took the lead in defining a Democratic legislative program (including a controversial tax increase), pressured committee chairs to move legislation or face removal, and aggressively used the speaker's authority over House procedures to advance measures he considered important priorities (Palazzolo 1992, chap. 6; Rohde 1991, 105–119; Sinclair 1995, chap. 4). Wright's speakership represented the highest point of the postreform reemergence of the office. But it also proved short-lived. In the midst of controversy over alleged violations of House ethics rules, Wright's political support among House Democrats quickly eroded, leading to his resignation in 1989 (Barry 1989). His successor, Thomas Foley of Washington, would prove to be a more restrained and conventional speaker (Rohde 1991, 184–189) and also the final Democratic speaker after forty years of unbroken Democratic control of the House.

## The Political Context of the Gingrich Speakership

The unexpected Republican sweep in the 1994 election transformed the political context for leadership in the House. This outcome, in which Republicans won majorities in both the House and Senate, was described by electoral analyst Gary Jacobson (1996, 203) as a "political earthquake" that would "send aftershocks rumbling through national politics for years to come." The forty-year period of unbroken Democratic control of the House that preceded the election was unprecedented in American history (Fenno 1997, 1).[5] The 1994 elections not only produced the first Republican majority in decades but for many House Republicans provided striking confirmation of the effectiveness of Newt Gingrich as a leader and party strategist.

Gingrich had worked tirelessly for over a decade to focus Republican Party strategy on the goal of winning the House majority, had conceived the idea of the "Contract with America" as the platform on which Republicans would run, and was credited by many for being personally responsible for the victory. This was especially true of the large group of junior members in the Republican majority. Of the 230 Republicans elected to the 104th Congress, almost one-third were freshmen and a majority (53 percent) had served four years or less in the House.[6] Although confidence in the new speaker would be shaken by later events, as a result of the 1994 electoral victory Gingrich held "an extraordinarily high level of trust among junior Republicans in the early part of the 104th Congress" (Rohde 2000, 6; see also Sinclair 1999, 443–444, 441–442). It is also important to note that the Republican majorities in the House produced by the elections of 1994 and 1996 were narrow (thirteen and ten seats, respectively). These majorities were smaller than any during the preceding forty-year run of Democratic control (Jacobson 1996, 222–223) and meant that Speaker Gingrich and the House Republican leadership had very little margin for error either in assembling majorities to pass legislation or to lose seats and still maintain majority status in each election cycle after 1994.

An important feature of the political context in the House during the Gingrich speakership that represented continuity from the preceding period of Democratic control was high levels of partisanship. The outcome of the 1994 election continued and even advanced a pattern of ideological homogeneity within and polarization between the parties in the House. A disproportionate number of Democrats who lost in 1994 were from the moderate and conservative wing of the party, while the seventy-three freshman Republicans were mostly conservatives who pulled their party further rightward (Aldrich and Rohde 1997–98, 562–564; Gimpel 1996, 12–14; Sinclair 1999, 434). As shown in figures 5.1, 5.2, and 5.3, roll call voting in the House during the 104th and 105th Congresses witnessed the highest levels of partisan cohesion and unity within the Republican majority in decades as well as a sharp increase in ideological polarization between the parties. The vertical lines in the figures indicate the Congresses of the Gingrich speakership. From the perspective of contextual theories, these are conditions that should produce assertive party leadership, and scholars taking this approach have cited these conditions as the primary cause of Gingrich's activism as speaker (Aldrich and Rohde 1997–98; Rohde 2000; Sinclair 1999).

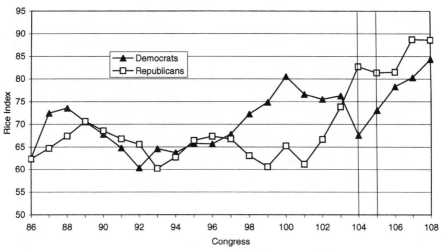

Figure 5.1. Party Cohesion (Rice Index), 86th to 108th Congresses (1959–2005).
*Source:* Cooper 2006.

Two additional important features of the political context during the Gingrich speakership were divided party government resulting from election outcomes in 1994 and 1996, and the issues on the congressional agenda. The importance of divided party government was obscured initially by the unusually weak political position in which Democratic president Bill Clinton found himself after Republicans took control of Congress in 1995 (see Jones 1999, 82–87, 115–134). But Clinton's politically adept use of the prerogatives of the presidency brought this factor very much back into play by the end of the first year of the Gingrich speakership. Finally, while there was some continuity in the agenda from the first two years of the Clinton administration in terms of attention to budget deficits and issues such as welfare reform, the House Republicans' "Contract with America" and initiative to balance the federal budget within seven years dramatically shifted the congressional agenda in a more conservative direction focused on tax cuts, restraining federal spending, and devolution of authority to the states. Although Clinton recovered politically after 1995 and succeeded in using the power of the presidency to move the agenda somewhat more to the center, by the final year of the Gingrich speakership the president would again be on the defensive as a result of scandal and the initiation of impeachment proceedings in the House.

In the early period of the 104th Congress, the political context offered unusually favorable conditions for assertive leadership by Speaker Gingrich. As we have seen, his Republican majority demonstrated high levels of unity in voting throughout the

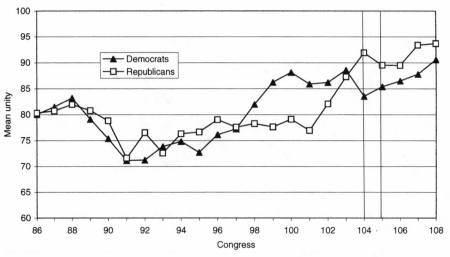

Figure 5.2. Mean Party Unity Scores, 86th to 108th Congresses (1959–2005). *Source:* Cooper 2006.

period Gingrich served as speaker. These contextual conditions, while important for understanding leadership politics during these years, do not provide a complete explanation for the leadership politics of the Gingrich speakership. First, through his efforts at building a Republican majority and defining an agenda for the new Republican House, Gingrich himself played a major role in shaping both his followers' preferences and legislative outcomes once Republicans took control. Second, while aggregate voting measures indeed show high levels of party unity among House Republicans throughout the 104th and 105th Congresses, closer analysis reveals that Republican members' preferences were initially ill defined or even seriously divided on a number of major initiatives Gingrich advanced as speaker. To understand the politics of the Gingrich speakership we need to begin by looking at Gingrich's goals as speaker and why these might have inclined him to lead aggressively not only on issues on which his followers' preferences were homogeneous but also on others about which their preferences were unclear or divided.

## Newt Gingrich's Goals as Speaker

Newt Gingrich was a professor of history before he was a politician, and his goals as speaker were grounded in his understanding of history. In a 1996 interview, Gingrich explained that he had begun to consult history as a guide to political practice as early as his undergraduate days: "History is the only academic discipline dense

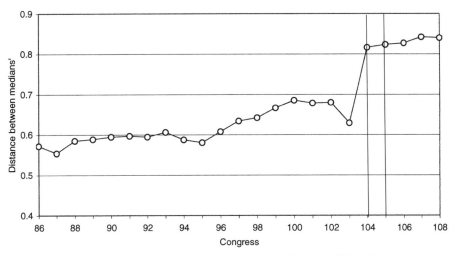

Figure 5.3. Ideological Polarization: Distance between Parties' Median NOMINATE Scores, 86th to 108th Congresses (1959–2005). *Source:* First-dimension DW-NOMINATE party medians, Poole 2006.

enough and confusing enough to reflect real life . . . Anything that can draw lines, any so-called social science, by self-definition is wrong. I was a political science major at Emory University when I dropped out of college for a year to run a congressional campaign in north Georgia . . . We lost, but I learned at the end of that race that everything the political scientists told me was silly, and everything I learned from history was useful" (Ambrose 1996, 74). Regarding the relationship between his academic and political careers, Gingrich explained: "I studied history in order to be a political leader, so for me it was very practical work" (ibid.). Gingrich's dissertation adviser during his graduate studies at Tulane University has said that Gingrich was already focused more on a political than an academic career (Bruck 1995, 53–54). He had talked of running for Congress since high school, and after teaching for four years at West Georgia College, mounted his first campaign for the House in 1974 (Steely 2000, 11, 24–64).

Gingrich's writings and other public statements offer a view of history in which nations encounter challenges to their survival. Some rise to meet these challenges and are renewed; others experience irreversible decline. The outcomes of these crises depend in large part on the ability of political leaders to guide and mobilize their societies. One characteristic of great leaders is a willingness to take risks to secure national renewal. In one autobiographical account, Gingrich recalls as a teenager having followed closely Charles de Gaulle's role in resolving the crises of the French

Fourth Republic. "This personal exposure to a nation in agony left an indelible impression on me," he writes. "I recognized that nations can undermine themselves through inadequate policies and moral collapse. Weak leadership and a refusal to confront problems rapidly lead to national decay. Successful leaders must be prepared to gamble everything—as de Gaulle did many times during his career" (Gingrich 1995b, 16).

Prior to becoming speaker in 1995, Gingrich had spent over a decade organizing around the goal of transforming the United States from a "liberal welfare state" into a "conservative opportunity society." As he described this program in a book written in the 1980s, it would involve smaller government with less centralized bureaucratic control made possible through new information technologies and a focus on decentralization, individual initiative, and entrepreneurship (Gingrich 1984). In Gingrich's view, President Reagan had come up short in achieving the conservative transformation that was needed in the United States because Reagan's horizon as a leader had been defined by opposition to liberalism rather than a positive vision of a new order in American politics. "The great failure of the modern Republican party, including much of the Reagan administration," Gingrich wrote in 1984 (122), "has been in its effort to solve problems operationally or tactically within the framework of the welfare state . . . Real change occurs at the levels of vision and strategy." Gingrich reiterated this theme in a 1995 interview: "You have to blow down the old order in order to create the new order. Reagan understood how to blow down the old order, but wasn't exactly sure what the new order would be" (Williams 1995, 212).

When Gingrich became speaker in 1995, his overriding goal was to succeed where President Reagan had failed, by creating a "new order" in the United States. In his own words: "My main goal was to move the city [Washington, DC] as far as I could compatible with maintaining the majority . . . I had no interest in being a managing majority of the old order. So my first goal was to drive the system as hard as I could, to reshape the way the system worked on things like a balanced budget, attitudes about tax cuts, welfare reform and to try to move institutional relationships a fair distance but in a way that was congruent with electing the majority" (Gingrich 2003).

Along with this extraordinarily ambitious goal of leading a transformation of American politics, before he became speaker Gingrich repeatedly demonstrated his willingness to challenge conventional wisdom and take political risks to advance his political goals. After two unsuccessful campaigns he was elected to the House from a west Georgia congressional district in 1978.[7] Almost immediately upon arrival in Washington Gingrich began discussing plans for Republicans to win control of the House by aggressively confronting the majority and nationalizing congressional elections around themes such as pervasive corruption in the Democratic-controlled Congress (Mann and Ornstein 2006, 64–65). By the early 1980s Gingrich was a founding member of the Conservative Opportunity Society (COS), which became the organizational base for Republican "bombthrowers," who focused on confronting the Democratic majority and highlighting interparty differences in pursuit of majority status.[8] COS members would later dominate the House Republican leadership, but at the time the organization was founded it was shunned by the party's top leadership and much of its membership. As one GOP leader interviewed by Connelly and Pitney (1994, 27) described the divide in the Republican Party in the 1980s: "The cleavage is between those favoring confrontation, the risk-takers, and the responsible partners in governing."[9] Senior Republicans at the time "warned incoming freshmen to steer clear of COS if they hoped to advance their careers in the House" (Balz and Brownstein 1996, 121).

Gingrich also acted independently of his party's leaders and risked his status in the party by taking on Democratic speaker Jim Wright during the 100th Congress (1987–1989), when he repeatedly accused Wright of serious ethical lapses and worked doggedly to attract media attention to Wright's behavior. In light of the seriousness of Gingrich's charges, Minority Leader Robert Michel of Illinois asked Gingrich to allow his evidence against Wright to be reviewed by a group of Republican colleagues. Even after the review produced a unanimous decision that there was no evidence of serious wrongdoing, and therefore no grounds for the party to call for an inquiry, Gingrich was undeterred, pressing the attack and orchestrating press coverage until the House Ethics Committee finally launched an investigation that led to Wright's resignation in June 1989 (Barry 1989, 602–606). Gingrich's explanation for his actions (offered at the time to journalist John Barry) was that Wright was in the process of consolidating power and becoming a highly effective Democratic speaker and that bringing down Wright would advance Republican electoral prospects by associating Democrats with political corruption in the public mind (ibid., 161–162, 362–369). Well before the outcome of his efforts was clear Gingrich explained: "Wright's a useful keystone to a much bigger structure. I'll just keep pounding on his ethics. There comes a point where it comes together and the media takes off on it, or it dies" (ibid., 369). When in the interim House Republicans experienced what they considered unfair and heavy-handed treatment by Speaker Wright, Gingrich's stature in the Republican conference grew for having taken the lead in confronting the Democratic speaker.

Gingrich progressed from outsider to elected leader within the House Republican Party in just over a decade, narrowly winning election as minority whip in 1989.[10] Demographic and ideological changes in the House Republican conference aided his rise, but Gingrich's path to leadership also demonstrated a strong propensity for taking big political risks and challenging established ways of doing things. As Peters (1997, 302) observes, "Gingrich has always sought to impose himself upon institutions rather than to allow institutions to impose themselves upon him." Regarding Gingrich's leadership of House Republicans during the period before he became speaker, Connelly and Pitney (1994, 63) note: "As a leader, Gingrich goes beyond merely servicing members' desires as he finds them. Preaching about 'the necessary revolution,' he tries to change what members want."

Gingrich had also studied the theory and practice of orchestrating change in organizations, and as a means to achieving his political agenda he was committed to producing institutional change in the House. "One of my goals," he stated early in his first year as speaker, "is to make the House co-equal with the White House" (Gettinger 1995, 1206). In Gingrich's view, producing change on this scale would involve strengthening party organization in the House (Peters 1997, 302–303). In the years before Republicans won control of the House, Gingrich had always sided with the "party activists" against the "committee guys" in battles within the Republican minority (Connelly and Pitney 1994, 20, 24–26). Gingrich also believed that producing large-scale policy and institutional change would require changing members' expectations about how the House worked rather than simply responding to them. As longtime Gingrich ally Vin Weber explained: "Newt felt that if they were to achieve a real realignment of the country, it would take more than gaining a majority. It would mean changing the expectations of members of Congress in a very fundamental way. It would mean changing their expectations about their schedule, their work habits, and ultimately their expectations about what is possible politically" (Drew 1996, 36).

In addition to these broad political and institutional goals Gingrich was personally strongly committed to two more specific policy goals—balancing the federal budget and cutting taxes. At a time when many of his most conservative allies were downplaying the importance of budget deficits, Gingrich devoted an entire chapter of his 1984 book *Window of Opportunity* to the topic, "Why Balancing the Budget is Vital." The case he made for budget balance was partly economic—that reducing government borrowing would reduce interest rates and pressures for government to cause inflation. But over a decade before he became speaker, Gingrich advocated a balanced budget initiative primarily because it could serve as a vehicle for effecting the broader transformation he was seeking to bring about in American politics. In his 1984 treatment of the issue, Gingrich made the case for enacting a balanced budget as a political strategy to shift the terms of the national political debate in a direction favorable to conservatives. Establishing balanced budgets as the norm in

American politics, Gingrich argued, would be the only effective way of restraining the spending growth on which the liberal welfare state and its supporting (Democratic) political coalition depended (Gingrich 1984, 184–204).

A second policy goal Gingrich strongly favored over the years before he became speaker was cutting taxes, which he viewed as the signature political issue for the Republican Party. During the 1980s he became an outspoken critic of tax increases to reduce budget deficits and was one of a group of House conservatives who successfully pushed for a plank in the 1984 Republican platform ruling out future tax hikes.[11] In one of his most visible actions as minority whip, Gingrich broke publicly with President George H. W. Bush in 1990 and refused to support a budget package that included tax increases and eliminated a capital gains tax reduction that had previously passed the House. He later sharply criticized Bush's decision to abandon cuts in capital gains taxes and reverse ground on his "no new taxes" pledge.

Gingrich's criticism of President Bush was framed much more in terms of political strategy than economic policy: "Giving up the tax pledge was a terrible error, because it struck at the core of people's respect for politicians . . . Losing that trust was a more serious consequence of Bush's raising taxes than any damage done to the economy" (Myerson 1991, 14). "This was a defining moment in [the Bush 41] presidency, and in the conservative movement. Because in the end, we either believed in cutting taxes or we were like liberal Democrats. I mean, I don't think there's any space for tax increasing Republicans . . . Raising taxes, I think kills conservatism" (Gingrich 1999). Gingrich's personal views on economic policy are well summed up by his self-description as "a balanced-budget supply-side Republican" (Ambrose 1996, 116). During a period when the conventional wisdom held that policymakers had to choose between deficit reduction and tax-cutting, and that actually attempting to balance the budget was a political nonstarter because of the massive tax increases or spending cuts that would be required, Gingrich's personal view was that a major political breakthrough in the direction he favored could occur only if Republicans attempted to balance the budget and cut taxes simultaneously.

Given his interest in history as a guide to political practice and a view of history in which political leaders are of central importance, it is hardly surprising that Gingrich's writings and speeches teem with references to historical figures from whom he claims to have drawn lessons. What is surprising for someone who aspired to and ultimately achieved the office of speaker of the House of Representatives is how few of these models were legislative leaders. When asked in a 1996 interview if he was using former House speakers as models for his approach to leadership, Gingrich responded:

No, but there are pieces that you take from each of them. There are tiny bits of Henry Clay; there are tiny bits of Sam Rayburn; some of Tom Reed, who is probably the closest to the model I follow. But in terms of who I really model off of, there are two very different tracks: One is political and the other is managerial. On a managerial track, I model off of Peter Drucker, W. Edwards Demming, George Marshall, Dwight Eisenhower—where you try to figure out how to run big systems, how to get things to work, how to get things to happen.

Politically, I probably start with Washington and Jefferson and then come up through Jackson, Lincoln, Theodore Roosevelt, McKinley and Mark Hanna, Franklin Roosevelt and Reagan—trying to understand what is effective political leadership. (Ambrose 1996, 74)

By his own account Gingrich's models were not legislative leaders but business executives who had transformed large organizations, military leaders who succeeded in organizing successful campaigns, and presidents who mobilized and drew authority from broad popular movements. In November 1994, just before he became speaker, Gingrich gave a speech at a Washington symposium at which he described the leadership model he intended to follow. The leader's job would be to define a positive "vision" and strategies to achieve this vision, then delegate authority to others to carry out projects and tactics (Gingrich 1994, 183–184). Gingrich also stated he intended to link his leadership to a popular base by means of a second, "listen-learn-help-lead" model: "so the job of the leader is to think about things, develop a vision and strategies and projects and tactics, then go back out and listen to the people and find out whether or not in fact they're on the same wavelength" (ibid., 185).

Gingrich's principal models at the time he became speaker were thus executives who managed transformative change from the apex of institutional hierarchies. Yet he believed that transformative leadership also required drawing authority from a popular, grassroots movement. "The most accurate statement of how I see the speakership," Gingrich explained early in 1995, is "somebody who could somehow combine grassroots organizations, mass media, and legislative detail into one synergistic pattern" (Cloud 1995). Dan Meyer (1997), who served as the new speaker's first chief of staff, noted: "I have heard Newt say being speaker of the House is his third most important job. The first was defining the movement, the direction we are going; the second was being leader of his party; the third was being speaker of the House." Gingrich's extraordinarily high visibility in the media, especially during his first year as speaker, fits well with this view of the leader simultaneously directing an organization while mobilizing and communicating with a mass base.[12]

A final point, which Gingrich himself made in an interview reflecting back on his speakership some years later, is that risk-taking and pushing the limits of what followers would accept were essential elements of the transformative mode of leadership he believed was needed to achieve his goals. Contrasting his approach with the "maintaining" leadership of Democratic speaker Sam Rayburn, Gingrich explained: "Maintaining leaders are inherently different than transforming leaders. Transforming leaders are inherently more isolated, more aggressive, more risk taking—operating more off an intuition about the future, where maintaining leaders operate more off an intuition about their members. Rayburn, who was a brilliant maintaining leader, would never have taken risks that would have alienated his members. He would have intuited the margins to which he could go and he wouldn't have gone beyond them" (2003).

When Republicans unexpectedly won control of the House of Representatives in the 1994 elections, a political leader with extraordinarily ambitious goals and a history of risk-taking behavior in pursuit of those goals became speaker. Gingrich had also engaged in an active effort to shape his followers' expectations and preferences and commit his followers to an agenda that would both advance his political goals and maximize Republican unity. As a result, the favorable political context Gingrich encountered for assertive leadership at the outset of his speakership was partly a consequence of his own actions to advance his goals while still a member of the Republican minority.

## Shaping the Context for a Republican Speakership

Newt Gingrich's longstanding efforts to organize Republicans to win the majority in the House led many Republican members to believe that Gingrich personally had played a major role in bringing about the historic Republican victory in 1994.[13] The result was a remarkable degree of authority and leeway for the speaker in the months immediately after the breakthrough election. The "Contract with America" organized by Gingrich in advance of the 1994 election also played a major role in defining the context within which Gingrich led the House during the early period of his speakership. While the Contract proved to be of modest importance in the election campaign, it became much more important after the election as an instrument of agenda control by Speaker Gingrich and the Republican leadership.

By 1994 Gingrich had been working relentlessly for over a decade to persuade House Republicans to focus on winning the majority as well as to develop and recruit Republican candidates who shared his vision. Though it is difficult to determine just how many members of the Republican conference might have been influenced by recruitment efforts undertaken by Gingrich's GOPAC organization, tapes conveying Gingrich's ideas and strategic advice had been sent to thousands of Republican candidates since the late 1980s (Balz and Kovaleski 1994). As Peters (1996, 4) notes: "During the 1992 and 1994 election cycles many GOP House candidates attended GOPAC training seminars, and almost all listened to GOPAC audio tapes featuring strategic advice, campaign themes, and general philosophy by Newt Gingrich." Among the members who acknowledged being influenced by Gingrich's efforts were John Boehner of Ohio and Roger Wicker of Mississippi. Said Boehner: "I started getting tapes in 1986 or 1987. I thought, this is great . . . If it weren't for the tapes, I probably wouldn't have run for Congress" (Balz and Kovaleski 1994). Wicker, who was elected leader of the big Republican freshman class in the 104th Congress, has stated that he listened attentively to GOPAC tapes over a seven- to eight-year period and that "a great deal of the philosophy I brought to Washington was shaped by Newt Gingrich" (Balz and Brownstein 1996, 146).

Gingrich had also provided important leadership in the effort by House Republicans to win the majority by raising money for Republican candidates and developing campaign strategy. As the 1994 election approached, Gingrich (at this point minority whip and presumptive Republican leader in the next Congress) and Bill Paxon of New York reinvigorated the Republican National Campaign Committee (RNCC) and targeted its resources toward Republican challengers. Gingrich requested that senior Republicans raise money to help fund challengers and signaled to those in line for committee leadership positions that their financial support for Republican candidates would be a factor in determining those appointments (ibid., 48–49; Garrett 2005, 78–80, 89). The results of these efforts were impressive. In 1992, only 12 Republican incumbents were active in fundraising for the RNCC and they raised only about $50,000; by 1994, 130 House Republicans engaged in fundraising and produced over $6 million in contributions (Gimpel 1996, 11). Gary Jacobson (1996, 216) points out that Republican challengers in 1994 had an average level of experience compared with challengers in previous election cycles but were better funded than Democratic challengers. These differences mattered, as Jacobson (ibid., 218) found that campaign spending was a significant variable explaining votes won by Republican challengers in 1994. Republican candidates also benefited from an aggressive Gingrich-led effort to nationalize the election and mobilize Republican constituencies. "Republican leaders did an outstanding job of organizing and mobilizing the groups in their coalition and of coaching their candidates in the art of using the party's themes effectively against Democrats. Newt Gingrich earned his speakership" (ibid., 211).

A second way in which Gingrich's efforts before the 1994 election shaped the leadership context in the House was his role in conceiving and overseeing the development of the Republican "Contract with America." In keeping with the strategy Gingrich had advocated since his election to Congress in 1978, the Contract was partly a campaign device intended to nationalize the 1994 congressional election. But even before the September 1994 unveiling of the Contract in an event on the Capitol steps, Gingrich was characterizing it as part of his postelection planning to define an agenda for the early months of a Republican-controlled House (Cohen 1994, 2200). Voter surveys and interviews with Republican candidates suggest that the Contract supplied some themes for Republican campaigns but probably did not have a major impact on voters in the election (Gimpel 1996, 21–26; Jacobson 1996, 209; Rae 1998, 42–44). The actual work of drafting the Contract was delegated to Republican Conference Chair Richard Armey and Republican leadership staff, led by Armey staffer Kerry Knott. But virtually every observer who has looked closely at the development of the Contract agrees that Gingrich conceived the idea, set it in motion, and played an important role by defining the framework for deciding which issues would be included. Other members and staff played important roles in developing the actual document, but Mayhew (2000, 24) has it right: "without Newt Gingrich, no Contract with America."[14]

In late January 1994, House Republicans approved a plan proposed by Gingrich and his staff to develop a ten-point positive agenda for the fall campaign. Also adopted at the same party retreat was a "vision" statement incorporating five themes: individual liberty, economic opportunity, limited government, personal responsibility, and security at home and abroad (Gillespie and Schellhas 1994, 4–5; Gimpel 1996, 17). Later in 1994, Armey and his staff surveyed Republican members and candidates, asking them to rank a list of preselected issues related to these themes for inclusion in a "Republican 100 Day Agenda" (Bader 1996, 185–187). During the summer, working groups of Republican members and staff drafted legislative language and polling was conducted on how best to frame the issues that had been chosen (ibid., 187–188). Armey established a participatory process in which rank-and-file Republicans were given opportunities to participate in drafting the content of the measures (Sinclair 1999, 427, 429). Actual participation in the drafting of the Contract items was fairly limited because, as one Gingrich staffer, Jack Howard, put it, "most people thought it was a PR stunt" (Garrett 2005, 71; see also Gimpel 1996, 19–20).

Gingrich delegated responsibility for developing the content of the Contract but continued to oversee the process. One of the guiding principles he laid down was that the Contract would not include issues that divided moderate and conservative Republicans, including abortion and school prayer. To enforce this condition, Gingrich intervened and "clashed fiercely" with Armey to keep a school prayer provision out of the document (Balz and Brownstein 1996, 38–39; see also Balz 1994). As one longtime Republican leadership staffer described Gingrich's role: "He was very good on the 'Contract with America' getting people together and finding common ground, but he was also pushing the system in that direction. By creating the limits he would lead everyone to the conclusion he wanted to lead them to . . . it was 'small d' democracy but it was also very *led* democracy" (Hellman 2002).

According to staff who were involved in the process, Gingrich and Armey had a relatively free hand in determining the content of the Contract, not because Republican members agreed on all of the policies it contained, but because few believed they would actually be in a position to implement it after the election. According to Gingrich staffer Jack Howard, Gingrich told his staff at the beginning of the process, "If we can get 20 to 30 percent of the members to buy in to this, you might have 10 percent who will be hard-core against but the rest will just sort of go along . . . We just really need about 20 percent of the core" (quoted in Garrett 2005, 70). According to Howard, the main participants were "an energetic but fairly small band of conservatives and then just a bunch of people who kind of went along" (ibid.). Armey staffer Kerry Knott (2005) confirmed this account. "We were able to develop the Contract largely because the people who were going to be in a position to actually *fulfill* the Contract didn't believe it was going to happen. So they gave us a free hand to put it together largely outside of the committee structure."

Thus Gingrich did not dictate the specific content of the Contract but took the lead in defining its main themes and overseeing its development to ensure that issues sure to evoke strong divisions between conservative and moderate Republicans were excluded. The accounts of staff involved in the process also make clear that he and other Republican leaders were not responding to a unified group of party followers in developing the document. The Contract was primarily a leadership-driven strategy, and broad agreement among Republicans to support the document was secured in part because few took it seriously or believed it would be implemented after the 1994 election.

Nonetheless, when the 104th Congress convened in January 1995 all but seven of Gingrich's Republican followers had committed in writing to spend the next three months addressing the agenda set forth in the document. Getting all the legislative measures included in the Contract to a vote in the House within 100 days would require active direction of the legislative process by the Republican leadership. Because of their belief that Gingrich had played such a crucial role in leading them into the majority, many House Republicans were also disposed to give the new speaker broad authority and discretion on both organizational and policy matters as the 104th Congress convened. As freshman Republican Jon Christensen of Nebraska proclaimed after the 1994 election: "I trust the leadership with everything . . . I trust their decision-making and their vision for the country" (Cloud 1994, 3322). Trust in Gingrich was also high among senior members, including moderate Republicans. As Sherwood Boehlert (R-NY) explained during the early months of the 104th Congress: "I have no doubt that we are in the majority today because of Newt Gingrich. People would ask why a Rockefeller Republican could support a conservative firebrand from Georgia. I'd say, he's brilliant, he's innovative, he's focused, he's disciplined. And there's another factor: I want to be in the majority" (Drew 1996, 106).

Gingrich's top staffers at the time were struck by the extraordinary influence his successful efforts in leading Republicans into the majority conferred on him at the outset of his speakership. Gingrich's chief of staff Meyer (1997) commented: "People credited him with winning the majority . . . He had tremendous authority at that point to do things. He was not challenged at that point."[15] By the end of the first year of the 104th Congress other political factors over which the speaker had little control began to define the political context for leadership in the House. But as Gingrich took over the leadership of the House in late 1994, his earlier efforts to shape the political context paid off by giving him unusually broad authority to influence both organizational and policy decisions. With extraordinarily ambitious policy and institutional goals and an understanding of leadership in which achieving large-scale change requires taking risks and pushing limits, Gingrich wielded that authority to the fullest.

## The Politics of the Gingrich Speakership

The examination of the politics of the Gingrich speakership focuses on four cases during the two Congresses Gingrich served as speaker (104th and 105th, 1995–1998). The first case involves changes in the organization of the House that were decided immediately after the 1994 election. Even before he was formally chosen as speaker, Gingrich broke with established practice for assigning chairs of standing committees and announced rules changes that altered the relationship between standing committees and the majority party leadership. The second case is Gingrich's leadership on the legislation contained in the "Contract with America." Particular attention will be paid to House passage of tax cuts that Speaker Gingrich called the "crowning jewel" of the Contract and to the passage of historic welfare reform legislation, which began as part of the Contract. The fourth case is the House Republicans' drive to balance the federal budget within seven years. Launched in

February 1995 while Gingrich and his Republican followers were at the height of their success in dominating the national agenda, two politically damaging government shutdowns and an election in which President Clinton was returned to office would intervene before legislation securing this goal was enacted in 1997. Finally, the analysis will consider why support for Gingrich's transformative mode of leadership had eroded to the point in late 1998 that he was effectively forced from office by his followers only four years after leading them back into the majority.

In each case the primary focus is on tracing the politics of leader-follower interactions in the processes by which these outcomes occurred. Two questions are of central importance. When Speaker Gingrich took the initiative on these issues, was he acting in response to what he knew to be widespread agreement or homogeneous preferences among his Republican followers? Or did Gingrich also actively use the prerogatives of the office to attempt to influence outcomes in situations where opportunities were present to advance his goals but his followers' preferences were uncertain or seriously divided?

## *Organizational Innovation: Fusing Party and Committee Leadership*

In late 1994 and early 1995, the new Republican majority adopted wide-ranging changes in the organization of the House. These changes included altering rules affecting the prerogatives of leadership, the number and operation of committees, floor deliberations and scheduling, as well as other changes to make congressional operations more transparent.[16] Arguably, the most important organizational changes adopted immediately after Republicans won the majority were rules changes that effectively increased the control of party leaders over standing committees to a degree that exceeded anything attempted by even the most active of the preceding Democratic speakers.[17] Two Gingrich-led initiatives were of crucial importance in moving the organization of the House in this direction. First, almost immediately after the election Gingrich established a clear precedent that committee leadership positions in the Republican House would be awarded based on ability and willingness to advance the party's legislative goals rather than seniority. Second, Gingrich and his staff initiated a restructuring of the committee assignment process that gave the Republican leadership effective control of committee appointments. A third important change, which reinforced the shift toward greater leadership control of committees was adoption of a new rule establishing six-year term limits for committee chairs. As Sarah Binder has argued, the result of these organizational changes was to create a new "fusion" of "partisan agenda control within the committee system" (2005, 12). Along with a continuation of the close cooperation between the party leadership and the Rules Committee that had developed under previous Democratic speakers, these new rules established the institutional framework for a new, more centralized form of party government in the Republican House in which the speaker and his top lieutenants routinely direct, intervene in, or alter committee action on legislation.

Two of the three organizational changes that increased the control of the party leadership over committees were initiated by Gingrich during the immediate postelection period in late 1994. Before the new Republican majority had even met in Washington, Gingrich asserted the authority to name committee chairs for the 104th Congress and announced a plan to restructure the House Republicans' committee assignment body to increase dramatically the influence of the speaker and top party leadership (Foerstel 1994). Among the appointments Gingrich announced were Robert Livingston (LA) to chair the Appropriations Committee, Thomas Bliley (VA) to chair the Commerce Committee, and Henry Hyde (IL) to chair the Judiciary Committee. Each of these appointments involved skipping over the most senior Republican on the committee—Livingston was actually the fifth-ranking Republican on the Appropriations panel. While the Republican leader had previously been given authority to name Republican members of the Rules Committee, no authority to name committee chairs had been conferred on Gingrich by the Republican conference (Aldrich and Rohde 1997–98, 549). At the same time he announced the appointments of committee chairs he also made public his intention to restructure the Republican committee assignment body—to be renamed the Steering Committee—in such a way that would more than triple the voting power of the Republican leader in the committee assignment process (Foerstel 1994; Jacoby 1994a).[18]

Aldrich and Rohde's (1997–1998, 550) account makes clear that the not-yet-speaker was acting ahead of any clear signal from his party conference or the newly elected Republican members: "Unlike the case of the Democrats 20 years earlier this was not an instance in which pressure from freshman insurgents played a major role . . . Virtually none of the newly-elected freshmen had come to town; they could not have been consulted about the choices, much less have initiated or urged them. Well before the Republican Conference could meet, and before any formal change in the method of choosing committee chairs could be considered, Gingrich and his allies asserted the power to choose the chairs of the committees that were most important to them." Changes in the formal structure of the Republican committee assignment process Gingrich announced in late November 1994 were also developed with little consultation with the Republican rank and file. While some groused to the press about how the new process would reduce the influence of their states or regions, the reaction of sophomore Ernest Istook of Oklahoma sums up the response of most Republicans: "It's mostly been treated by people as a done deal" (Jacoby 1994a).

The question of how to handle selection of committee chairs had been discussed in advance of the election among Gingrich and his staff. Richard Armey's staff had also been working closely with the Gingrich staff on organizational matters during this period (Swinehart 1996). Immediately after the election, Gingrich circulated a memo among Republican members critiquing the existing committee selection process and indicating that chair appointments would go to those willing to support and work for "the team" rather than to the most senior committee member (Swinehart 2005; see also Evans and Oleszek 1997, 88–89). After conferring with a small group of activist allies (including Armey, Bill Paxon, Tom DeLay, and John Boehner), a series of meetings and conference calls were organized by Gingrich to discuss organizational matters with Republican members. According to the staff who organized these discussions, their purpose was not consultation but to put Republican members on notice about how the appointments would be made. "Immediately after the election we had conference calls between the ranking [committee] members and the leadership stressing that there was no guarantee that anybody would be given the job [of chairing a committee]" (Swinehart 1996). As Gingrich's chief of staff Meyer (1997) explained: "What it boiled down to was Newt's viewpoint that we needed to have activists as committee chairs. It wasn't an ideological bent to it at all. It was we need people who can be aggressive and activist oriented." "In each case," Gingrich explained in 1995, "I thought they would bring a level of aggressiveness and risk taking that we would need in these very important positions" (Gingrich 1995b, 121).

The new committee assignment process was also developed primarily by Gingrich and his staff. Leonard Swinehart, the Gingrich staffer who took the lead in drafting the plan for the new Steering Committee, recalled that consultation with the Republican membership was limited to informal discussions with a small group of members: "I interviewed ten members . . . kind of a conglomeration of past and future leaders" (1996). Regarding the purpose of the new arrangement, Swinehart explained: "That was a takeoff on what the Democrats had done. We put some refinements in and we put control of more votes in the hands of Newt and the leadership" (ibid.). "There is no secret behind it at all, it was control. We decided to take it away from the . . . regions, away from others' ability to manipulate it and have us [the leadership] manipulate it. Plain and simple" (2005).

Gingrich and his staff sought little guidance and experienced few constraints from the Republican conference in developing these rules changes. Said Meyer (1997) of the decision to skip over senior members in appointing committee chairs:

"No one organized against it. I attribute that to the fact that no one thought we were going to win the majority except for Newt . . . Right or wrong, they said we've got this majority because of Newt. And so he had *tremendous* authority at that point to do these things. He was not challenged at that point . . . Most people didn't expect to become the majority so it wasn't like there was a lot of forethought, like should we become the majority we want to shift power from committees to the leadership." When the new Steering Committee proposal came before the Republican Conference for approval in early December 1994, only two members objected (Aldrich and Rohde 1997–98, 555).

A third important rules change in the area of party-committee relations in the House was the enactment of a six-year limit for committee and subcommittee chairs. This change was supported by Gingrich but cannot be attributed primarily to his leadership in the postelection period. While in the minority, Republicans had adopted a similar rule limiting their members to six years' service in the ranking minority position on committees (Cohen 1994, 2202; Evans and Oleszek 1997, 89). A six-year term limit for chairs had been included among a package of congressional reforms in the Contract and was endorsed again by the Republican conference in December 1994. This provision also had strong support among the seventy-three freshmen Republicans (Gugliotta 1994; Rae 1998, 69–70). In an early sign of the independence of the junior members, after the election freshman Republican Lindsey Graham of South Carolina and others pushed for a term limit on the speakership as well, and an eight-year term limit on that office was added to the package of rules changes (Evans and Oleszek 1997, 90–91; Jacoby 1994b). Gingrich would not serve long enough to see the effects of either rule come into play (and the term limit for the speakership would be waived for his successor, Denny Hastert of Illinois). But the term limit on committee chairs would prove highly effective in limiting the tendency that had been seen during the long period of Democratic control for chairs to establish independent power bases on committees, and it helped create powerful incentives for members aspiring to future committee leadership openings actively to support party goals.

The rules changes Gingrich advanced were approved by the Republican Conference in early December 1994. Thus in retrospect we can infer that Gingrich's actions were not contrary to the goals or preferences of his Republican followers. But it is also clear that Gingrich was not acting in response to widespread agreement or homogeneous preferences among his followers about how the new Republican House should be organized. Recall that none of his Republican followers had ever served in the majority, almost one-third were new members, and a majority had two years' service or less. Surely, among many of these members clear preferences about the organization of the House had yet to be formed (Sinclair 1999, 445–446). Nothing in the political context required Gingrich to take the actions he took. Instead, Gingrich took advantage of his position after the unexpected Republican victory to advance his goal of strengthening the control of party leaders over committees before his followers had even been given an opportunity to register their views.[19]

Commenting in November 1994 on the institutional changes he had announced, Gingrich explained the organizational innovations in relation to his goal of transformative change: "We wanted to maximize the opportunity for substantial change. This is a city which is like a sponge. It absorbs waves of change, and it slows them down, and it softens them, and then one morning they cease to exist" (Cloud 1994). As two of the most knowledgeable students of institutional reform in the House conclude regarding the organizational changes that occurred at the beginning of the 104th Congress: "Some shift in power from the committee system to the Speaker's office would have occurred even without Gingrich because of the significant preference homogeneity within the new House majority. However . . . the scope and magnitude of the Republican reorganization owed much to the political entrepreneurship of Gingrich" (Evans and Oleszek 1997, 172). The consequences of these organizational changes were quickly demonstrated as Gingrich and the Republican leadership then drove the measures contained in the Contract through the House committee system in the early months of 1995.

## *Delivering on the "Contract with America"*

The House Republicans' "Contract with America" involved pledges to pass a package of institutional reforms on the first day of the 104th Congress and to hold "full and open debate" and "a clear and fair vote" on the ten legislative measures outlined in the document within 100 days. As shown in table 5.1 below, the ten legislative measures contained in the Contract included budget and economic issues, social policy, legal and regulatory matters, national defense, and term limits for members of Congress. Once the Contract items were translated into actual bills and resolutions, the task facing Speaker Gingrich and the Republican leadership involved bringing over thirty separate measures before the House for a vote. From January through April 1995 action on the Contract measures dominated the agenda of the House. The attention of the press and public was so focused on Speaker Gingrich and House Republicans that President Clinton felt the need to affirm at an April 18 news conference, "The president is relevant here" (Purdum 1995).

In keeping with the leadership model he had articulated before becoming speaker—the leader defines vision and strategy then delegates implementation to others—once Republicans took control of the House Gingrich delegated primary operational responsibility for managing the Contract issues to others in the Republican leadership. As Chief Deputy Whip (and later speaker) Denny Hastert (IL) described the division of labor on the Contract measures: "Newt, of course, was the intellectual force behind all this, the conceptualizer. [Majority Leader Richard] Armey was the scheduler. [Majority Whip Tom] DeLay and I had to deliver the votes" (2004, 119). As the Contract bills were being debated and voted on, Gingrich intended to focus on communications and longer-term planning and strategy, especially for the budget initiative that would come next (Gingrich 1995b, 127; Owens 1997, 254). Others have provided detailed accounts of the blizzard of activity that was required to get the dozens of Contract measures before the House for a vote.[20] The primary objective here is to take a broad overview of the Contract process, focusing on the patterns of leadership politics involved in getting the Contract measures passed. Closer attention is given to two of the Contract measures—welfare reform and tax cuts—on which serious divisions emerged among House Republicans. A second objective is to assess the extent to which the Gingrich-designed Contract strategy actually proved consequential in producing change in public policy.

The process of getting all of the Contract measures to a vote in early 1995 was leadership-driven. Majority Leader Armey took primary responsibility for managing the schedule, and Armey, his staff, and Gingrich's staff closely monitored committee and floor action on the Contract measures, intervening when necessary to keep action on schedule, review major revisions in content or mediate conflicts that threatened to derail timely action. With such active direction from the Republican leadership and close to half of the Contract measures falling within the jurisdiction of the Judiciary Committee, Chairman Henry Hyde of Illinois began referring to his position as "the sub-chairman" (Drew 1996, 100; Owens 1997, 254). Committee chairs who balked at advancing Contract bills were put on notice that continuing to hold their positions would depend on cooperation with the leadership. When one Republican committee chair informed Speaker Gingrich that it would not be possible to meet a leadership-imposed deadline, Gingrich responded: "If you can't do it, I will find someone who will" (Rosenstiel 1995). Several Contract measures were also developed outside the normal committee process in leadership-appointed task forces (Deering 1999; Evans and Oleszek 1997, 132). With about one-fifth of the Contract measures the Republican leadership also intervened to revise legislation at the postcommittee stage or during floor consideration (Owens 1997, 256, 258–259). For example, in one case Republican leaders overturned a bipartisan compromise on student surveys that had been approved by the Government Reform Committee, restoring the original Contract provision by means of a leadership-sanctioned amendment when the bill came to the House floor (Cassata 1995).

As promised, all of the Contract measures reached a floor vote before the 100th day of the 104th Congress. In this respect the Contract was a remarkable success as an agenda control mechanism and provided striking evidence of Gingrich's effectiveness in shaping the context of the early period of Republican rule. As Dan Meyer (1997), explained: "In Newt's mind—and he was always quite up front about it—[the Contract] had two purposes. One was an agenda for the campaign. But two, it was even more a governing document. His view of it was if we won the majority it would in essence be a roadmap for the first 100 days. Give us something to do until we figured out just how we were supposed to operate as a majority." The Republican leadership not only delivered on the preelection pledge to vote on all the Contract measures within 100 days but lost only two major votes: a February 15 vote on an amendment that weakened the Contract provision on implementing a ballistic missile defense system; and the March 29 vote on proposing a constitutional amendment to limit congressional terms, which failed to receive the required two-thirds majority (see Garrett 2005, 203–205; Gimpel 1996, 71–75, 95–104).

In assessing the leadership politics of the Contract exercise, extraordinarily high levels of Republican unity in votes on Contract measures indicate that Gingrich's Republican followers probably were in strong agreement on most of the Contract issues. On the thirty-three votes identified by Congressional Quarterly (1995) as final passage votes on Contract measures, Republicans averaged 98 percent unity in support; on only one of the final passage votes (the congressional term limits amendment) did Republican unity fail to reach 90 percent (Jones 1999, 120–121). The highly assertive leadership supplied by Speaker Gingrich and his lieutenants on the Contract measures thus appears consistent with contextual leadership theories in which leaders are said to provide aggressive leadership in situations when their followers' preferences are homogeneous (Sinclair 1999).

Still, the view that Speaker Gingrich and the Republican leadership were acting as agents of a unified Republican majority does not fully capture the causal process at work in leadership politics on these issues for two reasons. First, the extraordinarily high level of Republican unity was itself partly a product of the agenda control strategy Gingrich had imposed in the development of the Contract. Second, even though we observe a pattern of unity in roll call votes on final passage, serious divisions were present among House Republicans on some of the most important Contract measures. Recall that Gingrich had insisted that the Contract be limited to issues on which there was broad support among Republican incumbents and candidates (Bader 1996, 185–190; Gimpel 1996, 18–19). Statements by moderate Republicans after the election suggest that some remaining policy disagreements within the party on Contract issues were also muted because many Republicans believed after the election that a mandate existed not simply to debate and vote on but to enact the Contract measures (Cassata 1995; see also Jones 1999, 95–115). Donald Wolfensberger (2000, 186), the senior Republican staffer on the House Rules Committee at the time, observes that the Contract "papered over . . . continuing fissures within the party among various factions (fiscal conservatives, supply-siders, social conservatives, and the more moderate Northeast/Midwest wing)."[21] At least some portion of Republican unity in support of the Contract measures should therefore be attributed to Gingrich's successful electoral and agenda control strategies.

Serious divisions within the party nonetheless emerged on some important Contract measures. These issues provide important evidence on whether strong agreement among his followers was in fact the necessary condition for assertive leadership by Speaker Gingrich or whether Gingrich also used the prerogatives of the speakership to advance his goals and influence outcomes in situations where his followers were divided. The two most important issues that evoked serious splits among Gingrich's followers during the early months of the 104th Congress were welfare reform and the tax cuts included in the Contract. Welfare reform was one of the most far-reaching policy proposals in the Contract, while the tax measure over which controversy developed (a $500-per-child tax credit) involved over $100 billion in reduced tax revenue over five years. These issues merit a closer look in order to understand how Speaker Gingrich responded and how his leadership affected outcomes on Contract measures when divisions developed among his followers.

*Really Ending Welfare as We Know It.* Newt Gingrich had long been an advocate of welfare reform and devolution of programs from the federal bureaucracy to lower levels of government, as these had been major elements of his "conservative opportunity society" program (see Gingrich 1984, 134–135, 141–142, 177–181). By the time Gingrich became speaker in 1995, support for major changes in federal welfare policy was present among the public and across much of the political spectrum. President Clinton had made a pledge to "end welfare as we know it" in the 1992 election campaign, by which he meant reforming the existing Aid to Families with Dependent Children (AFDC) program to require beneficiaries to work after two years and set limits on how long welfare benefits could be received, while also providing funding for training, child care, and subsidized jobs. But Clinton's welfare reform proposal died in a House committee, never coming to a vote in the Democratically controlled 103rd Congress (Weaver 2000, chap. 9). By the time Gingrich became speaker, House Republicans—as well as many Democrats—were in agreement on the need for major changes in welfare policy. But as the author of the definitive study of the politics of welfare reform in the 1990s, R. Kent Weaver, notes, "Republicans were far from united over which approach or package of welfare reform approaches to emphasize" (ibid., 253).

When Republicans took control of the House in 1994, Speaker Gingrich could not have led on the issue of welfare reform by advancing a Republican consensus because none existed. As Weaver documents, even though public support for change in the existing welfare system was strong, Gingrich and Republican leaders were faced with hard choices on welfare reform because there was no single approach around which Republicans cohered (ibid., 384). What the actual process of developing the Contract welfare reform measure in the House shows is that Gingrich—or other Republican leaders acting with his support—intervened at a number of crucial points to shape the content of the legislation. And each time Gingrich intervened he pushed for a more radical break with the policy status quo, even though it was unclear whether a majority of Republicans actually favored these moves. The result was passage of legislation by the House that dramatically shifted the terms of the debate on welfare reform in a more conservative direction, and final enactment of a welfare reform measure that moved welfare policy further from the status quo than many thought possible at the beginning of the process. Yet this case also provides evidence of the limits of House leadership, as Speaker Gingrich later found himself having to reverse course when the legislative strategy he preferred for dealing with the Clinton White House lacked sufficient support among his followers.

The welfare reform provisions in the "Contract with America" grew out of earlier efforts by House Republicans to develop a Republican alternative to the Clinton proposal in 1993–1994. During the 103rd Congress a Republican task force chaired by Pennsylvania Republican Rick Santorum developed legislation that included more stringent work requirements and time limits for welfare recipients than those in the Clinton plan. The Santorum bill also included provisions intended to deter illegitimate births by requiring states to deny additional benefits to women who have additional children while on the welfare rolls (termed a family cap) and prohibit cash benefits to unwed mothers under eighteen, although states would be allowed to enact exemptions from these provisions. That Santorum's plan (HR 3500) reflected the preferences of the overwhelming majority of House Republicans was indicated by the fact that 162 of the 175 Republicans serving in the House in the 103rd Congress signed on as cosponsors (Balz and Brownstein 1996, 276–277; Weaver 2000, 235–237). However, shortly after it was introduced in late 1993 the Santorum bill began to attract criticism from social conservatives for being an insufficiently ambitious alternative to the Clinton policy and needing stronger measures yet to deal with illegitimacy. Gingrich (at this point the Republican whip) was among those proposing that the Santorum plan be revised to make the bill a stronger and more distinctive Republican proposal (Balz and Brownstein 1996, 279). In April 1994, a new Republican alternative that moved in the direction Gingrich favored was introduced by James Talent of Missouri and Tim Hutchinson of Arkansas. Titled "The Real Welfare Reform Act of 1994," the Talent-Hutchinson bill capped welfare expenditures, disallowed state exemptions to a family cap and provisions to deny benefits to underage mothers (setting the age for eligibility at twenty-one rather than eighteen), and required more beneficiaries to be moved to work more quickly (Balz and Brownstein 1996, 279–280; Weaver 2000, 237).

Once a decision was made in 1994 to include welfare reform in the "Contract with America," Republicans had to decide which of the two competing plans would be used as the starting point for the Contract provision. As Balz and Brownstein report, even though the provisions in the Santorum bill had received almost unanimous endorsement by House Republicans only months before, Gingrich and Conference Chair Richard Armey rejected using the more moderate plan: "Santorum and the other task force members, citing their 162 sponsors, urged Armey to simply write their bill into the Contract. But Gingrich and Armey had converted to the view that the original bill was inadequately ambitious. 'That was a minority bill,' Armey told the task force members dismissively. 'We need to come at it from the perspective of a majority'" (Balz and Brownstein 1996, 281).

Armey convened a new working group to draft the Contract language that included Santorum and three Republican moderates (Nancy Johnson of Connecticut, Mike Castle of Delaware, and Dave Camp of Michigan) but also included Talent and Hutchinson. Armey also directed the group to meet with representatives of social conservative groups who were strong advocates of the stricter illegitimacy provisions. After a contentious drafting process, the Contract measure that emerged from the group moved significantly in the direction of the Talent-Hutchinson version. Unlike the Santorum bill, which actually increased welfare expenditures, the Contract version capped spending on AFDC and a number of other programs and ended the status of these programs as "entitlements" under federal law. No exemptions would be allowed to provisions requiring states to deny benefits to beneficiaries who had additional children and to unwed mothers under eighteen. The new bill also contained strict work requirements and time limits for eligibility for welfare benefits (ibid., 281–283; Weaver 2000, 260–264). Republican moderates, including Ways and Means Committee members Nancy Johnson and Clay Shaw of Florida (Ways and Means had jurisdiction over the welfare programs in the House) remained strongly opposed to portions of the Contract bill (Weaver 2000, 265). But Republican moderates "conceded the argument because few of them thought the Republicans would win back the House—or that the leadership could force them to stand with the Contract if they did" (Balz and Brownstein 1996, 283; see also Weaver 2000, 265).

Of course these expectations proved wrong. In addition to new Republican congressional majorities in both houses of Congress, the 1994 election brought eleven new Republican governors as well. Just after the election, Gingrich and incoming Senate Republican leader Bob Dole participated in a Republican governors' conference in Williamsburg, Virginia, at which a number of governors made appeals for Congress to convert federal social programs into block grants that would transfer money to the states with fewer federal strings attached. The governors also signaled willingness to accept lower federal funding levels in exchange for greater flexibility in administering the programs. According to one House staffer, "When Gingrich came back from Williamsburg, the message was block grants" (Balz and Brownstein 1996, 284). In a move that resulted in yet another major revision in the Republicans' welfare reform proposal, Gingrich invited a group of Republican governors to participate directly in negotiations with members and staff of the Ways and Means Committee in January 1995 to revise the bill that would go forward under the Contract. Agreement was reached to turn the major federal welfare programs into block grants and end their entitlement status, with spending levels to be frozen for five years, but also greater flexibility allowed to states to determine how the programs would be structured (Vobejda 1995; Weaver 2000, 268–269). House Republicans had the field clear to set the agenda for welfare reform proposals at this point because the Clinton White House, while continuing to express support for welfare reform in principle, offered no new proposal; Clinton's advisers had concluded that it would be better to wait before offering a White House bid and believed House Republicans were too internally divided to pass a welfare reform bill of the type being proposed by the governors (Weaver 2000, 273).

In addition to objections of Republican moderates to spending cuts and restrictions on benefits that were now incorporated in the Contract version, the direction favored by the governors—devolution of welfare programs to the states as block grants with few strings attached—now clashed with the goals of Republican social conservatives who favored strict federal guidelines on who could receive benefits. As Weaver explains the resulting political situation in early 1995: "Speaker Gingrich's January deal with the governors put the House Republicans in an awkward position. Their leadership had agreed to two distinct and incompatible deals on welfare reform: the deterrence and new paternalism approach of the original Personal Responsibility Act [the Contract measure] and the devolution approach negotiated with the governors. The later deal had the advantage of being given the imprimatur of the Speaker as having superseded the original act. But the Personal Responsibility Act was closer to the preferences of many House Republicans" (ibid., 269–270).

The two approaches were reconciled in a sometimes contentious process within the Ways and Means Committee during February, with many of the provisions favored by social conservatives appearing in the final version (bans on benefits to mothers under eighteen, a family cap, strict time limits for eligibility) along with the lower spending levels and the transformation of federal programs for the poor including AFDC from entitlements to block grants. Republican moderates secured some minor changes in the legislation (lifting the ban on benefits when a mother turned eighteen, for example), but the bill that came before the House for a vote in March mostly combined provisions from the Contract version with the radical devolution approach that emerged from the involvement of the Republican governors in the process. In the meantime, some antiabortion groups began to attack the bill on the grounds that provisions intended to deter illegitimacy would have the effect of encouraging more abortions. That Gingrich and the Republican leadership had pushed the process to the limits of what his followers would support was indicated when fifteen Republicans voted against the rule to debate the bill; the rule passed (217–211) only because three Democrats voted in favor. As Gingrich observed at the time, this was not a situation in which there was broad agreement or homogeneous preferences among a large majority of Republicans: "There was no natural coalition you could put together. Whatever you did would lose you other people" (Drew 1996, 143). On the vote on final passage on March 24 Republicans closed ranks and the bill passed 234–199 with only five GOP members voting in opposition. Some Republican moderates agreed to support the bill in part because they believed a more centrist bill would emerge from the Senate. "I don't have to condition my support on perfection in the House vehicle. We all know the Senate will look at it closely," explained James Greenwood of Pennsylvania (Congressional Quarterly 1996, 7–43).

The version of welfare reform passed by the Senate in September 1995 was indeed less sweeping in the number of benefit programs it converted to block grants, the flexibility allowed states regarding whether to deny benefits to teenage mothers and institute a family cap, and the budgetary savings it would produce. But the Senate version still represented a dramatic break with the status quo by terminating the sixty-year-old entitlement status for the AFDC program and converting it into a block grant to the states, along with including stiff work requirements and time limits on eligibility for benefits. After President Clinton endorsed the Senate version as it neared passage, the bill was approved 82–17 with bipartisan support.

House-Senate negotiations resulted in two bills being sent to the president, a huge budget balancing reconciliation measure that incorporated welfare-related changes that lowered spending by $81.5 billion over seven years and a separate measure that included the programmatic changes agreed to in AFDC, child welfare and nutrition, food stamps, and other programs. Citing unacceptable provisions included with welfare reform in both measures, President Clinton vetoed them in late 1995 and early 1996 respectively (Congressional Quarterly 1996, 7–44–52; Weaver 2000, 294–320).

Congressional Republicans were then faced with the strategic choice of sending a stand-alone welfare reform bill to the president or continuing to link welfare reform to other programmatic and budgetary issues Clinton had committed to oppose (Weaver 2000, 323–325). Republicans reintroduced welfare reform legislation in both houses in May 1996, initially joining the measure to reforms in the Medicaid program. The welfare reform provisions resembled those of the bills passed the previous year, including transformation of AFDC into block grants to the states and an end to the federal entitlement to benefits. Senate Majority Leader Bob Dole of Kansas, soon to receive the Republican nomination for the presidency, favored keeping the two issues linked, reportedly in anticipation that another Clinton welfare reform veto would weaken the Democratic president's position in the upcoming campaign.

Speaker Gingrich also supported this strategy (Drew 1997, 58, 98). However, because few of the Contract measures had been enacted into law at this point and the Republican initiative to balance the budget (discussed below) was in disarray after repeated Clinton vetoes, support grew among House Republicans for changing strategy to secure a major legislative achievement on which to run in the fast-approaching 1996 election (Garrett 2005, 144–146; Pianin 1996a; Weaver 2000, 325–326). When Gingrich publicly reaffirmed that the welfare reform and Medicaid measures would remain linked in late June, almost one hundred Republican members signed a letter calling on the Republican leadership to introduce a separate bill (Hume 1996; Katz 1996). Not long after Gingrich's announcement an unnamed House Republican leader told the *Washington Post*, "Newt went off on his own," and that the issues would likely be decoupled (Pianin 1996b). And, in what Congressional Quarterly (1997, 6–11) termed "a dramatic reversal," Republican leaders announced on July 11 that a separate welfare reform bill would be passed. By the end of July both houses passed the stand-alone measure and President Clinton announced he would sign it. After many twists and turns, this major plank in the Contract became law in August 1996.

The politics of welfare reform provide important evidence about the causal processes underlying leadership politics on the "Contract with America" measures. First, Republican unity found in votes on final passage did not always represent underlying agreement on policy. As Weaver (2000, 291) argues, if most Republicans were dissatisfied with the status quo on welfare policy at the time Gingrich became speaker, "there were deep substantive divisions among House Republicans on some elements of the Personal Responsibility Act." Second, Gingrich's repeated moves to push the Contract welfare measure further and further from the status quo occurred in the context of these deep divisions and had important policy consequences. "Just as striking as the Republicans' feat in keeping their coalition together," adds Weaver (2000, 292–293), "was their ability to move Congressional Democrats, and President Clinton, so far to the right." Finally, if Gingrich was successful in shifting the terms of the welfare reform debate through the use of agenda control and persuasion despite divisions among his followers over welfare policy, he still encountered limits and was forced to reverse field when he tried to persist in a strategy of continued confrontation with the White House when enough of his followers decided they were ready to see welfare reform enacted into law.

*The "Crowning Jewel" Tax Cuts.* The second Contract issue on which serious divisions emerged among House Republicans was the size of tax cuts included in the plan. Major income tax provisions were included in two of the ten Contract bills. HR 6, "The American Dream Restoration Act," included a $500-per-child tax credit for families with annual incomes up to $200,000, reduction of the "marriage penalty," and expanded availability of tax-sheltered IRAs. The second measure, HR 9, "The Job Creation and Wage Enhancement Act," provided for reductions in capital gains taxes for individuals and corporations, more favorable tax treatment of capital investment by large and small businesses, and reductions in estate taxes. The Ways and Means Committee reported out the Contract tax provisions on March 14, 1995.

In early April, as the Republicans were on the verge of delivering on their pledge to vote on all of the Contract measures within 100 days, the provision providing for a $500-per-child tax credit for families with incomes up to a cap of $200,000 emerged as one of the most divisive issues in this early period of the 104th Congress. President Clinton and congressional Democrats had sharply criticized the measure as providing an unneeded tax cut for the rich, and key Republican senators including Budget Committee chair Pete Domenici (NM) and Finance Committee chair Bob Packwood (OR) were publicly questioning the wisdom of enacting tax cuts while large budget deficits continued to loom (Gimpel 1996, 108; Rubin 1995a). As Gingrich (1995, 135) characterizes the controversy: "For the last three weeks of the Contract, the big issue became whether the Republicans would cave in to class-warfare rhetoric and set a lower cap. This was a much bigger issue than it appeared." Majority Leader Armey had already intervened to quell a move by Ways and Means Republicans to lower the income cap to $95,000 during committee consideration of the tax bill (Gimpel 1996, 109). Then, before the bill could be brought to a vote on the House floor, 102 House Republicans signed a letter requesting the leadership to allow a vote on an amendment to reduce the income cap for families receiving the tax credit from $200,000 to $95,000.

Thirty-five of the seventy-three Republican freshmen were among the signatories calling for the smaller tax cut, but this was no backbench revolt. Ten committee chairs and thirty-nine subcommittee chairs also signed. Included among the committee chairs were two Gingrich had handpicked over their more senior committee colleagues, Commerce Committee chair Thomas Bliley (VA) and Judiciary Committee chair Henry Hyde (IL). Stated Hyde: "I want something that defangs Democrats' charges that we are the party of the rich" (Rubin 1995a). By some accounts Gingrich initially appeared open to discussion of scaling back the tax cuts (Drew 1996, 171–177; Killian 1998, 74). But within days of the release of the letter he took a hard line in favor of the original provision. In a town hall meeting broadcast by satellite, the speaker emphasized the importance of sending a clear signal to voters about Republican support for lower taxes: "All I can say is that I was there when people told President [George H. W.] Bush it was OK to raise taxes; I was there when people told President Clinton he could raise taxes, and it destroyed his majority" (Rubin 1995a).

With almost half (102 of 230) of the Republican conference publicly stating a preference for a smaller tax cut, House Republicans were deeply split on the issue. Speaker Gingrich acknowledged in a March 28 speech to a business group, "The tax bill is in some trouble" (Rubin 1995b). Yet rather than backing off on the issue or leaving the House free to work its will by allowing a floor vote on the smaller tax cut, Gingrich instead declared the Contract tax bill with the higher income cap the "crowning jewel" of the Contract (Gingrich 1995a) and used his authority as speaker to enforce an up-or-down vote on the measure. As the vote approached, the speaker stated that he intended to frame the choice for his followers as one of either accepting the higher $200,000 income cap on the child tax credit or repudiating their party's position on tax cuts on the final major vote of the first 100 days of Republican rule. As Gingrich explained to reporters, "You're now going to go to these guys and say, 'On final passage, why don't you kill the *piece de resistance* of the entire Contract so you can go home on the 7th of April and have every Republican in your district ask you if you've lost your mind'" (Pianin 1995). "We were anxious," said Republican Rules Committee member John Linder (GA) about the vote on the rule to debate the bill. "We did not think we had the votes for the rule up until maybe a half hour before. That was what [Majority Whip] Tom DeLay calls not just counting the votes but growing the votes. Very close" (Linder 1995). Gingrich's strategy worked; both the rule and the bill passed the House on April 5 (by votes of 228–204 and 246–188, respectively), with only eleven Republicans voting no. Even Greg Ganske (IA) and Pat Roberts (KS), two of the leaders of the effort within the conference to lower the income cap, voted in favor.

The politics of the Contract tax cuts also show that Speaker Gingrich's leadership on the "Contract with America" measures was not limited to acting as an agent for highly unified followers. In this case Gingrich was able to influence the outcome by persuading a large bloc of Republican members to alter their policy preferences, or at least alter the policy outcome for which they were willing to vote, which is what ultimately matters in congressional politics. As Henry Hyde, one of the committee chairs who opposed the larger tax cut, explained: "At times like these, many of us subordinate our preferences to the greater good of the team" (Rubin 1995c). In the face of a major divide in the Republican conference over how large a tax cut was best for the "team" and despite the risk of losing control of the final major vote of the Contract period, Speaker Gingrich chose to use the prerogatives of the speakership to shape the outcome in the direction of his own strongly held personal goal of associating the Republican Party with big tax cuts. "Maintaining the Contract's original provision in the face of this internal pressure," writes James Gimpel (1996, 119), author of the most detailed account of the passage of the Contract measures, "was probably the most remarkable exhibition of leadership power during the first 100 days." The final outcome on the Contract tax cuts, however, would not be determined until a balanced budget agreement could be reached with President Clinton during the next Congress.

*The Contract and Policy Change.* Together with welfare reform and major tax cuts, all but one of the Contract measures passed the House in early 1995. But as Richard Fenno (1997, 37) has commented, passing the Contract measures in one chamber of Congress "was not synonymous with governing the country." Gingrich's often-stated goal of transforming national policy justifiably established a high standard for evaluating his leadership. Early on, Speaker Gingrich also set a tone of disdain for legislative compromise. In November 1994, he had proclaimed regarding the Contract measures: "We will cooperate with anyone, and we'll compromise with no one" (Cooper 1994). Fenno and others have argued persuasively that Gingrich's leadership on the Contract issues, while successful in orchestrating action inside the House, created expectations among his politically inexperienced followers and the public that later caused serious problems for his speakership and for his party

(Fenno 1997; Jones 1999, chap. 2). Among the criticisms that have been leveled at Gingrich's Contract strategy is that too little attention was paid to the broader political context beyond the House. "It took no cognizance of the Senate with its distinctive procedures and its different ideological makeup, nor did it comprehend the president with his bully pulpit" (Fenno 1997, 21). Working from models of executive leadership patterned in part on military leaders and corporate CEOs, Gingrich had not factored into his strategy the complexity of the politics of separation of powers in the American constitutional order (Connelly and Pitney 1999).[22]

The remainder of the chapter will show that many of these criticisms of Speaker Gingrich's leadership are on target. If Gingrich proved remarkably successful in winning House approval for major policy changes during his first year as speaker, he was in political trouble almost continuously after the first year, and by associating Republicans with a strident, confrontational partisanship undoubtedly contributed to President Clinton's political recovery and reelection in 1996 (Fenno 1997; Jones 1999). Even so, the imprint of the Contract exercise during early months of the Gingrich speakership on public policy was considerable.

First, by means of the Contract exercise and a balanced budget initiative also announced early in 1995 (discussed below) Gingrich and the House Republicans succeeded in decisively altering the terms of the policy debate in Washington in a more conservative direction. Welfare reform was only one policy area in which this occurred. As Charles O. Jones observes:

> One major effect of the hundred-day blitz was to set a new, more conservative agenda in place. It was no longer a question of whether there would be welfare reform but how restrictive it would be. The goal of balancing the budget was no longer debated, the issue was how and when. Devolution to the states was not at issue, only how and how much ... As the president sought to reestablish a more active role in the national policy process, he would have to orient himself to this revised agenda. Whether or not the House Republicans could expect to have their way beyond their own chamber, they had created the context within which politics would be played out in 1995. (1999, 121)

By early 1996 President Clinton had embraced the Republican goal of enacting a balanced budget, even declaring, "The era of big government is over." As Gingrich (2003) later described the response of the Republican-controlled Senate to the new agenda: "One of the great miracles of that period is look how far in '95 and early '96 we carried the Senate. The Senate didn't sign the Contract, the Senate wasn't a part of the Contract, most of the Senators thought we were crazy, but they couldn't figure out how to get off the bus."

Table 5.1 addresses the question of how often Speaker Gingrich and House Republicans actually did have their way beyond their own chamber on the measures included in the Contract. As this table shows, many Contract measures indeed failed to be enacted because of lack of support in the Senate or vetoes cast by President Clinton. These included the constitutional amendment to require a balanced budget as well as measures prohibiting foreign command of American troops in U.N. missions, and creating a new national product liability law. However, when the fate of all of the Contract measures is traced out through the end of the Gingrich speakership in 1998, the record of Contract legislation enacted into law still is substantial. Sixteen bills originating in the Contract or containing major Contract provisions had been signed into law by 1998. Some were relatively minor measures, but among these public laws were restrictions on unfunded mandates on the states, major personal and business tax cuts, welfare reform, an increase in funding for ballistic missile defense and a line-item veto.[23] Whatever political problems followed from Gingrich's Contract strategy, the evidence is clear that the Contract was consequential in leading to some major changes in public policy.

## Going to Zero: Enacting a Balanced Budget

The Contract had called for enactment of a balanced budget amendment to the Constitution that would take effect in 2002 (or the second fiscal year after ratification) but did not specify how the budget would be balanced. Before bringing the balanced budget amendment to a vote, House Republican leaders had declined to specify how the budget could be balanced out of concern that enumerating the required program cuts might threaten passage of the measure (Gimpel 1996, 45). Gingrich, however, had been arguing for over a decade that balancing the federal budget could serve as an important strategic vehicle for advancing the broader, transformative policy agenda he favored. In this case we find Speaker Gingrich again acting well ahead of any clear expression of his followers' preferences in an effort to shape those preferences in a direction consistent with his own goal of using a balanced budget initiative to drive more sweeping change in federal programs.

Gingrich reaffirmed his interest in the budget as a means of driving large-scale policy change in his first speech to House Republicans after being nominated for the speakership: "We have to have a dialogue about the budget because the budget is the transformational document for this system. When you've changed the budget, you've really changed government, and until you change the budget, you've just talked about changing government" (Congressional Quarterly 1995, 57D). In a March 1995 interview, he reiterated this point: "I regard getting to the balanced budget as the fulcrum to move the whole system. It's the only thing that gives you

TABLE 5.1
*Action on Contract Measures, 104th and 105th Congresses (1995–1998)*

| Contract Item | Final Status | Institution that Failed to Approve if Not Enacted |
|---|---|---|
| Congressional Reforms | Enacted | |

*Major provisions:* require existing federal laws to apply to Congress; reduce number of committees and committee staffs; term limits for committee chairs; ban proxy voting; require 3/5 vote for tax increases

*Enacted:* all provisions implemented through changes in House rules and legislation ending exemptions of Congress from 11 federal workplace and safety laws (PL 104-1)

| | | |
|---|---|---|
| Balanced Budget and Line-Item Veto | Partially Enacted | Senate |

*Major provisions:* propose constitutional amendment to require a balanced budget and legislation to give the president a line-item veto

*Passed House:* balanced budget amendment (HJ Res 1); line-item veto (HR 2)

*Enacted:* Line-item veto (PL 104-130), but invalidated by the Supreme Court on June 25, 1998

*Not Enacted:* proposed balanced budget amendment; failed to receive required two-thirds vote in the Senate in the 104th Congress (SJ Res 1) and again in the 105th (SJ Res 1)

| | | |
|---|---|---|
| Anti-Crime Measures | Partially Enacted | Senate |

*Major provisions:* restitution to crime victims, changes in exclusionary rule, limitations on death penalty appeals, grants for prison construction, changes in funding for anticrime programs to block grants; expedited deportation of criminal aliens

*Passed House:* HR 665, 666, 667, 668, 728, 729

*Enacted:* limitations on death penalty appeals, deportation of criminal aliens (PL 104-132); and deportation of criminal aliens (104-208)

*Not Enacted:* victim restitution (HR 665) passed Senate, no conference; exclusionary rule reform (HR 666) died in Senate committee; prison and sentencing measures (HR 667) died in Senate committee; law enforcement block grants (HR 728) died in Senate committee

| | | |
|---|---|---|
| Welfare Reform | Enacted (with Revisions) | |

*Major provisions:* prohibit benefits to minor mothers and mothers who have additional children while on welfare; reduce welfare spending; 5 year time limit for benefits; end benefits for noncitizens; require welfare recipients to work

*Passed House:* HR 2491 passed Senate, vetoed by President Clinton, December 6, 1995; HR 4 passed Senate, vetoed by President Clinton, January 9, 1996; repassed as HR 3734 and passed Senate in 1996

*Enacted:* PL 104-193

| | | |
|---|---|---|
| Measures to Strengthen Families | Partially Enacted | Senate, Presidential Veto |

*Major provisions:* child support enforcement; tax incentives for adoption, require parental consent for children's participation in certain surveys; stronger child pornography and sex crime legislation; tax benefits for home care of family members

*Passed House:* adoption (HR 3448), sex crimes (HR 1240), family privacy surveys (HR 1271), child support (HR 3734), family care (HR 2491)

*Enacted:* child support enforcement (PL 104-193); penalties for child pornography and sex crimes against children (PL 104-71); tax credits for adoption (PL 104-188)

*Not Enacted:* family privacy surveys (HR 1271) died in Senate committee; tax benefits for care of family members (HR 2491) vetoed by President Clinton, December 6, 1995

| | | |
|---|---|---|
| Tax Cuts for Families | Partially Enacted | Presidential Veto |

*Major provisions:* $500-per-child tax credit; reduce "marriage penalty"; expand Individual Retirement Accounts

*Passed House:* HR 1215; HR 2491; HR 2014 (105th Congress)

*Enacted:* child tax credit, expanded IRAs (PL 105-34 105th Congress)

*Not Enacted:* Reduction in marriage penalty. (HR 2491) passed Senate, vetoed by President Clinton, December 6, 1995

National Security Provisions          Partially Enacted          Senate, Presidential Veto

*Major provisions:* prohibit foreign command of U.S. troops in U.N. missions; develop a missile defense system to protect U.S. territory; prohibit cuts in defense spending from being used to fund other programs

*Passed House:* funding for missile defense with amendment to restrict scope; restrictions on foreign command of U.S. troops (HR 7); measure requiring deployment of missile defense system over the U.S. by 2003 (HR 1530); increase ($1 billion) in appropriations for missile defense (HR 4328, 105th Congress)

*Enacted:* increase in funding for missile defense programs (PL105-27, 105th Congress)

*Not Enacted:* prohibition of foreign command in U.N. missions, budgetary rules to protect defense programs (both died in Senate committee); deployment of missile defense system by 2003 (HR 1530) passed by Senate, vetoed by President Clinton, December 28, 1995

Social Security and Taxation
of Senior Citizens          Partially Enacted          Senate

*Major provisions:* repeal 1993 increase in social security benefits subject to taxation; increase earnings limits for beneficiaries; tax incentives for long-term care insurance

*Passed House:* HR 2491, passed Senate, vetoed by President Clinton on December 6, 1995; increase in earnings limits (HR 3136) and long-term care provisions (HR 3103) repassed

*Enacted:* increased earnings limit (PL 104-121), long-term care tax provisions (PL 104-191)

*Not Enacted:* provision to repeal increased taxation of social security benefits failed to pass Senate, dropped in House-Senate conference (HR 2491), November 1995

Capital Gains Tax Cut
and Regulatory Reform          Partially Enacted          Senate

*Major provisions:* cut capital gains taxes and revise other business tax provisions; reduce unfunded mandates on states; reduce federal paperwork for individuals and small businesses; require federal agencies to use cost/benefit analysis and reimburse property owners for loss of value due to regulations

*Passed House:* unfunded mandates (HR 5); business tax measures and regulatory reform (HR 9 —individual bills were HR 830, 925, 926, 1022), omnibus tax bill containing capital gains tax cut (HR 1215); budget reconciliation measure including tax measures in HR 1215 (HR 2491) passed Senate, vetoed by President Clinton, December 6, 1995, repassed as HR 2015 (105th Congress); business tax provisions (HR 3488)

*Enacted:* limitations on unfunded mandates (PL 104-4); reduce federal paperwork (PL 104-13); business tax provisions (PL 104-88); capital gains tax reduction (PL 105-34, 105th Congress)

*Not Enacted:* Some regulatory reform measures (included in HR 9) failed to pass the Senate

Legal Reforms          Partially Enacted          Senate, Presidential Veto

*Major provisions:* national product liability law with limits on punitive damages; restriction on shareholder suits against firms; apply loser pays rule to legal fees in certain federal lawsuits

*Passed House:* product liability (HR 956); shareholder suits (HR 1058); loser pays rule (HR 988)

*Enacted:* limitations on shareholder suits (PL 104-67)

*Not Enacted:* loser pays legislation (HR 988) failed to pass Senate; revised product liability measure (HR 956) passed Senate, vetoed by President Clinton, May 2, 1996

Term Limits          Not Enacted          House, Senate

*Major provisions:* proposed constitutional amendment to limit House and Senate members to either 6 years' service for House members and 12 years for Senators or 12 years for both

*Passed House:* No. Failed to receive required two-thirds vote in House in both 104th (HJ Res 73) and 105th (HJ Res 2) Congresses; failed to come to a floor vote in the Senate during either the 104th (SJ Res 21) or 105th (SJ Res 16) Congresses

---

SOURCE: Bader 1996, appendix E; Gimpel 1996; Congressional Quarterly 1996, 1–10; *CQ Weekly* (various issues); THOMAS (http://thomas.loc.gov/).
NOTE: All bill numbers are for the 104th Congress unless otherwise indicated.

the moral imperative to change the whole structure of the welfare state" (Williams 1995, 211).

But in early 1995, House Republicans—including new Budget Committee chair John Kasich (OH), one of the most committed deficit hawks in the party—understood that the goal in formulating the first Republican budget would be to enact sufficient spending reductions to offset the Contract tax cuts and defense spending increases and establish a "glide path" toward budget balance at some unspecified future date. The Contract provided: "We will instruct the House Budget Committee to report to the floor and we will work to enact additional budget savings . . . to ensure that the federal budget deficit will be less than it would have been without these bills" (Gillespie and Schellhas 1994, 11). Kasich stated that this glide path strategy, which would still involve hundreds of billions of dollars in spending cuts, was difficult but "doable" (Drew 1996, 128). Kasich made it clear in early 1995 that he did not believe it was politically feasible for Republicans to enact the tax cuts and defense spending increases set forth in the Contract and commit to a date certain for balancing the budget (Drew 1996, 127–128; Dewar 1995).

Without even consulting Kasich, at a February 14 press briefing, Speaker Gingrich asserted that the House would pass a budget that would be balanced within seven years (Maraniss and Weisskopf 1996, 37). Gingrich's chief of staff Dan Meyer (1997) explained:

> We had passed the balanced budget amendment and it went over to the Senate and it was hitting some rough water . . . Specifically, some of the Democrats were arguing . . . if the Republicans think we should have a balanced budget, how are they going to do it? And someone posed that to Newt and he said, "They're right, we will produce a budget this year that balances in seven years." He just said it. I can remember John Kasich was on the phone in about a nanosecond saying, "Where in the hell did *that* come from?" . . . I can remember Arne Christensen who was doing our budget work calling me and saying, "Did you hear what Newt just said?"

The next day in a meeting with Kasich and the House GOP leadership, Gingrich announced that the goal for the budget was now to balance it within seven years. Kasich objected that it was not possible. Gingrich then called for an informal show of hands, and all but Kasich supported the proposal. "Motion carries," Gingrich announced. "You're outvoted, John. We're going to zero" (Hager and Pianin 1997, 18–19; see also Drew 1996, 128; Maraniss and Weisskopf 1996, 37–38).[24] Before undertaking any further consultation with Republican members, the speaker made a formal announcement of the seven-year balanced budget goal to the press the following morning (*Washington Post* 1995).

As one leadership staffer described the abrupt shift in budget strategy in early 1995: "It was Newt way out there on his own. The Senate had not bought into this yet. All he had was almost a flip vote in the House leadership the day before—it wasn't like there was a big deliberate discussion of the question—but he announced the policy publicly the next day so that nobody could back away from it" (Drew 1996, 128–129). Leonard Swinehart (1996), Gingrich's staffer responsible for overseeing the House floor at the time, stated: "It was his idea totally. It was clearly top down. It was his sole decision." Dan Meyer added: "Newt just did it. He just announced it. Which was his operating style. His view was that . . . the job of a CEO is to move the goalposts and force the institution to accommodate that, because otherwise everybody would tell you why it can't be done" (1997). When asked about the decision to push for a balanced budget, Gingrich (2003) explained:

> When I was first Speaker we'd do dinners in the Capitol [with corporate CEOs] and I would ask them—we would spend two, three hours at a time—and I would ask them if you were trying to balance the budget, if you were to look at the scale of change we are trying to get, given the changes you've done as a CEO and how you run your own company, what is your advice. And it was very consistent. Set very big goals. Set very short time limits. And delegate like crazy. And don't ask any experts because we'll all be wrong, we'll be too timid. And I mean, CEO after CEO after CEO said [this]. So, when you got to these kinds of decisions I said OK, so let me get this straight. We are going to set very big goals, we are going to set very short time limits, and all the experts who know we can't do it are barred from the room.

Though Gingrich drew strong support for balancing the budget from members of the large Republican freshman class (Rae 1998, 76, 93–95, 100, 206; Fenno 1997, 41–44), there is no evidence that he consulted them or anyone else before establishing the balanced budget goal by means of an impromptu show of hands among a small group of top Republican leaders. And at the time Gingrich made the commitment public, the prospects of enacting a balanced budget were far from certain. Several senior Republican committee chairs whose expertise was needed to develop a balanced budget had already publicly expressed ambivalence about the policy changes that would be required to reach this goal (Pine 1995; Connolly 1995).

As one Republican leadership staffer described the political situation when Gingrich announced the balanced budget goal: "We [House Republicans] were all for a balanced budget amendment. Being for a constitutional amendment to balance the budget is pretty easy. It polls well and all that. But . . . [Gingrich] made the decision that we're going to *actually* balance the budget which means that we're going to have to make all these cuts and do all of these things. Now no one, when they did the Contract with America, had bought into that; that we would actually make the spending cuts and hit balance" (Hellman 2002). Said Majority Leader Armey's chief of staff Kerry Knott (2005): "Making that step to actually force the process to bend to a seven-year balanced budget was a *huge* risk . . . Most of the freshman class probably would have said, sign me up. But the members who'd been around for a while, who knew how difficult it would be—what it would mean on the appropriations side, what it would mean on entitlement spending and the political risks . . . Those who'd been around for a while knew this was going to be really, really hard. And Kasich, while agreeing in principle, went back and forth for *months:* 'Was this doable?'" Budget Committee chair Kasich commented in late February 1995, after the decision had been made by the leadership to go to zero: "There have been countless meetings with countless discussions. I try to let them know the enormity of the situation. I have my doubts about whether they're [fellow Republicans] going to come through or not. I don't know yet" (Drew 1996, 129).

Gingrich set up a budget steering group consisting of Kasich, Appropriations Committee chair Robert Livingston, Ways and Means Committee chair Bill Archer (TX), Majority Leader Richard Armey, and himself to coordinate the enormous task of passing the legislation that would be involved in meeting the goal of balancing the budget while enacting major tax cuts. Gingrich encouraged the others to work to develop consensus within the party on how to reach the goal, at one point admonishing them to avoid imposing decisions from the top (ibid., 130–132). In drawing up the budget resolution that would provide the framework for the policy changes needed to reach balance, Kasich encountered serious resistance within the party to cuts that would be required in transportation and agriculture programs (Maraniss and Weisskopf 1996, 38–44, 48–52).

The House voted 238–193 on May 18 to pass a Republican budget plan that met the seven-year balanced budget goal. Eight Democrats joined all but one Republican in voting in favor of the budget resolution. The plan mandated just over one trillion dollars in reduced spending over the seven-year period, including reductions of $288 billion in Medicare, $187 billion in Medicaid, $219 billion from farm programs and other nonhealth entitlements, and $192 billion from other domestic programs. With $287 billion in revenue foregone from the Contract tax cuts, the package would net $756 billion in total deficit reduction (Congressional Quarterly 1996, 2–21–24). The Senate passed a budget package later in May that was similar except for a smaller tax cut. A final budget resolution mandating $894 billion in total deficit reduction cleared both houses on June 29. The plan passed the House 239–194, with only one Republican voting no.

Speaker Gingrich personally took charge of a Republican task force that worked through the summer to develop changes in the Medicare program needed to meet the goal of reducing projected Medicare spending by $270 billion over seven years (Evans and Oleszek 1997, 122–123).[25] The eight-person group consisting of members from the Republican leadership and the Ways and Means and Commerce Committees developed a plan to increase premiums, hold down costs to providers, and allow beneficiaries to opt into private managed care plans as well as set up medical savings accounts. Said Commerce Committee chair Thomas Bliley, a member of the task force, "This bill, right from the start, was written in the speaker's office" (Pianin and Yang 1995).

President Clinton had played very little role in budget politics in early 1995 other than criticizing the Republicans' approach. In April, as the Republican balanced budget plan was taking shape, Clinton asked his staff, "How do we get in this thing?" (Drew 1996, 216). Just after the Republican plan cleared the House in May, the president decided the answer was to introduce his own balanced budget plan, although he announced he would support a plan to reach balance in ten rather than seven years. Congressional Republicans had succeeded in pulling the president onto their turf. As Clinton told his cabinet on June 13, just before he delivered a televised address outlining his ten-year plan: "The ticket to admission to American politics is a balanced budget" (ibid., 234). The Clinton plan also called for over $1 trillion in deficit reduction but proposed substantially smaller savings in the Medicare and Medicaid programs. Clinton and his advisers were also in no hurry to negotiate because they doubted Republicans had the political will to enact the massive spending reductions that would be required to meet their own seven-year plan, especially those in the popular Medicare program (ibid., 312–313).

House Republicans, on the other hand, were supremely confident that they could impose their budgetary priorities on the White House. In June Clinton had vetoed one of the first Republican budget measures rescinding $17 billion in spending from the previous year's budget. But he then signed a slightly modified version a few weeks later, leading some Republicans—including Gingrich—to believe Clinton would acquiesce on a larger budget package as well (ibid., 213; Swope 1997). Speaker Gingrich encouraged this view of Republicans' ability to prevail in a test of wills with the president. As he told a reporter in the summer of 1995: "The collision with the White House is a project but it's only a tiny part of what we're doing. I mean we'll do that *en passant*" (Drew 1996, 276–277).

Both the White House and the speaker had calculated wrong. By late October the House and the Senate passed massive reconciliation bills implementing the balanced budget plan including the Medicare reductions and major tax cuts. After the Republicans proved successful in passing the legislation to implement their budget, initial negotiations between congressional Republicans and the White House began in early November. But little headway was made. Final approval of the Republican budget package came on November 17 in both chambers. But Republicans had not passed most of the annual appropriations bills funding government operations, and failure to reach agreement with the White House on the terms of a short-term spending measure resulted in what would be the first of two government shutdowns.[26] Earlier in 1995, Gingrich had signaled repeatedly that he would be willing to shut down the government if necessary to impress on the White House the determination of Republicans to see their budget implemented (ibid., 214; Garrett 2005, 119; Jones 1999, 126). Implicit in this strategy was the calculation that the president would receive most of the blame for shutting down the government because he would be seen as obstructing enactment of a balanced budget. This proved to be an even more serious miscalculation and a misunderstanding of how the extraordinary politics of early 1995 had altered the political context. As Jones (1999, 117) observes, "With agenda setting having shifted to Capitol Hill, Republicans could expect accountability to be sited there as well." And this is precisely what happened.

Even so, Gingrich's confrontational strategy kept pulling President Clinton closer to the Republican position. The agreement reached to end the first shutdown on November 19 included a commitment by the president to accept the goal of budget balance within a seven-year time frame, provided less-severe cuts would be enacted in health, education, and environmental programs. But with opinion polls now showing public blame for the shutdowns falling primarily on Republicans, President Clinton vetoed the massive Republican budget reconciliation bill on December 6. Clinton attacked the measure for providing tax cuts for the wealthy and making harmful cuts in Medicare and other programs. Senate Majority Leader Robert Dole was now ready to abandon the shutdown strategy and keep the government open while continuing to negotiate with the White House. Gingrich had encountered resistance from some conservative Republicans, especially some of the freshmen, in ending the first shutdown (Drew 1996, 333). When Speaker Gingrich raised the possibility with House Republican leaders of keeping the government running while negotiating with Clinton he met with strong opposition (ibid., 350–351). With budget talks between the White House and Congress again at an impasse, House Republicans refused to support another short-term spending measure, causing a second government shutdown to begin on December 15. When the president signaled willingness on December 19 to negotiate a new seven-year budget plan—this time using budget numbers from the Congressional Budget Office as Republicans were demanding, Gingrich again raised the possibility of reopening the government. But the Republican conference refused to change direction and was now almost unanimous in support of maintaining the shutdown until the president actually agreed to submit a balanced budget (ibid., 352; Koszczuk 1995b).

In early January as the Republicans' public standing continued to deteriorate, Speaker Gingrich finally succeeded in persuading House Republicans to change course. Senate Majority Leader Dole won passage of a stopgap resolution in the Senate on January 2 to end the shutdown (Hager 1996). House Republicans initially rejected the Dole move, but on January 4 Speaker Gingrich proposed a new continuing resolution (short-term spending bill) to reopen the government. After a Republican Conference meeting could not reach agreement on how to proceed, the next day Gingrich convened the Conference and argued forcefully that the party position would be to pass a revised continuing resolution conditioned only on the president's submission of a seven-year balanced budget plan (Peters 1997, 308). To critics who objected that the speaker was backing down, he responded: "You don't like the job I'm doing as speaker, run against me" (Drew 1996, 361; see also Hager 1996). All but fifteen Republicans voted in support of the speaker's proposal. As Gingrich (2003) explained: "There was a morning that Dole couldn't go any further, and that's the morning we changed, because you couldn't go any further. But it was very important that it not be us and it was very important that we not prejudge whether Clinton would break and I think, in retrospect, there was every reason to believe Clinton might have broken."

After the second shutdown ended, the president again moved in the Republicans' direction, introducing a seven-year budget plan on January 6 based on Congressional Budget Office numbers. As Fenno (1997, 40) notes, "When the government reopened, the president offered a budget that had moved closer to the Republicans than anyone thought possible." But the two sides remained far apart on the programmatic changes that would be required to produce the massive spending reductions required to reach balance (Sinclair 2000, 201). By late January little progress had been made in negotiations with the White House and Republicans gave up on reaching a broad budget agreement with President Clinton for the remainder of 1996. "We do not believe it's now possible to get a budget agreement," said Gingrich. "I don't expect us to get a seven-year balanced budget agreement with President Clinton in office" (Congressional Quarterly 1996, 2–63).

Although Gingrich and the House Republicans would ultimately win the budget war, in the confrontation with President Clinton that began in late 1995 they lost the battle for public support. As Republican leadership staffer Kerry Knott (2005) put it: "Events started to overtake us . . . We never quite regained the momentum we had." Gingrich's standing with the public and with his House followers had also taken a big hit. A petulant comment made during the first government shutdown, suggesting that it was partly payback for a perceived snub from the president on a return flight from Israeli Prime Minister Yitzhak Rabin's funeral, provided an easy target for Democrats wanting to characterize Republicans as irresponsible and raised concerns within the party about the speaker's judgment (Koszczuk 1995a). The speaker's shift away from a strategy of confrontation with the White House in late 1995 also drove "a wedge between the leadership and the freshmen that had not existed during the Contract period when they had both been operating in harmony" (Rae 1998, 123). For the remainder of 1996 House Republicans became focused on issues on which both they and the president could agree to legislate in order to provide evidence to the voters of their ability to govern. The result was a surge in legislative productivity that included welfare reform, health insurance legislation, immigration reform, a major telecommunications regulation bill, and an increase in the minimum wage. As Jones (1999, 170) has noted, this was "a striking record for a session that began as one of the most conflictual in modern times."

The 1996 election, which thinned the House Republican majority for the 105th Congress from 19 to 10 seats and returned Bill Clinton to the White House, was interpreted by most in the party as a signal that they needed to continue to focus on delivering results. "We find ourselves here with a Democratic president and a Republican Congress," Gingrich said in a November 20 speech after being renominated as speaker, "and we have an absolute moral obligation to make this system work. If the last Congress was the 'Confrontation Congress,' this Congress will be the 'Implementation Congress'" (Yang 1996).

New negotiations with the White House on enacting a balanced budget commenced in the spring of 1997. Prospects for a deal were enhanced by movement that had already occurred on both sides during the 1995–1996 negotiations and by strong economic growth that narrowed the deficit and made the spending cuts required to reach balance smaller (Palazzolo 1999, 43–44). Daniel Palazzolo's (1999) detailed analysis of the politics of the 1997 balanced budget agreement shows that Speaker Gingrich played a less central role in the final round of negotiations, delegating greater authority to House committee chairs to shape the agreement—especially Budget Committee chair John Kasich. "In 1997, Gingrich adopted a more traditional style of House leadership: managing the internal workings of the process, delegating policy details to committee chairs, weighing in at the final stages of key decisions, and working as a 'middleman' to mediate differences between committee chairs and party factions" (Palazzolo 2000, 16). One of the speaker's most high-profile moves in the negotiations misfired when Gingrich publicly advanced the idea in March of reaching agreement with the White House on deficit reduction first, then taking up the tax cuts in the Republican proposal later. Gingrich's statement provoked a firestorm of criticism from Republican conservatives, and he reversed course to support keeping the tax cuts and deficit reduction packages linked (Palazzolo 1999, 69–70, 76).

By May the main outlines of an agreement were in place, and bipartisan majorities approved new budget plans in the House and Senate in early June. Two budget reconciliation bills—one containing the deficit reduction measures and one the tax cuts—were approved by late July, and President Clinton signed both into law on August 5, 1997. Republicans agreed to accept a number of Clinton's spending priorities—including increased funding for children's health care, higher welfare spending, and education tax cuts—and settled for smaller tax cuts than had originally been proposed. New revenues from economic growth also reduced the overall size of the final deficit reduction package required to reach balance to $263 billion over five years. But as Palazzolo (1999, 189) found, "The big ticket items in the budget . . . are Republican priorities." These included the $500-per-child tax credit; expanded individual retirement accounts and capital gains tax reductions that had originally been proposed in the Contract (collectively the largest tax cut since the first term of the Reagan administration); a 12 percent reduction ($115 billion) in projected Medicare spending over five years along with expanded options for beneficiaries including medical savings accounts; and holding overall spending in domestic nonentitlement programs below the rate of inflation for five years ($140 billion in savings) (Congressional Quarterly 1998, 2-47-61).

Improved economic conditions made balancing the budget a less heroic task in 1997 than it had been in 1995. But given the political difficulty of enacting hundreds of billions of dollars in spending reductions—including those in the popular Medicare program—it is hard to imagine that a balanced budget would have been enacted during the 105th Congress had Senate Republicans and President Clinton not embraced that goal in 1995. The initiative in defining that goal came from House Republicans, and Speaker Gingrich was the figure who convinced them to take this on. There is no evidence that Speaker Gingrich's followers were in agreement on pursuing such an ambitious budgetary plan in early 1995, or that they had even been consulted before Gingrich announced they would enact a balanced budget in February of that year. But there is clear evidence that long before he became speaker Gingrich had been strongly committed to advancing a balanced budget as a vehicle for transforming the direction of national governance. Gingrich made some serious strategic miscalculations about how to achieve this goal—especially regarding the effects of shutting down the government in late 1995—and these miscalculations combined with other problems that began to undermine his support among House Republicans. But the evidence is clear that his actions were consequential in defining the goal of budgetary balance at the outset of the 1995–1997 budget debates and that he did so more by shaping his followers' preferences rather than responding to them. Gingrich also left an imprint in the policy changes advanced through the balanced budget through the leadership role he took on the House Medicare task force in 1995.

Other measures were enacted during the 105th Congress—including an overhaul of the Food and Drug Administration, a funding package to keep the Amtrak system running, and a massive surface transportation bill. But House Republicans ended the Congress frustrated with their own leadership and having set a course to impeach the president for only the second time in American history. They had failed in the effort to enact another round of tax cuts, were unable to reach agreement with the Senate on a budget for 1999, and ended the second session of the 105th Congress by passing a huge omnibus appropriations measure negotiated by their leadership and the White House that broke the spending limits from the previous year's budget agreement and was considered by many a capitulation to the president's spending priorities. As the 1998 election approached, House Republicans had also initiated a formal inquiry into impeachment of President Clinton for misdeeds arising from the Monica Lewinsky scandal. The November 3 election, in which Republicans suffered electoral losses that narrowed their House majority to only six seats, proved to be the final act of the Gingrich speakership.

## Newt Fatigue: The Fall of the Transformative Leader

Newt Gingrich resigned the speakership when it became clear he would not be chosen by House Republicans to continue as leader of their narrowed majority. The same distinctive personal qualities and goals that help explain why Gingrich's leadership was so consequential for institutional and policy outcomes in Congress—his frenetic energy and willingness to test political limits and take big risks to achieve ambitious political ends—also created political problems that ultimately undermined the support among members on which all congressional leaders depend. As Arne Christensen (2005), who held a number of staff positions under Speaker Gingrich, including serving as his chief of staff, put it: "The general result was that you had at times a lot more creative policymaking, but also more strain on the system and ultimately, Newt fatigue." Speaker Gingrich's support among his Republican followers eroded and ultimately collapsed because of three sets of problems: grievances that had been accumulating among a wider and wider circle of Republican members over his approach to the office and erratic management of the House; allegations of ethics violations within the network of organizations he had created to communicate his ideas and support the effort to build a Republican majority; and finally what was seen as a failed electoral strategy for House Republicans in the 1998 election.

Reflecting back on his speakership in a 2003 interview, Gingrich emphasized: "I operated, very self-consciously, in a high-risk, high-demand model . . . I had no interest in being a managerial speaker." Said Gingrich's first chief of staff, Dan Meyer (1997): "He clearly wanted to be kind of above the day-to-day management. It just didn't work." Gingrich viewed himself as a national party leader and the leader of a conservative popular movement in addition to being speaker and for much of his speakership attempted to delegate day-to-day responsibility for managing the business of the House to Majority Leader Richard Armey. Gingrich's flirtations with a presidential bid added to concerns that he was not sufficiently focused on running the House (Katz 1998). As Gingrich proved between 1995 and 1997, the House speakership can sometimes be used as a position from which to drive change in American politics. But the speaker is held responsible by his followers for the management of the House. According to Denny Hastert of Illinois, who as chief deputy whip was in close communication with the Republican members, as early as the Contract exercise of the first 100 days: "Members began to complain that Newt thrived on chaos"; "Working for him was like being a graduate assistant to the professor who never slept" (Hastert 2004, 121, 147).

Gingrich also lost support because he came to be seen by his followers as too prone to change course unpredictably in response to pleading from members or to new ideas of his own.[27] Again to quote Hastert: "He had far-reaching visions, but something always got in the way of those visions. He would have good ideas; he was just amazing with good ideas. The problem was he would have three good ideas a day. He'd give me the job of following through on at least one of them. I'd still be working on this one idea that was, say, two weeks old when all of a sudden he'd change course. Whoever had talked to him last, he'd go off in that direction, and there was no consistency" (ibid., 147). Robert Livingston (2002), who chaired the House Appropriations Committee under Gingrich, offered a similar assessment: "He did enormous good for the Republican party and the . . . conservative movement. But when the need was there he could be pragmatic and not only cut a deal to solve his problem but doing it without telling or consulting anybody and drive everybody around him nuts. That was the big problem. He would change his mind so very, very quickly and with little or no consultation."

Probably most harmful to Gingrich from a political standpoint was the perception among some of the most committed Republican conservatives that he had abandoned the conservative "revolution" by changing course on the government shutdown strategy in late 1995 and later had proved too willing to compromise with President Clinton and accommodate party moderates in both the House and Senate. One result was an abortive "coup" attempt in July 1997, in which not only junior conservative backbenchers but also members of the Republican leadership actively discussed removing the speaker from office (Koszczuk 1997a, 1997b). Gingrich never fully regained their trust (see Fenno 2007, chap. 10).

A second set of problems that weakened the speaker's political support within the Republican conference were ethics charges that resulted in a formal reprimand from the House and a $300,000 penalty from the House Ethics Committee in January 1997. Critics charged that Gingrich had misused tax-exempt funds for partisan purposes and misled the Ethics Committee about interconnections between his partisan GOPAC organization and a "Renewing American Civilization" course for which the funds had been raised. The speaker admitted to submitting an inaccurate letter and agreed to the financial penalty (Congressional Quarterly 1998, 1–11–13). But together with the negative publicity Gingrich had garnered during the government shutdown, the ethics controversy caused some House Republicans to view the speaker as a growing political liability to the party. As a result a number withheld their votes in the January 1997 vote to reelect Gingrich speaker for the 105th Congress.

The development that brought the Gingrich speakership to an end was the outcome of the 1998 House elections. With President Clinton mired in the Lewinsky scandal and facing a sixth-year midterm election in which the opposition party normally scores major gains, Gingrich's political support collapsed when Republicans instead lost five seats. Gingrich's endgame strategy in the 1998 election had centered on running televised ads attacking Clinton. As Robert Livingston (2002), who was briefly in line to succeed Gingrich as speaker in 1998, explained:

> He'd gone after Clinton. And he'd done it with funds we'd all worked very hard to raise to support Republican members of Congress. I think the leadership of the Republican Party around the country and the members shared the belief by one or two days after the election that Newt had played his hand as hard as he could and lost. We had planned on picking up five seats and we lost fifteen. So a twenty-seat margin between what happened and what we were certain we were going to get just two months before the election. So there was tremendous disappointment with the outcome of the election. I can tell you because I was fielding calls and I talked with people. There were guys who said they wouldn't vote for Newt Gingrich for speaker under *any* circumstances. Period.

After conferring with other Republican leaders and learning he would not have the votes to be reelected speaker, Gingrich announced his resignation on November 6,

1998 (see Hastert 2004, 160–161). After four years of Gingrich's combative, centralized, high-profile, high-risk leadership style, House Republicans were ready for a return to a more conventional legislative leader.[28] When presumptive speaker Robert Livingston abruptly resigned from the House in December 1998, after revelations surfaced of indiscretions in his private life, Republicans quickly closed ranks in support of Denny Hastert of Illinois. When asked why Republicans had chosen Hastert, Republican Robert Ehrlich (2002) of Maryland responded: "It *had* to be Denny . . . He is the anti-Newt." Ehrlich added that Gingrich was a "polarizing politician," and after the Democrats engaged in a "demonization campaign" against him, the members "wanted calm. They wanted somebody who wanted one job not three, they wanted someone who could not be demonized by the Democrats." Newt fatigue had taken its toll.

## Conclusion

"I have an enormous personal ambition," Newt Gingrich told a Washington journalist a decade before he became speaker. "I want to shift the entire planet" (Romano 1985).[29] Once Gingrich became speaker of the House in 1995 he engaged in an extraordinarily ambitious effort to use the office of speaker to transform American politics. He also had developed an understanding of a type of transformational leadership he thought would be required to achieve his political goals and sought to put it into practice. Inevitably, Gingrich encountered the limits of leadership in the House and the American constitutional system. His tenure as speaker of the House was meteoric; he took Capitol Hill by storm, but four years later he had lost the procedural majority every legislative leader must have to remain in place. Contextual leadership theories that emphasize the importance of follower unity as the basis for strong leadership help explain why Gingrich was able to centralize authority and the problems Gingrich encountered when the unity of his followers began to fray and they became disillusioned with his leadership. However, the contextual perspective fails to capture the importance of Gingrich's successful efforts to shape his followers' preferences or to explain Gingrich's assertive leadership on issues on which his followers were divided. Here the conditional agency framework's emphasis on the leader's goals and propensity for taking risks to realize those goals helps explain some important features of the politics of the Gingrich speakership.

In the short space of four years Gingrich's leadership was consequential in three areas. First, he was the driving force for the establishment of a new, more party-centered institutional regime in the House of Representatives. Second, Gingrich succeeded in shaping his followers' preferences on public policy in a direction consistent with his own goals in a number of situations when Republicans were undecided or divided. The most important case is the 1997 balanced budget agreement that had its origins in Gingrich's unilateral decision to commit House Republicans to producing a balanced budget in February 1995. Yet Gingrich also played an important role in pushing House Republicans in the direction of supporting larger tax cuts and more radical reform of the welfare system.

Finally, Gingrich's aggressive, confrontational leadership style and the negative public reaction to that style that had set in by 1998 created the conditions for different types of leaders to come to the fore in the Republican Party. Initially for lack of a clear alternative, but later by choice, House Republicans selected Denny Hastert, a low-key, former high school wrestling coach with a collegial leadership style for speaker. Partly in response to the way Gingrich had led Congress, in seeking a standard-bearer in 2000, Republicans were drawn to George W. Bush because he had a record of fostering bipartisan cooperation in his home state of Texas and was seen as having a less hard-edged, less polarizing style of leadership.

In the final analysis it is hard to differ with Mayhew's assessment of Newt Gingrich: "We have as good a case as we are likely to see of a member of Congress operating in the public sphere with consequence" (Mayhew 2000, ix). And the former speaker may not be done yet. Commenting in 2006 about his interest in competing for the 2008 Republican presidential nomination, he explained: "If you're interested in defining the idea context and the political context for the next generation of Americans, which I am, the most effective way to do that is to be seen as potentially available" (Eilperin 2006).

# CHAPTER SIX

# *Conclusion*

## Congressional Leadership and Its Limits

> The Speaker is not the House of Representatives. The House of Representatives is not the government, or even the Congress. Ours is not a congressional system . . . Ours is, of course, a separated system of legitimate, coequal, and competing institutions.
>
> —*Charles O. Jones, 1999*

With each of the three House speakerships examined in this book, we find evidence that an individual leader was consequential for important outcomes in Congress. In each we also find cases of assertive, consequential leadership, not only in situations in which followers were in agreement about what they wanted to see happen in the House but also in situations in which followers' preferences were uncertain or even seriously divided. The central propositions of the contextual leadership theories are that leaders are motivated primarily by ambition to hold leadership positions in Congress and that a necessary condition for consequential leadership is for followers' preferences to be homogeneous on the issue to be decided. Each of the leaders examined in this book has been shown to have intensely held goals other than holding a leadership office in Congress, each proved willing to risk wielding the prerogatives of the speakership in support of those goals to influence decisions in situations when their followers' preferences were either unclear or seriously divided, and each succeeded in shaping congressional outcomes under those conditions. Thus there is clear evidence that the causal processes in leadership politics implied by the conditional agency framework were at work in some important policy and institutional outcomes in the Clay, Reed, and Gingrich speakerships and that the contextual leadership perspective provides an incomplete explanation of these cases.

Yet these cases also demonstrate that each leader also encountered limits to his ability to influence outcomes in the House. Speakers Clay, Reed, and Gingrich had little success in influencing outcomes when their followers' preferences on the issues to be decided were settled and homogeneous in opposition to the leader's goals. Each leader also encountered limits arising from the constitutional forms within which the House of Representatives must act. So while these cases show that the agency of congressional leaders can be consequential in American politics they also show that the agency of congressional leaders occurs within an institutional setting in which limits are always present. This concluding chapter will offer a brief review of the evidence from the politics of leadership in these cases, then address two broader questions posed by the findings of the study. The first question involves political science: in what manner and to what extent can we generalize about the politics of congressional leadership from these cases? The second question involves political practice: do these three leaders provide models of the type of leadership we need in Congress? Does Congress work more effectively as an institution when led by assertive, risk-taking leaders?

## Evidence from the Clay, Reed, and Gingrich Speakerships and Explanations of Congressional Leadership

As explained in chapter 2, the contextual theories of congressional leadership and the conditional agency framework differ on two key points: whether variation in leaders' goals and the intensity with which those goals are held need to be incorporated in explanations of leadership politics; and whether homogeneous follower preferences are a necessary condition for assertive, consequential leadership in Congress. As summarized in table 6.1 the evidence from these cases shows that Clay, Reed, and Gingrich each had goals beyond holding the House speakership. For two of the three leaders there is also clear evidence from the period before becoming speaker that these were goals held with sufficient intensity to produce tolerance for political risk when opportunities arose to advance these goals. Clay wanted to be president and to advance policies that would complete the work of the Founders by strengthening the union. He also became a strong proponent of early diplomatic recognition of newly independent republics abroad. However, because Clay became speaker so early in his political career the evidence we have of his tolerance for risk as a leader is mostly indirect (his taste for high-stakes card games and willingness to risk his life by dueling). In the years before he became speaker, Reed clearly demonstrated strong commitment to a number of public policy goals (especially maintaining protective tariffs and the gold standard) as well as the institutional goal of establishing responsible party government in the House and a willingness

TABLE 6.1
*Evidence on Leaders' Goals*

| Leader | Goals | Intensity of goals / risk tolerance |
|---|---|---|
| Henry Clay | *Policy:* increase economic interdependence among regions to strengthen the union; early recognition of newly independent republics<br><br>*Personal:* presidential ambition | Indirect evidence of risk tolerance in personal behavior before becoming speaker (dueling, gambling) |
| Thomas Reed | *Institutional:* establish majoritarian party government in the House<br><br>*Policy:* maintain high protective tariff and gold standard for the currency<br><br>*Personal:* presidential ambition | Strong commitment to policy and institutional goals and tolerance for taking political risks demonstrated in political behavior before becoming speaker |
| Newt Gingrich | *Institutional:* strengthen party control over legislative process; increase influence of the House in national policy-making process<br><br>*Policy:* transform national policy consistent with a "conservative opportunity society" model; use of balanced budget as a vehicle to drive programmatic change; tax cuts as signature issue for Republican Party<br><br>*Personal:* to be a transformational leader, change history ("move the planet") | Strong commitment to policy goals and tolerance for taking political risks demonstrated in political behavior before becoming speaker |

to take political risks to advance those goals. Newt Gingrich also demonstrated a propensity for taking political risks during his rise to power in the House and in pursuit of his goal of making history by transforming national policy and politics in conformity with a "conservative opportunity society" model.

The second major point of difference between contextual theories and the conditional agency framework concerns whether a high level of agreement among followers is a necessary condition for assertive, consequential leadership to occur in Congress. The conditional agency approach proposes that consequential leadership can occur under a wider range of political conditions (including situations where followers' preferences on the issue to be decided are uncertain or deeply divided) if the issue provides an opportunity for the leader to advance some goal he or she cares enough about to take political risks to advance it. Each explanation of leadership politics in turn implies a causal process that should be present in leader-follower interactions. For contextual theory, leaders who are concerned primarily with maintaining support to remain leader should use their powers assertively only when there is some clear indication that followers' preferences are homogeneous;

if followers' preferences are unclear or there is clear evidence of deep divisions on the issue, leaders are not expected to use the prerogatives of office assertively until broader agreement develops. For the conditional agency framework, on issues that provide opportunities for leaders to advance some intensely held goal, leaders may use the powers of office assertively to influence outcomes even when followers' preferences are uncertain or known to involve deep divisions.

The evidence on the processes of leader-follower interactions in each of the main cases examined within the three speakerships is summarized in table 6.2. Consistent with the contextual theories, each speaker did provide assertive leadership on some issues on which the evidence suggests followers' preferences were relatively homogeneous: Clay on prosecuting war with Britain during the Twelfth and Thirteenth Congresses; Reed on tariff legislation in the Fifty-first Congress; and Gingrich on many of the measures included in the "Contract with America." But there are multiple cases in which each speaker assertively wielded the prerogatives of the speakership and was consequential for outcomes on issues on which his followers' preferences were either uncertain or known by the leader to be seriously divided. Clay continued to assert the prerogatives of the speakership aggressively after 1815 to lead a deeply divided House on national policies he believed were needed to strengthen the bonds of union and achieved some measure of legislative success in those policies. We lack clear evidence that Clay viewed his own leadership on these issues as politically risky, although Clay did acknowledge publicly the tenuous nature of support for tariff legislation at one point. Through his active and skillful use of the office of speaker Clay also transformed the speakership into a more important leadership position during the early decades of House politics. In pursuit of the goal of establishing responsible party government, Reed pushed reform of House rules well beyond the changes his followers had actually agreed to support. He then used the speaker's authority under those new rules to advance legislation on the currency and electoral reform over which he knew serious divisions were present among his followers because the Republican Caucus was unable to reach agreement on endorsing the former bill as a party measure and was deeply split on the latter. The case of the Reed Rules is especially notable because the rules changes Reed orchestrated in 1890 established the majoritarian procedural foundations for the modern House and represent one of the most important institutional developments in the history of Congress.

Newt Gingrich led a new Republican majority in the 1990s that was unified in support of most of the conservative program embodied in the "Contract with America," but that unity in part reflected his own efforts to win a Republican majority and shape his followers' preferences in support of his policy goals. Before his

TABLE 6.2
*Summary of Causal Process Evidence on Decisions from Clay, Reed, and Gingrich Speakerships*

| | Opportunity to to advance leader's goals | Clear indication of homogeneous follower preferences before leader acts | Evidence leader was uncertain of support or aware of risk of defeat | Leader actively asserts the prerogatives of speakership to influence outcome |
|---|---|---|---|---|
| *Cases that fit contextual theory* | | | | |
| Clay | | | | |
| War measures (12th–13th Congresses) | NA* | yes | NA[a] | yes |
| Reed | | | | |
| McKinley tariff (51st Congress) | NA | yes | NA | yes |
| Gingrich | | | | |
| Most Contract bills (104th Congress) | NA | yes | NA | yes |
| | | | | |
| *Cases that fit conditional agency framework* | | | | |
| Clay | | | | |
| Tariff and internal improvements measures (14–16th, 18th Congresses) | yes | no | limited | yes |
| Reed | | | | |
| Reed Rules (51st Congress) | yes | no | yes | yes |
| Silver Purchase Act (51st Congress) | yes | no | yes | yes |
| Election reform (51st Congress) | yes | no | yes | yes |
| Gingrich | | | | |
| Organizational changes to increase party control over committees (104th Congress) | yes | no | no | yes |
| Contract Welfare Reform (104th Congress) | yes | no | yes | yes |
| Contract Tax Cuts (104th Congress) | yes | no | yes | yes |
| Balanced budget initiative (104th, 105th Congresses) | yes | no | yes | yes |
| | | | | |
| *Cases in which leader and follower preferences were in conflict* | | | | |
| Clay | | | | |
| Postwar foreign policy measures (14th–16th Congresses) | yes | yes | yes | no |
| Reed | | | | |
| Measures involving war with Spain and acquisition of new territories (55th Congress) | no | yes | yes | no |

*Not applicable. Leaders are assumed to have the same goal (office-holding ambition) in the contextual theories. With clear evidence of homogeneous followers' preferences there is no reason for the leader to judge taking action to be risky or uncertain.

followers had even assembled in Washington, Gingrich engineered rules changes that helped establish a new form of party government in the House in which standing committees were more subservient to the majority party and its leadership than at any point since the era of powerful speakers during the late nineteenth and early twentieth centuries. When House Republicans were clearly divided over how far to go in reforming welfare and how large a tax cut to pass to implement their Contract, Gingrich actively used the prerogatives of the speakership to push both outcomes in a direction consistent with his own policy goals. Gingrich also succeeded in defining budget balance within seven years as a goal for House Republicans in 1995 when no consensus on that goal existed among his followers, senior Republican leadership staff considered it extremely risky, and experienced legislators in his party thought it was impossible. But after the Republican majority in the Senate and the Democratic president embraced this goal, a balanced budget was enacted in 1997 involving hundreds of billions of dollars in spending reductions, major changes in the Medicare program, and a big tax cut. Interestingly, the causal mechanisms through which these three leaders influenced outcomes appear to have been primarily persuasion and agenda control; closer analysis of these and other cases might reveal that distribution of selective benefits or sanctions was important (especially in the tariff and budget measures), but little direct evidence of the importance of those mechanisms was found.

Each of these leaders also encountered limits arising from the fact that he was leading a body of elected representatives capable of acting independently of their leaders or because of constraints defined by a constitutional order of separated powers. As shown in the third group of cases in table 6.2, Speakers Clay and Reed both found themselves seriously at odds with their followers on foreign policy issues. Both appeared to recognize the limits of leadership in a situation in which their followers' preferences were homogeneous and fixed in opposition to their own. Clay held back in asserting the prerogatives of the speaker's office to advance his goal of early recognition of new Latin American republics in the face of consistent opposition to this policy from large majorities of his followers as well as from Presidents Madison and Monroe. Constitutional objections to federally funded internal improvements from Madison and Monroe (backed up by the presidential veto power) also limited his success in advancing his domestic program. In the face of overwhelming support for war with Spain and acquisition of new territories among his Republican followers in 1898–1899, Reed made almost no effort to influence outcomes on these issues despite the formidable powers that had been conferred on the speaker by the 1890s rules changes. Electoral reform legislation pushed through the House by Reed in 1890 failed to become law because a different constellation of political forces controlled the outcome in the Senate. Vetoes cast by President Clinton stopped a number of Contract measures and broke much of the force of the Gingrich-led agenda in late 1995 and early 1996. A more moderate Republican majority in the Senate also checked the extent of policy change resulting from the Contract. Also, on issues including welfare reform and the budget, Speaker Gingrich was at times forced to reverse course when his preferred strategies did not meet with the approval of his Republican followers.

These cases show that leaders' goals matter for understanding congressional leadership politics and that leadership can be consequential for outcomes in Congress in a wider range of political conditions than those in which followers are already in agreement about where they want to be led. But these cases also show congressional leadership always operates within limits. As Charles O. Jones (1999) reminds us, congressional leaders are dependent on majority support within their chambers and operate within a Madisonian constitutional system that normally requires agreement to be reached across both chambers of Congress and both ends of Pennsylvania Avenue for major changes in the direction of governance to occur.

## The Agency of Leaders in Congressional Politics

The patterns in leadership politics implied by the conditional agency framework—leaders with goals other than office-holding ambition inside Congress asserting active leadership on issues on which their followers' preferences are not homogeneous, yet succeeding in shaping outcomes—were thus found repeatedly within the three speakerships examined in the book. An outcome considered by many congressional scholars to be one of the most important institutional developments in the history of Congress—adoption of the Reed Rules in 1890—occurred precisely by means of this pattern in leadership politics. At a minimum the conditional agency framework helps explain how the procedural foundations of the modern House were put in place. But in judging the significance of evidence from the speakerships of Clay, Reed, and Gingrich for understanding congressional leadership, there remains the crucial question of how typical these cases are (for those who prefer the scientific jargon, the question of external validity). Can we generalize from this evidence of the independent agency of individual leaders in institutional and policy outcomes during the speakerships of Clay, Reed, and Gingrich to the importance of the agency of leaders for outcomes in congressional politics at other times?

First, these are all cases from the House of Representatives. The distinctive institutional features of the Senate suggest caution is in order in applying lessons about leadership politics from these cases to the upper chamber. Second, even when considering generalizations about leadership in the House of Representatives, there are some respects in which these speakerships probably are not typical cases. Speakers Clay, Reed, and Gingrich were selected for study in part because they stand out as some of the most activist leaders ever to serve in the House. If we think about placing House leaders along a continuum from highly risk-averse to highly risk-tolerant, these three individuals may well be at the high end of the continuum for risk-tolerance. Many House leaders—including prominent figures such as Speaker Sam Rayburn—are more risk-averse in their approaches to leadership. To the extent that this is true, the patterns in leadership politics found in these cases may not occur very frequently across the history of the House. Finally, the periods in which these three leaders served were also extraordinary in some respects. Henry Clay served during an early period in House politics when the procedures and institutional arrangements in the chamber were still relatively fluid and members had few bases of institutional power from which to push back against the speaker's initiatives (Peters 1997, 35–37). Thomas Reed and Newt Gingrich both served as leaders of parties that had been out of power for extended periods and were prepared to entertain institutional reforms and to legislate broad programs (Schickler 2001, 253–254). Both also assumed the office of speaker during periods when the speaker controlled institutional resources that conferred a high degree of control over the agenda of the House as well as selective rewards and sanctions.

If the distinctive features of these cases suggest that consequential leadership of the *scope* of that exercised by a Henry Clay or a Thomas Reed or a Newt Gingrich may be unusual in the House, there is much evidence to suggest that the conditions that gave rise to consequential leadership in these cases may occur frequently in congressional politics. First, within the conditional agency framework leaders assume the risks involved in acting independently of their followers because they have goals about which they care intensely beyond office-holding ambition in Congress. Research on Congress has repeatedly demonstrated that members have multiple goals beyond simply getting elected and holding office. Unless we are willing to believe the implausible scenario that members abandon goals other than holding office on being chosen as leaders, or that other goals are never intensely held, individuals who serve as congressional leaders will frequently have goals that encourage some degree of risk-tolerance with their leadership positions to influence outcomes when opportunities arise to advance those goals.

Second, disagreement—even serious division—among followers is a perennial condition leaders encounter in Congress. Even during periods when parties are relatively unified, issues emerge that divide partisan followers. Leaders have discretion about how to respond in these situations. Finally, there is much evidence that members do not have strong or fixed preferences on many of the issues that need to be decided in Congress (see chapter 2). If, as scholars such as Richard Fenno (1986) and R. Kent Weaver (2000) have documented, members' preferences can shift as new information or other influences emerge in the process of making decisions, surely leaders' positions are among the important sources of influence on what alternatives members ultimately choose to support. Even if the independent agency of leaders on the *scale* found in the Clay, Reed, and Gingrich speakerships may be infrequent in congressional politics, there still should be many decisions in which leaders attempt to influence policy and institutional outcomes on a narrower scale with consequences for the outcomes.

By assuming that leaders are always motivated by the goal of remaining leader and that members of Congress have fixed preferences on every issue, some theories of congressional politics in effect define away the possibility that the agency of leaders can matter. The evidence from the speakerships of Clay, Reed, and Gingrich shows that theories of congressional leadership that omit attention to leaders' goals and risk-tolerance risk missing important factors that may help explain how leaders act as well as the outcomes that occur in Congress. Political scientists seeking to understand and explain congressional leadership should look more closely at the actual processes involved in leadership politics during other periods as well; there is good reason to believe evidence of the agency of leaders will be found.

## Do Assertive Leaders Make Congress More Effective?

A final question raised by this study of Speakers Clay, Reed, and Gingrich is whether these speakers provide a model of the type of leadership under which Congress works most effectively. Although there are some very important differences in the approaches each of these speakers took in leading Congress, they shared an assertive, risk-taking approach to leadership. That quality helps explain why these leaders were consequential in shaping policy and institutional outcomes. But there remains the important question of how well the House performs its most important institutional tasks under this assertive mode of leadership. Does Congress work better under strong, risk-taking leaders?

Legislatures are distinctive political institutions made up of formal equals engaged in representing the interests and opinions in the political communities they govern, in deliberation and in lawmaking. Taking an institutional perspective attentive to the tasks the House of Representatives is expected to perform within the constitutional system, leaders in Congress should be held responsible for managing the House in a way that ensures that representation, deliberation, and lawmaking are all taking place. As discussed in chapter 1, this can be an extraordinarily challenging task because ensuring that representation and deliberation are occurring often complicates and slows down the task of reaching agreement among representatives to pass laws.

Of the three leaders in this study, Henry Clay probably comes closest to this institutional model of leadership. Partly because the institutional resources of the speakership were limited during this early period, Clay relied heavily on persuasion in the form of participation in House debates to shape outcomes in the direction he favored. Speakers Reed and Gingrich both had greater institutional resources at their disposal and both relied much more heavily on controlling the agenda of the House to advance their legislative goals. As we have seen, both were quite willing to use the institutional prerogatives of the speakership to frame decisions in ways that favored the outcomes they preferred in advance of consultation with their followers, to exclude representatives of the minority party from participation in shaping legislation, and when possible to drive their preferred alternatives through House decision-making processes with a minimum of debate.

Speakers Reed and Gingrich were both highly effective at times in orchestrating action by the House, but under both leaders efficient legislating sometimes occurred at the expense of representation and deliberation. As Peters (1997, 68) has noted, "Reed seems to have been more concerned with efficient government than with deliberative government." C. Lawrence Evans and Walter J. Oleszek (1997, 177) have written of the operation of the House under Gingrich's leadership that "there has been a downside to the GOP's decision to centralize power within the House and to expedite the decision-making process . . . the Republican changes have diminished the quality and thoroughness of deliberation on Capitol Hill" (see also Mann and Ornstein 2006).

Strong leadership in Congress is therefore not always an unalloyed good when it comes at the cost of the representative and deliberative capacities that the institution is uniquely capable of providing within the American constitutional system. But in the congressional setting, leaders who neglect representation and deliberation will usually pay a political cost for doing so. As Eric Schickler (2001, 273) notes, the political response to Reed's highly centralized and highly partisan mode of leadership in the Fifty-first Congress was "one of the most devastating defeats in congressional history" for his party. Voters narrowed Newt Gingrich's House majority in two successive elections, the second of which resulted in a collapse in his political support among his followers and ended his speakership. Leaders who neglect representation and deliberation to orchestrate legislative action they favor may be consequential for outcomes in Congress in the short term, but the structure of the institution and its place in the American constitutional system make it unlikely they will remain leaders in the long term.

## House Support for Speaker Henry Clay on Votes on Major Bills and Resolutions on which Clay Took a Public Position, 14th–18th Congresses

Speaker Clay's position reported first, followed by the vote of the full House. Votes reported as yeas-nays. Measures with an issue area identified in parentheses (tariff, internal improvements, or foreign policy) are those used to calculate the support scores reported in the text and shown in tables 3.1, 3.2, and 3.3. Votes reported for these measures include the vote by members of the committee of jurisdiction.

Roll call voting data are from ICPSR Study No. 4, Inter-university Consortium for Political and Social Research and Congressional Quarterly, Inc., *United States Congressional Roll Call Voting Records, 1789–1990* (Ann Arbor, MI: Inter-university Consortium for Political and Social Research).

+ Speaker Clay's position supported by the House in vote on final passage
– Speaker Clay's position rejected by the House on final passage

*14th Congress:* March 4, 1815–March 3, 1817
1st session: December 4, 1815–April 30, 1816

+ Direct taxation bill
 Clay position: floor speech (*Annals of Congress,* 14th Cong., 1st sess., 723–730, 746–747, 776–792)
   ICPSR vote #:  23: Clay: Y; House 109–16
         24: Clay: N; House 73–79
         26: Clay: N; House 67–86

+ Bill to change members' compensation from $6/day to $1,500/annum
 Clay position: floor speech (*Annals of Congress,* 14th Cong., 1st sess., 1174)
   ICPSR vote #:  45: Clay: Y; House 80–67

+ Bill to establish second Bank of the United States
 Clay position: floor speech (*Annals of Congress,* 14th Cong., 1st sess., 1127–1134)
   ICPSR vote #: 50: Clay: Y; House 80–71

+ 1816 Tariff bill (tariff)
 Clay position: floor speech (*Annals of Congress,* 14th Cong., 1st sess., 1237–1238, 1263, 1272)

ICPSR vote #:  59: Clay: N; House 65–63; Ways and Means 3–1
60: Clay: N; House 84–60; Ways and Means 3–1
61: Clay: Y; House 79–71; Ways and Means 1–3
63: Clay: N; House 86–56; Ways and Means 2–2
64: Clay: N; House 51–76; Ways and Means 3–1
68: Clay: N; House 51–82; Ways and Means 2–2
69: Clay: N; House 47–95; Ways and Means 1–2
70: Clay: Y; House 88–54; Ways and Means 2–2

2nd session: December 2, 1816–March 3, 1817

+  Bill to repeal annual salary and restore per diem compensation
Clay position: floor speech (*Annals of Congress,* 14th Cong., 2nd sess., 495–498, 714–715)
ICPSR vote #:  88: Clay: N; House 81–91
92: Clay: N; House 53–115
93: Clay: N; House 85–81
97: Clay: Y; House 138–27

–  Neutrality law prohibiting arming of ships in U.S. ports to aid South American independence efforts (foreign policy)
Clay position: floor speech (*Annals of Congress,* 14th Cong., 2nd sess., 742)
ICPSR vote #: 100: Clay: N; House 94–60; Foreign Affairs 6–0

+  "Bonus" bill creating a fund to support federally subsidized internal improvements from proceeds of Bank of the United States (BUS) charter and dividends (internal improvements)
Clay position: floor speech (*Annals of Congress,* 14th Cong., 1st sess., 866–868)
ICPSR vote #: 105: Clay: Y; House 86–84; Select "Bonus" 4–0

–  Attempt to override Madison veto of "bonus" bill (internal improvements)
Clay position: vote and floor speech (*Annals of Congress,* 14th Cong., 2nd sess., 1062)
ICPSR vote #: 122: Clay: Y; House 60–56; Select "Bonus" 4–0

*15th Congress:* March 4, 1817–March 3, 1819
1st session: December 1, 1817–April 20, 1818

–  Resolution proposing again to use BUS bonus to fund internal improvements. Main resolution failed 73–72 in Committee of the Whole (*Annals of Congress,* 15th Cong., 1st sess., 1249). Successive votes on narrower resolutions defining congressional authority (internal improvements).
Clay positions: floor speeches (*Annals of Congress,* 15th Cong., 1st sess., 1164–1180, 1359–1378)
ICPSR vote #:  41: Clay: N; House 77–87; Select Internal Improvements 1–3
42: Clay: Y; House 90–75; Select Internal Improvements 3–1
43: Clay: Y; House 82–84; Select Internal Improvements 2–2
45: Clay: Y; House 71–95; Select Internal Improvements 2–2

46: Clay: Y; House 81–83; Select Internal Improvements 2–2

47: Clay: Y; House 83–55; Select Internal Improvements 2–1

– Resolution to appropriate funds to send formal minister to "United Provinces of Rio de la Plata" (now Argentina) rather than commissioners proposed by President Monroe (foreign policy)

Clay position: floor speech (*Annals of Congress,* 15th Cong., 1st sess., 1468–1469)

ICPSR vote #:  53: Clay: Y; Foreign Affairs 3–2; House 45–115

2nd session: November 16, 1818–March 3, 1819

– Resolution censuring Andrew Jackson for actions taken during 1818 military campaign in Florida

Clay position: floor speech (*Annals of Congress,* 15th Cong., 2nd sess., 631–655)

ICPSR vote #:  91: Clay: N; House 108–62

92: Clay: N; House 107–63

94: Clay: Y; House 70–100

– Tallmadge amendment to Missouri statehood bill, banning importation of slaves, and emancipating children of existing slaves at age twenty-five

Clay position: floor speech (*Annals of Congress,* 15th Cong., 2nd sess., 1174–1175)

ICPSR vote #:  99: Clay: N; House 87–76

100: Clay: N; House 82–78

101: Clay: N; House 97–56

+ Taylor amendment restricting slavery in the Arkansas territory

Clay position: vote (#105) and floor speeches (*Annals of Congress,* 15th Cong., 2nd sess., 1223–1224)

ICPSR vote #: 102: Clay: N; House 70–71

103: Clay: N; House 75–73

104: Clay: Y; House 77–79

105: Clay: Y; House 89–88

106: Clay: Y; House 89–87

107: Clay: N; House 86–90

*16th Congress:* March 4, 1819–March 3, 1821

1st session: December 6, 1819–May 15, 1820

+ Missouri statehood bill

Clay position: floor speech (*Annals of Congress,* 16th Cong., 1st sess., 1210)

ICPSR vote #:  28: Clay: Y; House 90–87

29: Clay: Y; House 134–42

– Clay resolutions on treaty with Spain over Florida. Asserted power of Congress to decide disposition of territory and repudiated the treaty for dropping U.S. claims to Texas. Resolutions never considered on the House floor.

Clay position: floor speech (*Annals of Congress,* 16th Cong., 1st sess., 1691)
>    ICPSR vote #: no recorded vote

+   Baldwin Tariff bill (tariff)
Clay position: floor speech (*Annals of Congress,* 16th Cong., 1st sess., 1946, 1997, 2034–2052)
>    ICPSR vote #:  57: Clay: N; House 71–96; Manufactures 0–7
>                   69: Clay: N; House 79–92; Manufactures 3–3
>                   70: Clay: N; House 93–71; Manufactures 2–5
>                   71: Clay: Y; House 92–71; Manufactures 2–4
>                   72: Clay: Y; House 92–71; Manufactures 2–4
>                   73: Clay: N; House 70–90; Manufactures 0–7
>                   74: Clay: N; House 78–90; Manufactures 0–7
>                   75: Clay: Y; House 91–78; Manufactures 7–0

+   Clay resolution to send ministers to newly independent South American republics (foreign policy)
Clay position: floor speech (*Annals of Congress,* 16th Cong., 1st sess., 2223–2229)
>    ICPSR vote #:  92: Clay: Y; House 80–75; Select Foreign Affairs 1–4

Clay resigns speakership, October 28, 1820

*17th Congress:* March 4, 1821–March 3, 1823
Clay out entire Congress

*18th Congress:* March 4, 1823–March 3, 1825
1st session: December 1, 1823–May 27, 1824

+   Bill authorizing funding for national survey of roads and canals (internal improvements)
Clay position: floor speech (*Annals of Congress,* 18th Cong., 1st sess., 1021–1041)
>    ICPSR vote #:  13: Clay: Y; House 113–82; Select Roads and Canals 5–1
>                   15: Clay: N; House 86–113; Select Roads and Canals 2–5
>                   16: Clay: Y; House 115–86; Select Roads and Canals 5–2

+   Amendment to military appropriations bill requiring the consent of New York State for purchase of property at West Point
Clay position: vote
>    ICPSR vote #:  17: Clay: N; House 85–85

–   Resolutions in support of Greek independence and opposition to efforts by European powers to assist Spain against South American republics. Resolutions never considered on the House floor.
Clay position: floor speech (*Annals of Congress,* 18th Cong., 1st sess., 1103–1104, 1113–1115, 1170–1178)
>    ICPSR vote #: no recorded vote

+ Tariff of 1824 (tariff)
  Clay position: votes (#45, 78) and floor speeches (*Annals of Congress,* 18th Cong., 1st sess., 1898, 1962–2001, 2622–2634)
    ICPSR vote #:  35: Clay: Y; House 65–132; Manufactures 0–7
    45: Clay: Y; House 102–101; Manufactures 6–1
    57: Clay: Y; House 107–102; Manufactures 6–1
    74: Clay: N; House 97–97; Manufactures 1–6
    78: Clay: N; House 94–94; Manufactures 1–6

+ Bill to appropriate funds to improve navigation of Ohio and Mississippi Rivers (internal improvements)
  Clay position: floor speech (*Annals of Congress,* 18th Cong., 1st sess., 2558)
    ICPSR vote #:  69: Clay: Y; House 115–60; Select Navigation of Ohio and Mississippi 4–1

+ Bill fixing the western boundary of the Arkansas territory
  Clay position: floor speech (*Annals of Congress,* 18th Cong., 1st sess., 2758–2760)
    ICPSR vote #:  89: Clay: Y; House 70–58

2nd session: December 6, 1824–March 3, 1825

+ Appropriation for Cumberland Road (internal improvements)
  Clay position: floor speech (*Register of Debates,* 18th Cong., 2nd sess., 231–239)
    ICPSR vote #:  97: Clay: Y; House 97–72; Select Cumberland Road 6–0

*Preface*

1. The best single-volume historical treatment of the House speakership is Peters 1997. Other useful overviews of leading speakers and the development of the office include Remini 2006; Davidson, Hammond, and Smock 1998; and Cheney and Cheney 1996. For more specialized studies of House leadership and works focusing primarily on recent House leaders, see the works discussed in chapter 2.

*Chapter One • Leading Representatives*

1. The account of congressional leadership that comes closest to a "great man" perspective on congressional leadership is probably Richard and Lynne Cheney's *Kings of the Hill.* "In explaining the House by way of abstractions, one must also keep in mind the power of strong individuals to reshape the forms they find. The House has often had such individuals . . . and they have been most responsible for what the House of Representatives is" (1996, xiv).

2. In practice, rules in some legislatures (including the U.S. Senate) may require supermajorities to reach decisions on certain issues (ratification of treaties) or under certain conditions (a filibuster). But note that even in the U.S. Senate the formal requirement for passing legislation is a simple majority.

3. All page citations to the *Federalist* are from the New American Library edition (Hamilton, Madison, and Jay 1961).

4. On the requisites for legislative deliberation, see Bessette 1994, chap. 3. See also Mucciaroni and Quirk 2006.

5. For a thoughtful discussion of the multiple expectations and responsibilities of U.S. House speakers in addition to their roles as party leaders, see Green, forthcoming.

6. As Eric Schickler (2001, 42–43, 274–276) has pointed out in the case of the U.S. Congress, efficient lawmaking orchestrated by activist leaders can even prove hazardous to the political health of the majority party when the full range of interests in the party fails to be represented in legislation that gets enacted.

7. On the origins of the institutional design of the Senate and the different capacities expected of the House and Senate, see Wirls and Wirls 2004, especially 76–82 and 147–162.

8. For an account of how contemporary congressional leaders use narrowly targeted benefits to assemble coalitions for passage of legislation advancing broader national interests, see Evans 2004.

9. For a more detailed exploration of the treatment of political leadership in the *Federalist,* see Ceaser 1979, 52–61, and Strahan 2003.

## Chapter Two • *Explaining Congressional Leadership*

1. The section that follows focuses on recent work on elected leaders in the House of Representatives. For a more comprehensive overview that includes earlier works and research on other types of leaders in Congress, see Sinclair 1990.

2. Elsewhere Cooper has identified a number of other contextual factors in addition to electoral politics that can affect the development of leadership institutions and other organizational features of Congress, including workload and agenda, relations with the executive, and ideas about democratic decisionmaking. See Cooper 1977, 1981, 2001.

3. It is sometimes overlooked that Cooper and Brady acknowledge the importance of leaders' personal traits and skills as an influence on leadership power and style in the House. Their conclusion was not that leaders are unimportant in explaining leadership politics but that the influence of personal characteristics of leaders occurs within parameters defined by the institutional context (Cooper and Brady 1981, 423–424).

4. Rohde (1991, 38) does note that leadership selection processes in the House often elevate leaders who have been elected earlier to lower positions sometimes resulting in the presence of leaders whose orientations reflect expectations or conditions at an earlier time.

5. As we have seen, Rohde's analysis of House leadership is an exception to this mode of theorizing because Rohde's theory (1991, 2000) employs a principal-agent framework yet also incorporates personal characteristics of leaders as an important cause of leadership behavior under certain conditions.

6. Even less importance is assigned to leaders in another influential body of political science scholarship on Congress in which both policy outcomes and institutional arrangements are said to be determined primarily by the preferences of the median or pivotal member of the chamber. See Krehbiel 1991, 1998.

7. A second condition considered necessary for strong or consequential leadership in some contextual theories is the presence of major programmatic differences (or preference polarization) between the majority and the minority parties (see Aldrich and Rohde 1997–98, 2000). If there is bipartisan or universal agreement on issues it would be illogical to delegate authority to leaders to facilitate passage of measures sure to win approval anyway. I focus on follower unity or homogeneity in testing contextual theories because this condition is emphasized in all of the contextual theories as a necessary condition for active and consequential leadership to occur and conversely all of these theories imply that leaders will be less active and consequential for outcomes when followers' preferences are heterogeneous on the issue in question.

8. An exception is Cox and McCubbins's (2002, 2005) account of negative agenda power. In their theory majority party leaders *always* retain the power to block measures that divide the party. Although the analysis in this book may have implications for understanding nega-

tive agenda power, the focus is on positive actions by leaders to influence policy or institutional choices.

9. While the main proponents of contextual leadership theories all reject Krehbiel's (1993, 1999) argument that congressional parties are inconsequential for explaining outcomes in Congress, the logic underlying explicit or implicit arguments in contextual theories that individual leaders are (mostly) inconsequential for explaining outcomes in Congress seems at times to come close to—or even converge with—Krehbiel's theoretical position (see Cooper and Young 2002, 103–104). The conditional agency perspective advanced in this study is based on the view that both parties and individual leaders are consequential, for many of the same reasons. Perhaps the point is best made with a question: Don't the same features of congressional politics that make parties consequential for outcomes (multiple issue dimensions, opportunities to use agenda control to manipulate outcomes, inchoate member preferences on some issues) inevitably create opportunities for leaders to be consequential as well? Or, can parties matter in Congress yet party leaders not matter?

10. On the leeway that may exist for leaders because of the costs involved in removing them, see also Kiewiet and McCubbins 1991, 48, and Cox and McCubbins 1993, 131–132.

11. Although outside the time frame of his main analysis, Schickler (2001, 272–276) notes in an epilogue the importance of Gingrich's leadership in the institutional changes adopted in 1995 by the new Republican majority in the House.

12. Nor is any claim being made that leaders are always key actors in the adoption of policy or institutional changes. As Davidson points out in the case of institutional changes, leaders can serve as sponsors, resistors, or managers of change. For example, regarding the institutional reforms that occurred in Congress from the 1960s through the early 1990s, Davidson (1994, 174) observes: "Most often [elected leaders] served as managers or brokers of proposals made by others, mediating between reform factions and those members defending the status quo." On the roles of leaders in organizing institutional reform in Congress, see also Forgette 1997.

13. On the need for scholars to devote greater attention to the challenge of incorporating the agency of leaders in theories of congressional politics, see also Aldrich and Shepsle 2000.

14. This view of theory is similar to Arnold's (1990, 122) approach to theorizing about when Congress will enact legislation serving broad rather than narrow interests: "Although one cannot predict with certainty whether Congress will pass a specific program, one can still set forth the conditions under which Congress may approve a proposal that serves organized interests or that delivers narrowly targeted geographic interests, and the conditions under which Congress may break free of parochial concerns and enact a bill that serves more diffuse and general interests." As Bennett and George (2001, 138) note, these types of theories "constitute a theoretical middle ground between parsimonious general theories and rich explanations based on specific sequences of causal mechanisms in individual cases."

15. A defender of the view that office-holding ambition within the legislature should always be considered the dominant goal might argue that congressional followers will normally avoid selecting leaders with strong policy (or institutional) goals out of step with their own. In which case, leaders' policy (or institutional) goals are of little independent significance for explaining leaders' actions. But consider a situation in which the leader is chosen on the basis

of the leader's views on one set of issues, then the congressional agenda shifts to an entirely different set of issues. As will be seen in the discussions of the Clay and Reed speakerships in chapters 3 and 4, this is not just a hypothetical possibility, but a situation that has occurred more than once in the history of the House.

16. Hamilton addresses the political motive of fame when making the case against limits on the eligibility of the executive for reelection, but the logic of the analysis is applicable to any highly visible officeholder.

17. It is interesting to note that only one presidential aspirant who served as speaker, James K. Polk, has actually succeeded in winning the office.

18. As both Schickler and Pierson have argued, institutional arrangements in Congress are probably more complex and less coherent than implied by concepts of institutional equilibrium, and less resilient than implied by theories of path dependence (see Schickler 2001, 267–268; Pierson 2004, 154–155). I find these arguments sufficiently persuasive to have dropped earlier efforts to apply a punctuated equilibrium framework ("institutional time") to congressional leadership politics (see Strahan 2002). As I discuss below, certain political situations in the history of Congress do resemble "critical" moments or junctures in the sense that leaders encounter unusually broad opportunities to influence the course of institutional or policy change. But the same causes that allow leaders to influence outcomes during these relatively infrequent critical episodes are often present in congressional decisions of narrower scope as well. As a result, a framework that approaches leadership politics in terms of critical junctures (during which the agency of leaders is unusually important) and periods of institutional equilibrium (during which leaders have very limited leeway) may not do justice to the distinctive institutional setting of the legislature and risks missing the agency of leaders in the more normal course of congressional politics. I am indebted to both Joseph Cooper and Ronald Peters for their persistence in encouraging me to rethink this point.

19. A causal mechanism is "a component of a causal process that intervenes between agents with causal capacities and outcomes" (Bennett and George 2001, 139).

20. Following the approach of economic theories, some theorists of legislative politics view legislators' preferences as fixed and externally determined (usually by the electoral constituency), leaving little if any opportunity for persuasion to affect what happens within the legislature. For critiques of the view that legislators' preferences are fixed and externally determined, see Bessette 1994; Rohde 1995; Evans and Oleszek 1999; Sinclair 2002; Cooper and Young 2002; Cooper and Hering 2003; Behringer, Evans, and Materese 2006. On the problems involved in applying economic theories that assume fixed, exogenously determined preferences to politics more generally, see Wilson 1980.

21. The most important example of this type of multidimensionality in American politics was the interplay between economic development issues and the slavery question during the first half of the nineteenth century. See especially Riker 1980, 1982, 1986, and Weingast 1998.

22. Cooper and Brady (1981, 423) propose that the leader's skill may actually be *more* important in explaining outcomes during periods when the formal powers of the office are limited because the leader must attempt to influence members from a weaker position. But the point holds that leaders' opportunities to influence outcomes will be greater in periods where more agenda power and more rewards and sanctions are in the hands of leaders.

23. Contextual theories are correct in stating that more institutional resources tend to be

delegated to leaders during periods when party followers are unified. The point here is that those resources can also be brought to bear by risk-tolerant leaders to influence outcomes on issues on which followers are *not* unified.

24. A comment may be helpful at this point regarding one possible objection to the choice of cases for the study. Some methodologists in the social sciences have argued that selecting cases known to have high values on both the causal variable of interest (risk-tolerant leaders) and the outcome one is seeking to explain (institutional and policy changes) will make it impossible to evaluate causal hypotheses about relationships between these variables (see King, Keohane, and Verba 1994, 128–149). While focusing only on observations with high values on both the independent and dependent variables can indeed create serious inferential problems in research that relies primarily on patterns in covariation among variables *across observations* to evaluate causal hypotheses, these problems with causal inference do not arise in research that relies primarily on *within-case* causal process observations to evaluate the proposition that leaders can be important causal agents. As the authors of one of the best recent treatments of qualitative methods in political science have emphasized, "causal process observations involve a *different* approach to inference" (Collier, Brady, and Seawright 2004, 255; emphasis in the original). Causal process observations involve research that goes beyond assessment of correlations between variables to "focus on ideas or priorities that must be held by actors in order for the hypothesis . . . to be correct" and on "indispensable steps in the causal process without which the hypothesis does not make sense" (ibid., 258; see also Hall 2003, 391–398). While this book will employ some comparisons across the cases of the three leaders, the principal strategy for evaluating the competing claims of the conditional agency and contextual explanations of congressional leadership will involve causal process observations within cases observed during each leader's tenure.

25. One problem in attempting to evaluate the contextual theories is that none of these theories states precisely what level of agreement or homogeneity in followers' preferences is sufficient to evoke active leadership. Presumably it must be higher than a simple majority. To cite the historical example that was probably most important in the development of this theory—the reemergence of stronger Democratic leadership in the House of Representatives during the 1980s—liberals who favored stronger party leadership had been a numerical majority of the House Democratic party for over a decade before stronger leadership actually emerged in the chamber.

## Chapter Three • Henry Clay

1. Although both authors acknowledge Clay's strong attachment to the cause of maintaining the union, this view of Clay's motivation receives support in the two best biographies of Clay, Van Deusen 1937 and Remini 1991, especially the former.

2. See Shepsle 1989; Gamm and Shepsle 1989; Aldrich and Shepsle 2000, and Jenkins 1998.

3. Peterson (1987, 380–385) and Shankman (1999) also portray Clay more as a principled politician whose skill at political maneuvering has been overrated.

4. The contextual theories discussed in chapter 2 were developed primarily to explain leadership in the modern House. Because of the many important differences between the

House of the early nineteenth century and the modern House—especially the weak political parties during this early period and their virtual breakdown after about 1815—some aspects of these contextual theories do not apply to leadership in this period. However, as Rohde and Shepsle (1987) have argued, the presence of the essential institutional feature of a leader/agent elected by multiple principals should result in similar leadership politics even in this early period. According to them in this early period as well as in the modern House, when "there is a high degree of homogeneity of preferences . . . leaders vigorously use the tools they have been granted. As preference homogeneity declines . . . leaders tend to respond with caretaker, housekeeping strategies" (122).

5. This pattern of initial homogeneity among Clay's Republican followers' voting patterns during the Twelfth and Thirteenth Congresses followed by a significant decline in unity over the later Congresses Clay served as speaker has been documented using a variety of measures of roll call voting. Figure 3.1 indicates a decline in Republican cohesion (Rice Index) from scores in the 0.5–0.6 range (0.5 indicates an average of 75 percent of the party voting together) in the earlier Congresses to scores in the 0.2–0.3 range for the later ones (see also Binder 1997, 53–54). Although use of the NOMINATE measure of roll call voting can be problematic during this period (see Poole and Rosenthal 1997, 38–39, 52–53) a measure of party unity based on standard deviations of first-dimension D-NOMINATE coordinates shows a very similar pattern of declining homogeneity among Clay's followers (Jenkins 1998, 504–506).

6. Others who have argued that Clay transformed the office of the speakership include political scientists Nelson Polsby (1968, 155–156) and Elaine Swift (1998) and historians Merrill Peterson (1987, 51) and Robert Remini (1991, 79). Peters (1997, 34) argues that Clay was "the first strong speaker" but that his leadership was more personal than institutional and had limited lasting effect on the office itself. Stewart takes a similar view, characterizing Clay as an influential leader but one who had limited influence on the institutional development of the House: "a brilliant and dogged tactician, but not an institutional architect" (2004, 43).

7. The most systematic treatment of the politics of congressional decisionmaking surrounding the War of 1812 is found in two articles by Ronald L. Hatzenbuehler (1972, 1976). Other useful accounts include Mayo 1937, 385–525; Horsman 1962, 225–262; Brown 1964; Fritz 1977; Remini 1991, 72–93, 97–104; Stagg 1983, 86–153; and Stewart 2004, 18–27.

8. All citations to Clay's papers are to the University Press of Kentucky edition (Hopkins and Hay 1959–1991).

9. Clay reportedly came close to fighting two additional duels, one with Representative James Milnor, a Pennsylvania Federalist, during the period he was speaker, and another in 1841 with Democratic Senator William R. King of Alabama (Van Deusen 1937, 341; Remini 1991, 83, 575).

10. On political duels in the early years of American politics, see Freeman 2001, 167–180.

11. Clay also made reference to his reputation as a card player in an 1820 House speech attacking the strategy of the Monroe administration in negotiations with Spain over Florida. "In early life he had sometimes indulged in a species of amusement, which years and experience had determined him to renounce, which if the Committee [of the Whole] would allow him to use it, furnished him with a figure—Shall we enter on the game, with our hand exposed to the adversary, whilst he shuffles the cards to acquire more strength?" *Annals of Congress,* 16th Cong., 1st sess., 1730.

12. Although nominally of the same Jeffersonian Republican party, by 1820 Adams and Clay were rivals for the presidency, a fact that may have colored Adams's judgment of Clay.

13. For Clay's explanation of the reasons for his change of opinion regarding the constitutionality of the bank, see the speech he gave to his constituents on June 3, 1816 (*Clay Papers*, 2: 199–205).

14. On the importance of the problems experienced during the War of 1812 for the development of Clay's views on what later became known as the American System, see Brown 1985, 123–126, and Shankman 1999, 7, 49–74.

15. On Clay's views on slavery, see Colton 1846, 1: 186–209; Shankman 1999, 101–113; Remini 1991, 178–184; Howe 1979, 133–137.

16. The most comprehensive analysis of Clay's political ideas is Shankman 1999. Also helpful are Howe 1979, chap. 6; Brown 1985, chap. 5; Minicucci 2001; Larson 2001, chap. 4.

17. As Minicucci (2001) has shown, a program of interest-based nation-building had been embraced in different forms by both Jeffersonian Republicans and Federalists. Clay's distinctive contribution to this line of thought was his emphasis on the harmony of sectional and regional economic interests if a strong internal market could be fostered by national policy.

18. On Clay's view that the ultimate elimination of slavery would occur more quickly if the issue did *not* become a focus of national politics, see Shankman 1999, 102–110.

19. Gamm and Shepsle (1989, 52) acknowledge that they could find "no smoking gun" in support of their "leadership survival" explanation of Clay's postwar leadership. Instead they rely primarily on inferences from Clay's need for political support to be reelected speaker and the timing of changes in the House committee system to support their interpretation. On the problem of limited evidence from which to judge different interpretations of how Clay operated as speaker, see also Stewart 2004, 10–18.

20. Evidence on Clay's floor speeches was obtained from the *Annals of Congress* (1st–18th Cong.) and the *Register of Debates* (18th Cong., 2nd sess.). These sources provide the most comprehensive record of House debates during this period. The *Annals of Congress* (covering the years 1789–1824) are a reconstruction of the earliest floor proceedings and debates, assembled primarily from newspaper accounts. These volumes were compiled by the private publishers Gales and Seaton between 1834 and 1856. The *Register of Debates* (1824–1837), also published by Gales and Seaton, was the first contemporaneous record of congressional debates. Neither was a verbatim account of all floor remarks, but it seems unlikely that policy remarks by speakers would have gone unreported very often. We do know that the content of some of Speaker Clay's major speeches went unrecorded. However, when this occurred the *Annals* notes the point at which the speaker participated in the debate. This does not affect the accuracy of the count of floor speeches but does result in some underreporting of the total lines in the record taken up by the speaker's policy speeches. In cases where the record notes that the speaker stated a position in the debate but does not report his remarks, the speech was included in the count of policy speeches but is not counted in the total length of the speaker's remarks for that Congress. The two sources also vary in format, which requires that the measures of length of floor speeches be standardized to take into account these differences in formatting, using the format of the *Annals* as the baseline. For more detailed analysis of floor participation by all House speakers from 1789 to 1841, see Strahan, Gunning, and Vining 2006.

21. Support scores were calculated as the ratio of votes cast in support of Clay's position to total votes a member cast on all "Clay votes" (see appendix) in that issue area during a given Congress. Members who missed all votes in an issue area were dropped in the computation of chamber, regional, and committee means. A comment may be in order at this point about the choice not to employ the Poole and Rosenthal NOMINATE coordinates as a measure of members' preferences. First, by using issue-specific preference measures for these comparisons, problems of bias are avoided that can be introduced by the use of preference measures that are based on all roll call votes rather than those specific to issue areas (see Hall and Grofman 1990, and Hurwitz, Moiles, and Rohde 2001). Second, the highly volatile patterns in House voting during the second period of the Clay speakership provide a very poor fit with the assumptions on which the NOMINATE technique is based (Poole and Rosenthal 1997, 30–31, 38–39, 90–95). The issue-specific Clay support scores used here are also less than ideal measures. In some Congresses, the numbers of votes used to calculate these scores are very small. However, because the votes on which these scores are based were each selected on the basis of a careful survey of primary and secondary sources, what may be lost in the small numbers of votes is hopefully offset by the accuracy of those votes as indications of support for Speaker Clay's policy positions.

22. For additional discussion and analysis of the evidence on Clay's committee appointments during this period, see Strahan, Moscardelli, Haspel, and Wike 2000.

23. The mean percentage of new members for the Fourteenth through Eighteenth Congresses was 46.3 (Polsby 1968, 146). Turnover was especially high (59.2 percent) at the beginning of the Fifteenth Congress (1817–1819) because of an unpopular salary increase that had been approved in the previous Congress. Clay himself had a close election in 1816 as a result of the "salary grab" issue (see Remini 1991, 143–147; Skeen 1986).

24. Numbers in parentheses are mean regional support scores for Clay's positions on all votes in the issue area during all postwar Congresses.

25. The internal improvements support score for members from the Mid-Atlantic region drops significantly in the Eighteenth Congress primarily because of a shift in voting by the New York delegation (see table 3.1). During the Fourteenth and Fifteenth Congresses, while federal funding was being sought for the Erie Canal, most New York representatives voted in support of federally funded internal improvements. After the canal was funded locally, most New Yorkers began to vote in opposition to these measures. See Dangerfield 1952, 323; Sellers 1991, 78–79; Larson 2001, 73–80.

26. Three select committees exercised jurisdiction over internal improvements issues during the Eighteenth Congress. All three had majorities appointed from Mid-Atlantic and western states. For purposes of clarity in presentation, only the most important of these, the Select Committee on Roads and Canals, is included in table 3.2. For data on all of these select committees, see Strahan, Moscardelli, Haspel, and Wike 2000, table 4.

27. The one exception to this pattern was limited support shown by members of the Committee on Ways and Means on tariff votes during the Fourteenth Congress. Here it is important to emphasize that the speaker's discretion in making committee appointments was not unconstrained. Ways and Means had traditionally included a large southern contingent among its members (see Stewart et al. 1995, 27–28, table 8). Clay's unwillingness to disturb the longstanding influence of southern members on Ways and Means probably explains both the

relatively weak support on that panel for tariff legislation during the Fourteenth Congress and the shift in tariff jurisdiction to a new Committee on Manufactures discussed later in this chapter. After the shift in jurisdiction in the Sixteenth Congress the members of the Committee on Manufactures consistently provided much stronger support for Clay's positions on tariff legislation than did the chamber as a whole.

28. The one exception is the select Foreign Affairs Committee during the Fifteenth Congress, which registered mean support of 0.60 for Clay's foreign policy position, when mean support in the chamber was 0.28. This anomaly may reflect the fact that there was only a single foreign policy vote on which Clay took a position during this Congress and two committee members from the regions least supportive of Clay's views (Peterson Goodwyn of Virginia and Benjamin Orr of Massachusetts) failed to vote. Had these two committee members voted and voted no, the mean committee support score for this Congress would have been 0.43.

29. The House also passed a tariff bill in 1820, but the bill was rejected by the Senate by one vote. See Stanwood 1903, 180–193.

30. Clay presided over the creation of eleven of the standing committees created between 1811 and 1825, but only two of these were actually substantive legislative committees. Another five were created during his absences in the Thirteenth and Seventeenth Congresses. See Jenkins and Stewart 1998, 2002.

31. On referral of measures during this period, see Cooper and Young 1989, 70–71 and 103, n.2. Some important measures continued to be referred to select committees throughout this period, including most measures involving internal improvements.

32. "The principles which should regulate the execution of the duties of the incumbent of the Chair are not difficult to comprehend, although their application to particular instances is often extremely delicate and perplexing. They enjoin promptitude and impartiality in deciding the various questions of order as they arise; firmness and dignity in his deportment towards the House; patience, good temper, and courtesy, towards the individual members; and the best arrangement and distribution of the talent of the House, in its numerous subdivisions, for the despatch of the public business, and the fair exhibition of every subject presented for consideration. They especially require of him, in those moments of agitation from which no deliberative assembly is always entirely exempt, to remain cool and unshaken amidst all the storms of debate, carefully guarding the preservation of the permanent laws and rules of the House from being sacrificed to temporary passions, prejudices, or interests." *Annals of Congress,* 18th Cong., 1st sess., 795.

33. In his final speech to the House, Speaker Dayton acknowledged the divided vote on the resolution by taking a final jab at his opponents: "Permit me to say, that far from being displeased, I have been on the contrary, very much gratified at hearing that the resolution of thanks has not been passed, as a mere matter of form, unanimously. As in all public bodies, there have ever been found men whose approbation must be considered by the meritorious as a censure, so in this body, there are, unhappily, some whose censure will be regarded by all whose esteem I value, as the highest testimony of merit." *Annals of Congress,* 5th Cong., 3rd sess., 3054–3055.

## Chapter Four • Thomas Reed

1. Other major studies of House rules by Cooper and Young (1989, 94) and Binder (1997, 82–84, 125–126) also see the adoption of the Reed Rules as an important turning point in the history of Congress but emphasize that these reforms built on earlier rules changes that had enhanced the speaker's powers and allowed majorities greater control over the legislative process.

2. Republicans had control of all three branches from 1881 to 1883 (Forty-seventh Congress), but a perfect tie in strength with the Democrats in the Senate meant that actual control of that chamber was in fact tenuous and contested.

3. As Reed (1890b, 671–672) observed of contemporary districting practices: "Our apportionments of congressional districts are no means utterly fair; but there is a limitation to injustice beyond which no party dares to go, except in Indiana, where 4,000 majority in the State gives Republicans but three out of thirteen Congressmen." Democrats voiced similar complaints of Republican-controlled states.

4. Richard Valelly (2007) estimates that suppression of the black vote in the South may have cost Republicans as many as 15 to 19 seats in House elections of the 1870s and 1880s.

5. Jenkins and his colleagues also found that even after the economic interests of the districts represented by the parties became more distinctive in the mid-1890s, "nearly one-third of Republicans represented districts closer to the Democratic median [than to the median for their own party] in per capita manufacturing. This shows that the sharp polarization in party voting during these years was not simply a function of polarization in district political economy" (Jenkins, Schickler, and Carson 2004, 550). In other words, to the extent that homogeneity of preferences among party members is tied to the economic interests of their districts, this evidence shows there was less homogeneity of preferences among Reed's Republican followers than might be suggested by the high levels of party unity in voting during these years.

6. Unless otherwise noted, biographical information about Reed is drawn from McCall 1914 and Robinson 1930.

7. All of the Reed correspondence and diary entries cited in this chapter are from The Thomas Brackett Reed Collection in the George J. Mitchell Department of Special Collections and Archives at Bowdoin College. Letters are cited by date and last name of Reed's correspondent.

8. In correspondence during the middle years of his congressional service and in private musings recorded in his diary, Reed still sometimes expressed ambivalence about his choice of politics as a career. After winning reelection comfortably in 1882, he wrote a letter to his friend George Gifford laced with sarcastic commentary on the hypocrisy of Washington politics. "I have of late been much disgusted . . . If anyone were to come along now and offer me what I am fairly worth in some other business this country would run great risk of losing a statesman" (TBR to Gifford, December 30, 1882). Again uncertain of his prospects for reelection in 1884, he wrote: "If in your sweet seclusion you learn of my disaster mourn mildly for I am not sure that I shall at all. This business has many elements of boredom in it" (TBR to Gifford, April 23, 1884). "I am a fool to mix in politics," Reed wrote in his diary in 1885, "being swamped in trivialities. At present I prefer to study languages. But, however, it earns my

bread, not only my daily bread but also the bread of my old age, which will come" (TBR Diary, October 5, 1885, English translation, original passage in French, translator unknown).

9. For evidence of Reed's attention to local interests, see: the response from the War Department to Reed's request for attention to dredging a channel in Maine (War Department to TBR, December 3, 1881); references in his diary to efforts to help the previous occupant of his congressional seat secure an appointment in the Treasury Department and to conflicts with Maine senators Eugene Hale and William Frye over an appointment for the collectorship of Portland, Maine (TBR Diary, January 23–24, 1882); correspondence in 1885 with the Navy Department over staffing at the Portsmouth Navy Yard; and the response from the Treasury Department regarding Reed's request on behalf of the Maine delegation for the appointment of one General W. F. Wentworth to a position as Collector of Internal Revenue (Treasury Department to TBR, July 27, 1889).

10. Historians of the House have called attention to this episode primarily because it established an important precedent for using the Rules Committee to secure greater control over legislation. Interestingly, in the account of this episode found in Reed's diary, he focuses on the strategic challenge involved in dealing with the Senate on the tariff measure. His main concern was to structure the procedure so House Republicans would have maximum bargaining leverage with the Senate and would retain the option of killing the high-profile party measure if the final version remained unacceptable to the House Republicans. Reed writes (TBR Diary, 1883):

> It was evident that the Pennsylvania, Ohio, and New Jersey men were terribly aggrieved while most New England men, the Northwest and extreme West were furious to pass the bill . . . for a time the caucus ran wild but after two hours I got at them with the idea that while a good revision [of the tariff] was a good thing, a bad one was a bad thing and we must go slow and have no jumping out of the window until we found what story of the house we're in. [William] McKinley [R-OH] backed me up and we adjourned with only one resolution which left things in the hands of the Committee on Rules.

Reed explains that the resolution developed by the Rules Committee was structured to allow House action by a majority vote only to express *disagreement* with the Senate bill and request a conference. It intentionally did not allow the option of approving the Senate-passed bill by majority vote (see also Taussig 1892, 232–233). Reed does not claim authorship of the actual rule: "[George M.] Robeson [NJ] drew up a rule and [Speaker Warren] Keifer modified it and I presented it to the House." Reed explains his strategy was for House conferees to express objections to the Senate bill on constitutional grounds. (The tariff changes in the bill had originated in the Senate and been attached to an unrelated House-passed tax bill—arguably a violation of Article 1, section 7 of the Constitution.) This objection was to be raised for two reasons:

> The first was to give our people power with the Senate conferees by alarming them by the threat of beating the Senate Bill by the constitutional question whereby we should meet any idea the Senate people had that the House would carry their bill pure and simple without any changes. The second reason was that if no bill could be agreed on

by the conferees we could kill the Senate bill . . . It was a very close situation. We could not pass a bill which slaughtered Pennsylvania, Ohio & New Jersey for that would in time kill all of us. We could not very well refuse to make any and every effort to pass a Bill. Hence we had to have a string tied to the Bill with somebody standing with a little hatchet to cut it to pieces if it did not turn out a good little Bill.

Perhaps Joseph Cannon's assessment of Reed—that he was "never a politician"—does not do him full justice.

11. Reed also supported a proposal adopted during the Forty-ninth Congress to break up the power of the House Appropriations Committee (see Stewart 1989, 79–132). At the time he argued that assigning control over most appropriation measures to a single committee had contributed to the problem of congestion in the legislative process. Later he expressed regret in supporting a move that weakened control over spending measures (Robinson 1930, 118–122).

12. Said Randall in response to Reed's proposal to amend the rules in 1884: "The method of transacting business proposed by the gentleman from Maine will be recognized by all who were members of the last House [the Forty-seventh, which had a GOP majority] as substantially the same as was then pending and which the minority of that House prevented from consideration. In renewing it now [when the Democrats are in the majority] the gentleman from Maine exhibits his consistency and establishes his sincerity" (*Congressional Record,* 48th Cong., 1st sess., 869).

13. The only direct evidence we have on Reed's attitude toward political fame is a comment he made in a speech not long after he was first elected to Congress (1878): "We all know too sadly well that oblivion begins to devour the mightiest when dead, and has in all ages been so greedy as to overtake some men yet living. Human fame, even of those who are at pains to preserve their memories, is as evanescent as the cloud of a summer sky" (quoted in McCall 1914, 51).

14. Theodore Roosevelt's efforts went well beyond speaking with other Republicans in Washington. In a letter he sent to Reed from St. Paul in the fall of 1889, Roosevelt reports on a series of conversations with Minnesota politicians about Reed's prospects (including Republican Senator Cushman Davis), assesses support for Reed's candidacy among the members of the Minnesota delegation, and offers advice on how best to "manage" those not yet in his camp (Roosevelt to TBR, September 15, 1889).

15. The vote was Reed 85, McKinley 38, Cannon 19, David B. Henderson of Iowa (who succeeded Reed as speaker) 14, and Julius Caesar Burrows of Michigan 10.

16. The specific party measures Representative Mills cites as motivating Republican efforts to change the rules were new electoral laws that would tip the balance in federal elections toward their own party (1889, 669, 672). Other contemporary observers noted that Democrats at this point were determined to block Republican efforts to pass federal election legislation, as well as legislation on the tariff. See Joseph Cannon's comments in Busbey 1927, 172, and Dunn 1922, 25.

17. Four years earlier, when the Forty-ninth House convened under Democratic control in December 1885, Reed had argued that the rules of a previous Congress did not bind its successor and that the House should operate under common parliamentary or legislative law until new rules were formally adopted. Regarding the substance of common parliamentary

law, Reed stated: "I must confess that I hardly know what would be regarded as the legislative parliamentary law of this country. I suppose that the Speaker will have to evolve it out of his own knowledge of the subject, with such aid as we can give him by discussion on the floor" (*Congressional Record*, 49th Cong., 1st sess., 145).

18. Unfortunately no minutes or other formal records of House party caucuses from this period appear to have survived. However, based on Gerald Gamm and Steven Smith's research on party caucuses in the late nineteenth- and early twentieth-century Senate, we can have some confidence that journalistic reports are reasonably accurate accounts of what happened. Gamm and Smith placed newspaper accounts of party caucuses alongside minutes that have been found for these caucuses in the Senate (some as early as 1903) and found that the journalistic accounts "appear to have been remarkably accurate." "Since newspaper accounts of caucus meetings accurately report caucus business for the period for which we have access to conference minutes, we regard newspaper accounts as accurate for the other periods as well" (2006, 6, 31). It seems reasonable to draw the same inference for newspaper accounts of the party caucuses in the House during this same period.

19. A proposed change in the quorum rule would have been even more important—and more objectionable—to the Democrats than were the rules changes that were reported to have been discussed in their caucus. It is inconceivable that former speaker Carlisle or others would not have brought this matter up if they thought there was any possibility the Republicans were planning such a move. It is equally improbable, given the detail in which this and other caucus meetings were described in newspapers at the time, that discussion of a change in the quorum rule would have gone unreported if it had occurred.

20. The only formal resolution adopted during the Republicans' January 27 caucus called for all members to remain in Washington unless they were ill and to be in the Capitol whenever the House was in session ("New Code Is in Sight," *Washington Post*, January 28, 1890).

21. Note that the plan to which Republicans had agreed in their January 27 caucus failed when fewer than 165 Republicans (a quorum) were on the House floor for the first election case. If Reed's plan all along was to overrule the existing quorum rule (as I believe it was) the failure to achieve a quorum of Republican members on the first election case probably strengthened his hand by demonstrating to his Republican followers that they would be unable to control the outcome of the election cases without changing this rule.

22. In his autobiography, Joseph Cannon states that Reed had told him and William McKinley to be ready for parliamentary action on the floor but had not revealed his plan to them: "Neither Republican nor Democrat knew that Reed was ready to stage a revolution. He sent no word either to McKinley or me" (Busbey 1927, 175).

23. Although he did not refer publicly to any other precedents, Reed may also have taken inspiration from actions taken a few years earlier by the speaker of the British House of Commons to rein in minority obstructionism in that body. Reed later commented, regarding his British counterpart's decision (in 1881) to refuse dilatory motions or other use of the rules to obstruct business in the House of Commons: "He did it without the action of the House, with no precedent in his favor, and nothing to sustain him but the common-sense of the English people" (1890a, 538–539). I am indebted to David Mayhew for pointing out the possibility that Reed might have been influenced by these earlier parliamentary developments in the United Kingdom.

24. Schickler's (2001, 37–38) analysis of the 1890 rules change has shown that at least some Democrats shared concerns over the unwieldy order of business required by House rules and that there had been some Democratic support for the limited reforms Reed had proposed unsuccessfully earlier in the 1880s. It seems plausible that some Democrats might have supported more limited rules changes in 1890 as well.

25. On the rarity with which the American electoral system ever confers a clear policy mandate, see Jones 2005, 177–220.

26. Bensel's (2000, 124–131) analysis of party politics at the state level during the period 1877–1900 found that most Republican state party platforms also included planks favoring tariff protection. The exceptions were states in the West.

27. The final vote recorded was 120–117, but one Democrat opposed to the bill changed his vote to yea in order to be able to offer a motion to reconsider. Another Democrat who claimed he had not heard his name called attempted to have his voted added to the nays but did not succeed. Had this claim succeeded the vote would actually have been 119–119 and Reed would have had to cast his own vote to break a tie ("Leaders Push the Bill," *Washington Post*, June 6, 1890; Bensel 2000, 400).

28. For a richly detailed account of the politics surrounding the federal elections bill in 1890–1891, see Upchurch 2004. On Hoar's role as the leading proponent in the Senate, see Welch 1965 and Valelly 2007.

29. Valelly (2007) concludes that suppression of the black vote in the South probably did cost Republicans control of the House in the Forty-sixth (1879–1881) and Fiftieth (1887–1889) Congresses.

30. For a more detailed account of the arguments made by proponents and opponents of the measure in the House debate, see Upchurch 2004, 93–105.

31. An interesting feature of the prolonged Senate debate over the force bill was an effort led by Republican Senator Nelson Aldrich (RI) to change the Senate rules to allow limitations on debate to be established by a majority vote (see Binder 1997, 186–187; Valelly 2007; Upchurch 2004, 160–166). The failure in early 1891 of this attempt to emulate what Reed had achieved in the House sealed the fate of the federal election bill in the Senate.

## Chapter Five • Newt Gingrich

1. On Cannon's view of party government and approach to leadership, see Jones 1968; Peters 1997, 75–87; Rager 1998.

2. Longworth did break with the committee seniority system in one instance to punish a group of Republican progressives who failed to support the party's presidential nominee in 1924, but he made clear that "the seniority violations were an exception brought on by extreme circumstances" (Schickler 2001, 122; see also pages 129–132; Bacon 1998, 132–133).

3. The fact that Speaker Rayburn was generally risk-averse in his approach to leadership does not mean that he never advanced legislative measures he favored unless assured of success. Green (forthcoming) finds that Rayburn did on occasion act to influence legislative outcomes on issues that did not have the clear support of his Democratic followers, including natural gas regulation in 1949–1950 and reciprocal trade legislation in 1955. House Democrats were deeply split on both issues.

4. The literature on the 1970s reform era in Congress and its consequences is extensive. Good overviews include Cooper 1981; Davidson and Oleszek 1977; Dodd and Oppenheimer 1977, 1981; Mann and Ornstein 1981; Polsby 2004; Rieselbach 1986; Schickler 2001, chap. 5; Sheppard 1985; Sundquist 1981. On the consequences of reform for House leadership, see especially Jones 1981; Rohde 1991; Sinclair 1983, 1992, 1995.

5. The previous record had been sixteen years of unbroken party control, last achieved by Republicans from 1895 to 1911 (the first four years under Thomas Reed's leadership).

6. The Republican majority grew to 235 during the 104th Congress because five Democrats switched parties.

7. Gingrich ran twice against incumbent Democrat Jack Flynt before he won election to the House in 1978 (see Fenno 2000). For detailed accounts of Gingrich's campaigns and his relationships with the Georgia districts he represented over the course of his career in the House, see Steely 2000.

8. The best account of Gingrich's rise within the House Republican party is Connelly and Pitney 1994.

9. Conflicts between junior members seeking to develop a "majority party mentality" and more senior members who had become acclimated to minority status had been a recurring feature of House Republican Party politics since the late 1950s. See Jones 1970.

10. Gingrich won election as whip by only two votes. He drew disproportionate support from the most conservative members of the conference, junior members, those from the South and West, and those affiliated with groups oriented toward activism in pursuit of majority status (Harris 2006).

11. Gingrich's opposition to tax increases in the face of huge budget deficits in the 1980s makes clear that his interest in balancing the budget did not include achieving balance by raising revenues while leaving the existing mix of national programs in place—hence his widely quoted remark about Republican senator Bob Dole being the "tax collector for the welfare state" when Dole supported tax increases to reduce budget imbalances during these years (Dewar 1984). For Gingrich, a balanced budget was desirable mostly as a means of driving change in public policy, rather than as an end in and of itself.

12. Evans and Oleszek (1997, 118) have noted that "Gingrich's media tactics often parallel presidential communications strategies more than they do the public roles adopted by previous speakers." On Gingrich's extraordinarily high media visibility, see also Harris 1998.

13. Clearly, many factors other than Gingrich's leadership were important in the 1994 election outcome, including President Clinton's weak performance during his first two years in office and broader trends in party politics, some of which had been set in motion decades earlier. For an excellent analysis of the causes of the Republican victory in the 1994 House election, see Jacobson 1996. On Clinton's political missteps, see Jones 1999, chap. 2. On the developments in party politics in the South that were crucial to Republicans achieving majority status in the House in the 1990s, see Black and Black 2002, and Shafer and Johnston 2006.

14. On Gingrich's central role in conceptualizing and guiding the development of the Contract, see also Gimpel 1996, 16–21; Drew 1996, 28–33; Hastert 2004, 119; Balz and Brownstein 1996, 37–43; and Wolfensberger 2000, 162–167. The one dissenting account, which assigns greater importance to Richard Armey, is Garrett 2005, 69–104.

15. This effect had its limits. For example, freshman Mark E. Souder stated that he felt no

special obligation to support Gingrich's preferred candidate for whip, Bob Walker (R-PA). "He gave us our organizing vision, but we are not indebted to Gingrich personally" (Hook 1995, 48). The freshmen generally provided strong support for the speaker's institutional and policy initiatives, although from the very beginning they demonstrated willingness to act independently. For example, Republican leaders had to negotiate with the freshmen to get a balanced budget amendment—one of the items in the Contract—to the House floor (Drew 1996, 120–123).

16. This chapter discusses only one aspect of the extensive organizational changes implemented by the new Republican majority. For a more detailed treatment of the full range of organizational changes adopted by the Republican majority at the beginning of the 104th Congress, see Aldrich and Rohde 1997–98 and Evans and Oleszek 1997.

17. The movement toward a more centralized Republican organization in the 104th Congress built on earlier rules changes in the late 1980s, which had given the GOP leader authority to appoint minority members to the Rules Committee and increased influence in the Republican Committee on Committees. See Rohde 1991, 136–137; Connelly and Pitney 1994, 49–51.

18. With the existing Republican Committee on Committees, the top party leader controlled only about 6 percent of the total votes. In the new Steering Committee the speaker would control close to 25 percent of the votes. Another bloc of approximately 25 percent of the votes would be controlled by other party leaders (Evans and Oleszek 1997, 88–89; Jacoby 1994a).

19. Gingrich's postelection support was so strong among House Republicans that there appears to have been little sense on his part or that of his staff that these moves involved much political risk. One of Gingrich's senior staffers said he "was surprised at the extent to which members said Newt could operate with impunity . . . He had an opportunity on a few occasions to go way beyond what he did . . . He could have removed other people from chairmanships. He could have skipped around two or three other people. And he didn't. I remember talking with him about this and rules changes and he said if we overreach there will be a reaction to it" (Swinehart 1996). That Gingrich remained attentive to limits on leadership even at the height of his influence is also shown by his choice not to advance a plan for a major restructuring of committee jurisdictions after resistance developed among senior Republicans (Evans and Oleszek 1997, 93–101).

20. The most detailed treatment is Gimpel 1996. Other useful accounts of the politics of passage of the Contract measures include Balz and Brownstein 1996; Drew 1996; Fenno 1997; Jones 1999, chap. 3; Owens 1997; Rae 1998, chap. 3; Wolfensberger 2000, chaps. 11, 13.

21. Robin Kolodny (1999) also makes the case that high levels of unity in roll call votes during the 104th Congress sometimes masked ongoing policy divisions between moderate and conservative Republicans in the House.

22. Gingrich conceded these errors in his 1998 book *Lessons Learned the Hard Way:* "Looking back I see that part of the problem of our having overlooked the power of the President had to do with the way we had begun to define—or perhaps I should say had not begun to define—our strategy. A legislator and an executive are two very different things and for a time we had allowed ourselves to confuse the two" (10). "The House . . . is neither a corporation nor a military institution" (25).

23. The line-item veto legislation was later invalidated by the Supreme Court in June 1998.

24. This account was confirmed by two of Gingrich's top staffers (Meyer 1997; Swinehart 1996).

25. The $288 billion target for Medicare savings originally voted by the House was later cut back to $270 billion in negotiations with the Senate.

26. For specifics of the politics of the government shutdowns, see Drew 1996, 325–361, and Sinclair 2000, 194–203.

27. An informative account of the most important legislative missteps that fed the view that Gingrich was changing course without adequate consultation and stumbling in his management of the House is Wolfensberger 2000, chap. 12.

28. As Schickler has noted, a similar pattern followed Thomas Reed's speakership, when House Republicans chose the more collegial David Henderson of Iowa to be speaker for the Fifty-sixth Congress (Schickler 2001, 64–67, 275). Both Henderson and Hastert employed less assertive and more collegial modes of leadership than had their predecessors, but in neither case did the change in leaders result in a less *partisan* approach (see Owens 2005; Finocchiaro and Rohde 2004; Strahan and Palazzolo 2004, 107–111; Duff and Rohde 2006).

29. Gingrich may not have succeeded on quite this scale, but his model of leadership has been emulated in some far-flung places, including Mongolia, where the Democratic Union Party employed a "Contract with the Mongolian Voter" as the centerpiece of the June 1996 election that ended seventy-five years of control by the Communist Party (Thayer 1997).

*Personal Interviews*

Christensen, Arne. Staff assistant to Speaker Newt Gingrich for budget issues and Chief of Staff. March 18, 2005.

Ehrlich, Robert L. (R-MD). Member of the House of Representatives. July 10, 2002.

Gingrich, Newt. Speaker of the House of Representatives. January 22, 2003.

Hellman, Ralph. Staff assistant to Newt Gingrich, staff member for the Republican Policy Committee, Policy Director in the Office of the Majority Whip, and Policy Director for Speaker Dennis Hastert. July 11, 2002.

Knott, Kerry. Chief of Staff to Majority Leader Richard Armey. March 16, 2005.

Kutler, Edward. Senior staff member, Office of Speaker Newt Gingrich. July 2, 2002.

Linder, John (R-GA). Member of the House of Representatives. April 18, 1995.

Livingston, Robert (R-LA). Chair of the House Appropriations Committee. July 11, 2002.

Meyer, Daniel. Chief of Staff to Speaker Newt Gingrich. June 23, 1997.

Swinehart, Leonard. Senior Floor Assistant to Speaker Newt Gingrich. June 27, 1996, and March 17, 2005.

*Archival Collections*

Thomas Brackett Reed Collection. George J. Mitchell Department of Special Collections and Archives. Bowdoin College Library. Brunswick, ME.

*Published Works*

Adair, Douglas. 1974. "Fame and the Founding Fathers." In Trevor Colbourn, ed., *Fame and the Founding Fathers: Essays by Douglas Adair*. New York: Norton.

Adams, John Quincy. 1875. *Memoirs of John Quincy Adams Comprising Portions of His Diary from 1795 to 1848*. 12 vols. Charles Francis Adams, ed. Philadelphia: J. B. Lippincott & Co.

Aldrich, John H., and David W. Rohde. 1997–98. "The Transition to Republican Rule in the House: Implications for Theories of Congressional Politics." *Political Science Quarterly* 112 (Winter): 541–569.

———. 2000. "The Consequences of Party Organization in the House: The Roles of the Majority and Minority Parties in Conditional Party Government." In Jon R. Bond and Richard Fleisher, eds., *Polarized Politics: Congress and the President in a Partisan Era*. Washington, DC: CQ Press.

Aldrich, John H., and Kenneth A. Shepsle. 2000. "Explaining Institutional Change: Soaking, Poking, and Modeling in the U.S. Congress." In William Bianco, ed., *Congress on Display, Congress at Work*. Ann Arbor: University of Michigan Press.

Alexander, De Alva Stanwood. 1916. *History and Procedure of the House of Representatives*. Boston: Houghton Mifflin Co.

Ambrose, Stephen. 1996. "The Newt Frontier." *George* (August): 72–75, 113–116.

*Annals of Congress*. 1789–1824. 1st to 18th Congresses. Washington, DC: Gales and Seaton.

Argersinger, Peter H. 2001. "The Transformation of American Politics: Political Institutions and Public Policy, 1865–1910." In Byron E. Shafer and Anthony J. Badger, eds., *Contesting Democracy: Substance and Structure in American Political History, 1775–2000*. Lawrence: University Press of Kansas.

Arnold, R. Douglas. 1990. *The Logic of Congressional Action*. New Haven: Yale University Press.

Bacon, Donald G. 1998. "Nicholas Longworth: The Genial Czar." In Roger H. Davidson, Susan Webb Hammond, and Raymond W. Smock, eds., *Masters of the House: Congressional Leaders over Two Centuries*. Boulder, CO: Westview Press..

Bader, John B. 1996. *Taking the Initiative: Leadership Agendas in the Congress and the "Contract with America."* Washington, DC: Georgetown University Press.

Balz, Dan. 1994. "GOP 'Contract' Pledges 10 Tough Acts to Follow." *Washington Post* (November 20).

Balz, Dan, and Ronald Brownstein. 1996. *Storming the Gates: Protest Politics and the Republican Revival*. Boston: Little, Brown.

Balz, Dan, and Serge F. Kovaleski. 1994. "In Bush Budget Revolt, Gingrich Took the Reins." *Washington Post* (December 21).

Barry, John M. 1989. *The Ambition and the Power*. New York: Viking.

Baxter, Maurice G. 1995. *Henry Clay and the American System*. Lexington: University Press of Kentucky.

Behringer, Courtney L., C. Lawrence Evans, and Elizabeth R. Materese. 2006. "Parties, Preferences and the House Whip Process." Paper presented at the 2006 Annual Meeting of the Southern Political Science Association, Atlanta, GA, January 5–7, 2006.

Bennett, Andrew, and Alexander L. George. 2001. "Case Studies and Process Tracing in History and Political Science: Similar Strokes for Different Foci." In Colin Elman and Miriam Fendius Elman, eds., *Bridges and Boundaries: Historians, Political Scientists, and the Study of International Relations*. Cambridge: MIT Press.

Bensel, Richard Franklin. 2000. *The Political Economy of American Industrialization, 1877–1900*. Cambridge: Cambridge University Press.

Bessette, Joseph M. 1994. *The Mild Voice of Reason: Deliberative Democracy and American National Government*. Chicago: University of Chicago Press.

Binder, Sarah A. 1997. *Minority Rights, Majority Rule: Partisanship and the Development of Congress*. Cambridge: Cambridge University Press.

———. 2005. "The Republican Revolution at 10: Lasting Legacy or Faded Vision?" Congress Project Roundtable Discussion, Woodrow Wilson International Center for Scholars, Washington, DC (January 24). www.wilsoncenter.org/events/docs/repub-rev-trans.pdf.

Binkley, Wilfred E. 1962. *President and Congress*. 3rd rev. ed. New York: Vintage Books.

Black, Earl, and Merle Black. 2002. *The Rise of Southern Republicans*. Cambridge: Harvard University Press.

Brady, David W. 1988. *Critical Elections and Congressional Policymaking*. Stanford: Stanford University Press.

Brady, David W., Joseph Cooper, and Patricia A. Hurley. 1979. "The Decline of Party in the U.S. House of Representatives, 1887–1968." *Legislative Studies Quarterly* 4: 381–407.

Brady, David W., and Mathew D. McCubbins. 2002. "Party, Process, and Political Change: New Perspectives on the History of Congress." In David W. Brady and Mathew D. McCubbins, eds., *Party, Process, and Political Change: New Perspectives on the History of Congress*. Stanford: Stanford University Press.

Brown, George Rothwell. 1922. *The Leadership of Congress*. Indianapolis: Bobbs-Merrill.

Brown, Roger H. 1964. *The Republic in Peril: 1812*. New York: Columbia University Press.

Brown, Thomas. 1985. *Politics and Statesmanship: Essays on the American Whig Party*. New York: Columbia University Press.

Bruck, Connie. 1995. "The Politics of Perception." *New Yorker* (October 9): 50–77.

Busbey, L. White. 1927. *Uncle Joe Cannon: The Story of a Pioneer American*. New York: Henry Holt.

Carlyle, Thomas. 1901. *On Heroes, Hero-worship, and the Heroic in History*. Originally published 1841. Reprint Boston: Ginn & Co.

Carney, Dan. 1996. "As Hostilities Rage on the Hill, Partisan-Vote Rate Soars." *CQ Weekly* (January 27).

Cassata, Donna. 1995. "Republicans Bask in Success of Rousing Performance." *CQ Weekly* (April 8).

Ceaser, James W. 1979. *Presidential Selection: Theory and Development*. Princeton: Princeton University Press.

Cheney, Richard B., and Lynne V. Cheney. 1996. *Kings of the Hill: Power and Personality in the House of Representatives*. New York: Simon and Schuster.

Cloud, David S. 1994. "Gingrich Clears the Path for Republican Advance." *CQ Weekly* (November 19).

———. 1995. "Speaker Wants His Platform to Rival the Presidency." *CQ Weekly* (February 4).

Cohen, Richard E. 1994. "Hurricane Newt." *National Journal* (September 24): 2198–2202.

Collier, David, Henry E. Brady, and Jason Seawright. 2004. "Sources of Leverage in Causal Inference." In Henry E. Brady and David Collier, eds., *Rethinking Social Inquiry: Diverse Tools, Shared Standards*. Lanham, MD: Rowman and Littlefield.

Colton, Calvin. 1846. *The Life and Times of Henry Clay*. 2 vols. New York: A. S. Barnes.

Committee on Rules, U.S. House of Representatives. 1983. *A History of the Committee on Rules*. Washington, DC: Government Printing Office.

Congressional Quarterly. 1995. *Congressional Quarterly Almanac, 1994*. Washington, DC: Congressional Quarterly Inc.

———. 1996. *Congressional Quarterly Almanac, 1995*. Washington, DC: Congressional Quarterly Inc.

———. 1997. *Congressional Quarterly Almanac, 1996.* Washington, DC: Congressional Quarterly Inc.

———. 1998. *Congressional Quarterly Almanac, 1997.* Washington, DC: Congressional Quarterly Inc.

*Congressional Record.* 1873–. 43rd Congress to present. Washington, DC: Government Printing Office.

Connelly, William F., Jr., and John J. Pitney. 1994. *Congress' Permanent Minority? Republicans in the U.S. House.* Lanham, MD: Rowman and Littlefield.

———. 1999. "The House Republicans: Lessons for Political Science." In Nicol C. Rae and Colton C. Campbell, eds., *New Majority or Old Minority: The Impact of Republicans on Congress.* Lanham, MD: Rowman and Littlefield.

Connolly, Ceci. 1995. "Clay, Shaw, Bilirakis Anxious Over Cuts to Defense, Medicare." *St. Petersburg Times* (January 20).

Cooper, Joseph. 1962. *The Previous Question: Its Standing as a Precedent for Cloture in the United States Senate.* Senate Document 87–104. Washington, DC: Government Printing Office.

———. 1970. *The Origins of the Standing Committees and the Development of the Modern House.* Houston: Rice University Studies.

———. 1977. "Congress in Organizational Perspective." In Lawrence C. Dodd and Bruce I. Oppenheimer, eds., *Congress Reconsidered.* New York: Praeger.

———. 1981. "Organization and Innovation in the House of Representatives." In Joseph Cooper and G. Calvin MacKenzie, eds., *The House at Work.* Austin: University of Texas Press.

———. 2001. "The Twentieth-Century Congress." In Lawrence C. Dodd and Bruce I. Oppenheimer, eds., *Congress Reconsidered,* 7th ed. Washington, DC: CQ Press.

———. 2006. "House Party Voting Scores: Data for the 40th–107th Congresses." http://jhunix.hcf.jhu.edu/~jcooper/House_Party_Voting.xls.

Cooper, Joseph, and David W. Brady. 1981. "Institutional Context and Leadership Style: The House from Cannon to Rayburn." *American Political Science Review* 75: 411–426.

Cooper, Joseph, and Martin Hering. 2003. "Proximity Voting Versus Party Effects in Congressional Decision Making." Unpublished manuscript. Johns Hopkins University. www.jhu.edu/~polysci/faculty/cooper/proxyvoting.pdf.

Cooper, Joseph, and Cheryl D. Young. 1989. "Bill Introduction in the 19th Century: A Study of Institutional Change." *Legislative Studies Quarterly* 14: 67–105.

Cooper, Joseph, and Garry Young. 2002. "Party and Preference in Congressiuonal Decision Making: Roll Call Voting in the House of Representatives, 1889–1999." In David W. Brady and Mathew D. McCubbins, eds., *Party, Process, and Political Change in Congress: New Perspectives on the History of Congress.* Stanford: Stanford University Press.

Cooper, Kenneth J. 1994. "Gingrich: Cooperation, Yes. Compromise, No." *Washington Post* (November 12).

Cox, Gary W., and Mathew D. McCubbins. 1993. *Legislative Leviathan: Party Government in the House.* Berkeley: University of California Press.

———. 2002. "Agenda Power in the U.S. House of Representatives, 1877–1986." In David W. Brady and Mathew D. McCubbins, eds., *Party, Process, and Political Change: New Perspectives on the History of Congress.* Stanford: Stanford University Press.

———. 2005. *Setting the Agenda: Responsible Party Government in the U.S. House of Representatives.* New York: Cambridge University Press.

Dangerfield, George. 1952. *The Era of Good Feelings.* New York: Harcourt, Brace and Co.

Davidson, Roger H. 1981. "Subcommittee Government: New Channels for Policy Making." In Thomas E. Mann and Norman J. Ornstein, eds., *The New Congress.* Washington, DC: American Enterprise Institute.

———. 1994. "The Speaker and Institutional Change." In Ronald M. Peters, Jr., ed., *The Speaker: Leadership in the House of Representatives.* Washington, DC: CQ Press.

Davidson, Roger H., and Walter J. Oleszek. 1977. *Congress against Itself.* Bloomington: Indiana University Press.

Davidson, Roger H., Susan Webb Hammond, and Raymond W. Smock, eds. 1998. *Masters of the House: Congressional Leadership over Two Centuries.* Boulder, CO: Westview Press.

Deering, Christopher. 1999. "Learning to Legislate: Committees in the Republican Congress." In Nicol C. Rae and Colton C. Campbell, eds., *New Majority or Old Minority: The Impact of Republicans on Congress.* Lanham, MD: Rowman and Littlefield.

Derthick, Martha, and Paul J. Quirk. 1985. *The Politics of Deregulation.* Washington, DC: Brookings Institution Press.

Dewar, Helen. 1984. "Republicans Wage Verbal Civil War; Gingrich Leads Rebels." *Washington Post* (November 19).

———. 1995. "Republicans Face the Bitter Truth; Divisions, Democratic Defiance Complicate Already Arduous Agenda." *Washington Post* (January 23).

Dion, Douglas. 1997. *Turning the Legislative Thumbscrew: Minority Rights and Procedural Change in Legislative Politics.* Ann Arbor: University of Michigan Press.

Dodd, Lawrence C., and Bruce I. Oppenheimer, eds. 1977. *Congress Reconsidered.* New York: Praeger.

———, eds. 1981. *Congress Reconsidered,* 2nd ed. Washington, DC: CQ Press.

Drew, Elizabeth. 1996. *Showdown: The Struggle between the Gingrich Congress and the Clinton White House.* New York: Simon and Schuster.

———. 1997. *Whatever It Takes: The Real Struggle for Political Power in America.* New York: Viking.

Duckett, Alvin Laroy. 1962. *John Forsyth: Political Tactician.* Athens: University of Georgia Press.

Duff, Jeremy F., and David W. Rohde. 2006. "Rules to Live By: Agenda Control and the Use of Special Rules in the House." Paper presented at the Annual Meeting of the Southern Political Science Association, Atlanta, GA (January 5–7).

Dunn, Arthur Wallace. 1922. *From Harrison to Harding.* Vol. 1. New York: G. P. Putnam's Sons.

Eilperin, Juliet. 2006. "Gingrich May Run If No Front Runner Emerges." *Washington Post* (June 10).

Epstein, David F. 1984. *The Political Theory of the Federalist.* Chicago: University of Chicago Press.

Evans, C. Lawrence, and Walter J. Oleszek. 1997. *Congress under Fire: Reform Politics and the Republican Majority.* Boston: Houghton Mifflin.

———. 1999. "The Strategic Context of Congressional Party Leadership." *Congress & the Presidency* 26 (Spring): 1–20.

Evans, Diana. 1994. "Congressional Oversight and the Diversity of Members' Goals." *Political Science Quarterly* 109 (Autumn): 669–687.

———. 2004. *Greasing the Wheels: Using Pork Barrel Projects to Build Majority Coalitions in Congress.* New York: Cambridge University Press.

Fenno, Richard F., Jr. 1973. *Congressmen in Committees.* Boston: Little, Brown.

———. 1986. "Observation, Context, and Sequence." *American Political Science Review* 80 (March): 3–15.

———. 1990. *Watching Politicians: Essays on Participant Observation.* Berkeley, CA: IGS Press.

———. 1991. *The Emergence of a Senate Leader: Pete Domenici and the Reagan Budget.* Washington, DC: CQ Press.

———. 1997. *Learning to Govern: An Institutional View of the 104th Congress.* Washington, DC: Brookings Institution Press.

———. 2000. *Congress at the Grassroots: Representational Change in the South, 1970–1998.* Chapel Hill: University of North Carolina Press.

———. 2007. *Congressional Travels: Places, Connections, and Authenticity.* New York: Pearson Longman.

Finocchiaro, Charles J., and David W. Rohde. 2004. "Speaker David Henderson and the Partisan Era of the U.S. House." Paper presented at the History of Congress Conference, Stanford University (April 9–10).

Foerstel, Karen. 1994. "Gingrich Flexes His Power in Picking Panel Chiefs." *CQ Weekly* (November 19).

Follett, Mary Parker. 1896. *The Speaker of the House of Representatives.* New York: Longmans, Green.

Forgette, Richard G. 1997. "Reed's Rules and the Partisan Theory of Legislative Organization." *Polity* 29 (Spring): 375–396.

Formisano, Ronald P. 1981. "Federalists and Republicans: Parties, Yes—System, No." In Paul Kleppner et al., *The Evolution of American Electoral Systems.* Westport, CT: Greenwood Press.

Freeman, Joanne B. 2001. *Affairs of Honor: National Politics in the New Republic.* New Haven: Yale University Press.

Fritz, Harry W. 1977. "The War Hawks of 1812: Party Leadership in the Twelfth Congress." *Capitol Studies* 5 (Spring): 25–42.

Fuller, Herbert Bruce. 1909. *The Speakers of the House.* Boston: Little, Brown.

Gamm, Gerald, and Kenneth Shepsle. 1989. "Emergence of Legislative Institutions: Standing Committees in the House and Senate, 1810–1825." *Legislative Studies Quarterly* 14: 39–66.

Gamm, Gerald, and Steven S. Smith. 2006. "The Rise of Floor Leaders in the United States Senate, 1890–1915." Paper presented at the History of Congress Conference, Center for the Study of American Politics, Yale University (May 12–13).

Garrett, Major. 2005. *The Enduring Revolution: How the Contract with America Continues to Shape the Nation.* New York: Three Rivers Press.

George, Alexander L., and Andrew Bennett. 2005. *Case Studies and Theory Development in the Social Sciences.* Cambridge: MIT Press.

Gettinger, Stephan. 1995. "'Contract': Just a Step in Speaker's Plan." *CQ Weekly* (April 29).

Gillespie, Ed, and Bob Schellhas, eds. 1994. *Contract with America*. New York: Times Books.

Gimpel, James G. 1996. *Fulfilling the Contract: The First 100 Days*. Boston: Allyn and Bacon.

Gingrich, Newt. 1984. *Window of Opportunity: A Blueprint for the Future*. New York: Tor Books.

———. 1994. "Rep. Newt Gingrich, Washington Research Symposium, Washington, D.C., November 11, 1994." In Ed Gillespie and Bob Schellhas, eds., *Contract with America*. New York: Times Books.

———. 1995a. "The Contract's Crowning Jewel." *Wall Street Journal* (March 21).

———. 1995b. *To Renew America*. New York: HarperCollins.

———. 1998. *Lessons Learned the Hard Way: A Personal Report*. New York: HarperCollins.

———. 1999. *C-SPAN American Profile: Former Speaker Newt Gingrich*. Interview with Brian Lamb, July 30, 1999. Transcript retrieved from c-span.org.

Green, Matthew N. Forthcoming. "Presidents and Personal Goals: The Speaker of the House as Non-Majoritarian Leader." *Congress & the Presidency*.

Gugliotta, Guy. 1994. "In New House, Barons Yield to the Boss." *Washington Post* (December 1).

Hager, George. 1996. "A Battered GOP Calls Workers Back to Job." *CQ Weekly* (January 6).

Hager, George, and Eric Pianin. 1997. *Mirage: Why neither Democrats nor Republicans Can Balance the Budget, End the Deficit, and Satisfy the Public*. New York: Random House.

Hall, Peter A. 2003. "Aligning Ontology and Methodology in Comparative Research." In James Mahoney and Dietrich Rueschemeyer, eds., *Comparative Historical Research in the Social Sciences*. New York: Cambridge University Press.

Hall, Richard L. 1996. *Participation in Congress*. New Haven: Yale University Press.

Hall, Richard L., and Bernard Grofman. 1990. "The Committee Assignment Process and the Conditional Nature of Committee Bias." *American Political Science Review* 84: 1149–1166.

Hamilton, Alexander, James Madison, and John Jay. 1961. *The Federalist Papers*. New York: New American Library.

Hargrove, Erwin C. 2004. "History, Political Science and the Study of Leadership." *Polity* 36 (July): 579–592.

Harlow, Ralph Volney. 1917. *The History of Legislative Methods in the Period before 1825*. New Haven: Yale University Press.

Harris, Douglas B. 1998. "The Rise of the Public Speakership." *Political Science Quarterly* 113 (Summer): 193–212.

———. 2006. "Legislative Parties and Legislative Choice: Confrontation or Accommodation in the 1989 Gingrich-Madigan Whip Race." *American Politics Research* 34 (March): 189–222.

Hastert, Denny. 2004. *Speaker: Lessons from Forty Years in Coaching and Politics*. Washington, DC: Regnery Publishing.

Hatzenbuehler, Ronald L. 1972. "Party Unity and the Decision for War in the House of Representatives in 1812." *William and Mary Quarterly* 29: 367–390.

———. 1976. "The War Hawks and the Question of Leadership in 1812." *Pacific Historical Review* 43: 1–22.

Hinds, Asher C. 1907. *Hinds' Precedents of the House of Representatives of the United States*. Vol. 2. Washington, DC: Government Printing Office.

Hirshson, Stanley P. 1962. *Farewell to the Bloody Shirt: Northern Republicans and the Southern Negro, 1877–1893*. Bloomington: Indiana University Press.

Hook, Janet. 1995. "Conservative Freshman Class Eager to Seize the Moment." *CQ Weekly* (January 7).

Hopkins, James F., and Melba Porter Hay, eds. 1959–1991. *The Papers of Henry Clay.* Vols. 1–3, 10. Lexington: University Press of Kentucky.

Horsman, Reginald. 1962. *The Causes of the War of 1812.* Philadelphia: University of Pennsylvania Press, 1962.

Hoskins, Halford L. 1927. "The Hispanic American Policy of Henry Clay, 1816–1828." *Hispanic American Historical Review* 7: 460–478.

House, Albert V., Jr. 1935. "The Contributions of Samuel J. Randall to the Rules of the National House of Representatives." *American Political Science Review* 29: 837–841.

Howe, Daniel Walker. 1979. *The Political Culture of the American Whigs.* Chicago: University of Chicago Press.

Hume, Sandy. 1996. "GOP Keeps Together Welfare, Medicaid." *The Hill* (June 26).

Hurwitz, Mark S., Roger J. Moiles, and David W. Rohde. 2001. "Distributive and Partisan Issues in Agriculture Policy in the 104th House." *American Political Science Review* 95 (December): 911–922.

Jacobs, Lawrence R., Eric D. Lawrence, Robert Y. Shapiro, and Steven S. Smith. 1998. "Congressional Leadership of Public Opinion." *Political Science Quarterly* 113: 21–41.

Jacobson, Gary C. 1996. "The 1994 House Elections in Perspective." *Political Science Quarterly* 111 (Summer): 203–223.

Jacoby, Mary. 1994a. "Big States Losers in Gingrich's Plan for Committee on Committees." *Roll Call* (December 1).

———. 1994b. "Is Next GOP Reform Speaker Term Limit?" *Roll Call* (December 12).

Jenkins, Jeffery A. 1998. "Property Rights and the Emergence of Standing Committee Dominance in the 19th Century House." *Legislative Studies Quarterly* 23: 493–520.

Jenkins, Jeffery A., Eric Schickler, and Jamie L. Carson. 2004. "Constituency Cleavages and Congressional Parties: Measuring Homogeneity and Polarization, 1857–1913." *Social Science History* 28 (Winter): 537–573.

Jenkins, Jeffery A., and Charles Stewart III. 1998. "Committee Assignments as Side Payments: The Interplay of Leadership and Committee Development in the Era of Good Feelings." Paper presented at the 1998 Annual Meeting of the Midwest Political Science Association, Chicago.

———. 2002. "Order from Chaos: The Transformation of the Committee System in the House, 1810–1822." In David W. Brady and Mathew D. McCubbins, eds., *Party, Process, and Political Change: New Perspectives on the History of Congress.* Stanford: Stanford University Press.

Johannsen, Robert W., ed. 1965. *The Lincoln-Douglas Debates of 1858.* New York: Oxford University Press.

Jones, Charles O. 1968. "Joseph G. Cannon and Howard W. Smith: An Essay on the Limits of Leadership in the House of Representatives." *Journal of Politics* 30: 617–646.

———. 1970. *The Minority Party in Congress.* Boston: Little, Brown.

———. 1981. "House Leadership in an Age of Reform." In Frank H. Mackaman, ed., *Understanding Congressional Leadership.* Washington, DC: CQ Press.

————. 1999. *Clinton and Congress: Risk, Restoration, and Reelection.* Norman: University of Oklahoma Press, 1999.

————. 2005. *The Presidency in a Separated System.* 2nd ed. Washington, DC: Brookings Institution Press.

Katz, Jeffrey L. 1996. "GOP's New Welfare Strategy Has Democrats Reassessing." *CQ Weekly* (July 13).

————. 1998. "Can the Revolutionary Resist Running for President?" *CQ Weekly* (August 1).

Keller, Morton. 1977. *Affairs of State: Public Life in Late Nineteenth Century America.* Cambridge: Harvard University Press.

Kennon, Donald R., and Rebecca M. Rogers. 1989. *The Committee on Ways and Means: A Bicentennial History.* Washington, DC: Government Printing Office.

Kiewiet, D. Roderick, and Mathew D. McCubbins. 1991. *The Logic of Delegation.* Chicago: University of Chicago Press.

Killian, Linda. 1998. *The Freshmen: What Happened to the Republican Revolution?* Boulder, CO: Westview Press.

King, Gary, Robert O. Keohane, and Sidney Verba. 1994. *Designing Social Inquiry: Scientific Inference in Qualitative Research.* Princeton: Princeton University Press.

Kleppner, Paul. 1979. *The Third Electoral System, 1853–1892: Parties, Voters, and Political Cultures.* Chapel Hill: University of North Carolina Press.

Knupfer, Peter B. 1991. *The Union as It Is: Constitutional Unionism and Sectional Compromise, 1787–1861.* Chapel Hill: University of North Carolina Press.

————. 1992. "The Return of Henry Clay." *Reviews in American History* 20: 319–325.

Kolodny, Robin. 1999. "Moderate Success: Majority Status and the Changing Nature of Factionalism in the House Republican Party." In Nicol C. Rae and Colton C. Campbell, eds., *New Majority or Old Minority: The Impact of Republicans on Congress.* Lanham, MD: Rowman and Littlefield.

Koszczuk, Jackie. 1995a. "Train Wreck Engineered by GOP Batters Party and House Speaker." *CQ Weekly* (November 18).

————. 1995b. "Gingrich Struggling to Control Revolts among the Troops." *CQ Weekly* (December 23).

————. 1997a. "Frustration Sparks Rebellion, Discontent Fuels Smoldering Fire." *CQ Weekly* (July 26).

————. 1997b. "Gingrich, Aides Rediscover Unity, but Coup Attempt Still Echoes." *CQ Weekly* (November 22).

Krehbiel, Keith. 1991. *Information and Legislative Organization.* Ann Arbor: University of Michigan Press.

————. 1993. "Where's the Party?" *British Journal of Political Science* 23: 235–266.

————. 1998. *Pivotal Politics: A Theory of U.S. Lawmaking.* Chicago: University of Chicago Press.

————. 1999. "Paradoxes of Parties in Congress." *Legislative Studies Quarterly* 24 (February): 31–64.

Larson, John Lauritz. 2001. *Internal Improvement: National Public Works and the Promise of Popular Government in the Early United States.* Chapel Hill: University of North Carolina Press.

Lodge, Henry Cabot. 1889. "The Coming Congress." *North American Review* 149 (September): 293–301.

———. 1911. "Thomas Brackett Reed: The Statesman, the Wit and the Man." *Century Magazine* (January): 613–621.

Luce, Robert. 1924. *Legislative Assemblies*. Boston: Houghton Mifflin Co.

McCall, Samuel W. 1914. *The Life of Thomas Brackett Reed*. Boston: Houghton Mifflin Co.

McCarty, Nolan, Keith T. Poole, and Howard Rosenthal. 2002. "Congress and the Territorial Expansion of the United States." In David W. Brady and Mathew D. McCubbins, eds., *Party, Process, and Political Change in Congress: New Perspectives on the History of Congress*. Stanford: Stanford University Press.

McMurry, Donald L. 1922. "The Political Significance of the Pension Question, 1885–1897." *Mississippi Valley Historical Review* 9 (June): 19–36.

Mahoney, James, and Richard Snyder. 1999. "Rethinking Agency and Structure in the Study of Regime Change." *Studies in Comparative International Development* 34 (Summer): 3–32.

Mann, Thomas E., and Norman J. Ornstein, eds. 1981. *The New Congress*. Washington, DC: American Enterprise Institute.

———. 2006. *The Broken Branch: How Congress Is Failing America and How to Get It Back on Track*. New York: Oxford University Press.

Manzer, Robert A. 1996. "Hume on Pride and Love of Fame." *Polity* 18 (Spring): 333–355.

Maraniss, David, and Michael Weisskopf. 1996. *Tell Newt to Shut Up*. New York: Simon and Schuster.

Martis, Kenneth C. 1989. *The Historical Atlas of Political Parties in the United States Congress, 1789–1989*. New York: Macmillan.

Mayer, George H. 1964. *The Republican Party: 1854–1964*. New York: Oxford University Press.

Mayhew, David R. 2000. *America's Congress: Actions in the Public Sphere, James Madison through Newt Gingrich*. New Haven: Yale University Press.

Mayo, Bernard. 1937. *Henry Clay: Spokesman of the New West*. Boston: Houghton Mifflin Co.

Mills, Roger Q. 1889. "Republican Tactics in the House." *North American Review* 149 (December): 665–672.

Minicucci, Stephen. 1998. "Finding the Cement of Interest: Internal Improvements and Nation-Building, 1790–1860." Ph.D. diss., Massachusetts Institute of Technology.

———. 2001. "The 'Cement of Interest': Interest-Based Models of Nation-Building in the Early Republic." *Social Science History* 25 (Summer): 247–274.

Moe, Terry. 1984. "The New Economics of Organization." *American Journal of Political Science* 28 (November): 739–777.

Morgan, H. Wayne. 1969. *From Hayes to McKinley: National Party Politics, 1877–1896*. Syracuse: Syracuse University Press.

Mucciaroni, Gary, and Paul J. Quirk. 2006. *Deliberative Choices: Debating Public Policy in Congress*. Chicago: University of Chicago Press.

Myerson, Adam. 1991. "Miracle Whip: Can Newt Gingrich Save the Bush Presidency?" *Policy Review* 55 (Winter): 14–19.

Nielsen, George R. 1968. "The Indispensable Institution: The Congressional Party during the Era of Good Feelings." Ph.D. Diss., University of Iowa.

Ornstein, Norman J., Thomas E. Mann, and Michael Malbin. 1998. *Vital Statistics on Congress 1997–1998*. Washington, DC: Congressional Quarterly Inc.

Owens, John E. 1997. "The Return of Party Government in the US House of Representatives: Central Leadership–Committee Relations in the 104th Congress." *British Journal of Political Science* 27 (April): 247–272.

———. 2005. "Style, Skills, and Context: An Interactionist Exploration of Dennis Hastert's Speakership." Paper presented at the 2005 Annual Meeting of the Southern Political Science Association, New Orleans, LA.

Palazzolo, Daniel J. 1992. *The Speaker and the Budget: Leadership in the Post-Reform House of Representatives*. Pittsburgh: University of Pittsburgh Press.

———. 1999. *Done Deal? The Politics of the 1997 Budget Agreement*. New York: Chatham House Publishers.

———. 2000. "The Two Speakerships: Newt Gingrich's Impact on Budget Policy." *Extensions: A Journal of the Carl Albert Congressional Research and Studies Center* (Fall): 6–19.

Peters, Ronald M., Jr. 1996. "The Republican Speakership." Paper presented at the 1996 Annual Meeting of the American Political Science Association, San Francisco.

———. 1997. *The American Speakership: The Office in Historical Perspective*. 2nd ed. Baltimore: Johns Hopkins University Press.

———. 1999. "Institutional Context and Leadership Style: The Case of Newt Gingrich." In Nicol C. Rae and Colton C. Campbell, eds., *New Majority or Old Minority: The Impact of the Republicans on Congress*. Lanham, MD: Rowman and Littlefield.

———. 2004. "The Changing Speakership." In Walter J. Oleszek, ed., *The Cannon Centenary Conference: The Changing Nature of the Speakership*. Washington, DC: Government Printing Office.

Peterson, Merrill D. 1987. *The Great Triumvirate: Webster, Clay, and Calhoun*. New York: Oxford University Press.

Pianin, Eric. 1995. "Domenici to Attack Deficit and Ignore GOP Tax Cut; Decision Complicates Republican Program." *Washington Post* (March 29).

———. 1996a. "Despite Budget Settlement, Hill Republicans Remain Split over Spending." *Washington Post* (June 21).

———. 1996b. "GOP Budget Reforms Stew on Back Burner; House Freshmen Chafe at Leaders' Strategy." *Washington Post* (June 30).

Pianin, Eric, and John E. Yang. 1995. "House Passes Medicare Reform Bill; Clinton Vows to Veto GOP Measure Aimed at Saving $270 Billion." *Washington Post* (October 20).

Pierson, Paul. 2004. *Politics in Time: History, Institutions, and Social Analysis*. Princeton: Princeton University Press.

Pine, Art. 1995. "GOP's Defense Plans Are at War with Budget Goals." *Los Angeles Times* (January 20).

Polsby, Nelson W. 1968. "The Institutionalization of the U.S. House of Representatives." *American Political Science Review* 62: 144–168.

———. 1975. "Legislatures." In Fred I. Greenstein and Nelson W. Polsby, eds., *Handbook of Political Science*, vol. 5, *Governmental Institutions and Processes*. Reading, MA: Addison Wesley.

————. 2004. *How Congress Evolves: The Social Bases of Institutional Change.* New York: Oxford University Press.

Poole, Keith T. 2006. "NOMINATE Data: Party and Chamber Medians, 1st–108th Congresses (DW-NOMINATE Scores)." http://voteview.com.

Poole, Keith T., and Howard Rosenthal. 1997. *Congress: A Political-Economic History of Roll Call Voting.* New York: Oxford University Press.

Porter, Robert P. 1893. "Thomas B. Reed of Maine: The Man and His Home." *McClure's Magazine* (October): 375–386.

Purdum, Todd S. 1995. "Clinton Seeks New Welfare Bill, Saying G.O.P. Plan Is Too Harsh." *New York Times* (April 19).

Rae, Nicol C. 1998. *Conservative Reformers: The Republican Freshmen and the Lessons of the 104th Congress.* Armonk, NY: M. E. Sharpe.

Rager, Scott William. 1998. "Uncle Joe Cannon: The Brakeman of the House of Representatives." In Roger H. Davidson, Susan Webb Hammond, and Raymond W. Smock, eds., *Masters of the House: Congressional Leaders over Two Centuries.* Boulder, CO: Westview Press.

Reed, Thomas B. 1889a. "Rules of the House of Representatives." *Century Magazine* 37 (March): 792–795.

————. 1889b. "Obstruction in the National House." *North American Review* 149 (October): 421–428.

————. 1890a. "Reforms Needed in the House." *North American Review* 150 (May): 538–546.

————. 1890b. "Federal Control of Elections." *North American Review* 150 (June): 671–681.

————. 1890c. "Contested Elections." *North American Review* 151 (July): 112–121.

————. 1892. "Two Congresses Contrasted." *North American Review* 155 (August): 227–236.

————. 1895. "Historical Political Upheavals." *North American Review* 160 (January): 109–117.

————. 1896. "Introduction." In Calvin Colton, ed., *Works of Henry Clay Comprising His Life, Correspondence and Speeches.* Vol. 1. New York: Henry Clay Publishing Co.

————. 1897. "Empire Can Wait." *Illustrated American* (December 4): 713–714.

*Register of Debates.* 1824–1837. 18th to 25th Congresses. Washington, DC: Gales and Seaton.

Remini, Robert V. 1991. *Henry Clay: Statesman for the Union.* New York: Norton.

Rieselbach, Leroy N. 1986. *Congressional Reform.* Washington, DC: CQ Press.

Riker, William H. 1980. "Implications from the Disequilibrium of Majority Rule for the Study of Institutions." *American Political Science Review* 74: 432–446.

————. 1982. *Liberalism against Populism: A Confrontation between the Theory of Democracy and the Theory of Social Choice.* Prospect Heights, IL: Waveland Press.

————. 1986. *The Art of Political Manipulation.* New Haven: Yale University Press.

Risjord, Norman K. 1992. "Partisanship and Power: House Committees and the Powers of the Speaker, 1789–1801." *William and Mary Quarterly* 49: 628–651.

Roberts, Jason M., and Steven S. Smith. 2003. "The Evolution of Agenda-Setting Institutions in Congress: Path Dependency in House and Senate Institutional Development." Paper presented at 2003 History of Congress Conference, University of California–San Diego, San Diego, CA.

Robinson, William A. 1930. *Thomas B. Reed: Parliamentarian.* New York: Dodd, Mead.

Rohde, David W. 1991. *Parties and Leaders in the Postreform House.* Chicago: University of Chicago Press.

———. 1995. "Parties and Committees in the House: Member Motivations, Issues, and Institutional Arrangements." In Kenneth A. Shepsle and Barry R. Weingast, eds., *Positive Theories of Congressional Institutions.* Ann Arbor: University of Michigan Press.

———. 2000. "The Gingrich Speakership in Context: Majority Leadership in the House in the Late Twentieth Century." *Extensions: A Journal of the Carl Albert Congressional Research and Studies Center* (Fall): 4–7.

Rohde, David W., and Kenneth A. Shepsle. 1987. "Leaders and Followers in the House of Representatives: Reflections on Woodrow Wilson's *Congressional Government.*" *Congress & the Presidency* 14: 111–133.

Romano, Lois. 1985. "Newt Gingrich, Maverick on the Hill: The New Right's Abrasive Point Man Talks of Changing His Tone and Tactics." *Washington Post* (January 3).

Rosenstiel, Thomas. 1995. "Why Newt Is No Joke." *Newsweek* (April 10): 26.

Rubin, Alissa J. 1995a. "Unity Frays within House GOP over Family Tax Credit." *CQ Weekly* (March 25).

———. 1995b. "GOP Leaders Ready to Deal on Troubled Tax-Cuts Bill." *CQ Weekly* (April 1).

———. 1995c. "Finishing the 'Contract' in Style, House Passes Tax-Cut Bill." *CQ Weekly* (April 8).

Sabl, Andrew. 2002. *Ruling Passions: Political Offices and Democratic Ethics.* Princeton: Princeton University Press.

Schickler, Eric. 2001. *Disjointed Pluralism: Institutional Innovation and the Development of the U.S. Congress.* Princeton: Princeton University Press.

Sellers, Charles. 1991. *The Market Revolution: Jacksonian America, 1815–1846.* New York: Oxford University Press.

Shafer, Byron E., and Richard Johnston. 2006. *The End of Southern Exceptionalism: Class, Race and Partisan Change in the South.* Cambridge: Harvard University Press.

Shankman, Kimberly. 1999. *Compromise and the Constitution: The Political Thought of Henry Clay.* Lanham, MD: Lexington Books.

Sheingate, Adam D. 2003. "Political Entrepreneurship, Institutional Change, and American Political Development." *Studies in American Political Development* 17 (October): 185–203.

Sheppard, Burton D. 1985. *Rethinking Congressional Reform.* Cambridge, MA: Schenkman Books.

Shepsle, Kenneth A. 1989. "Studying Institutions: Some Lessons from the Rational Choice Approach." *Journal of Theoretical Politics* 1: 131–147.

Shepsle, Kenneth A., and Mark S. Bonchek. 1997. *Analyzing Politics: Rationality, Behavior, and Institutions.* New York: Norton.

Silbey, Joel H. 1991. *The American Political Nation, 1838–1893.* Stanford: Stanford University Press.

Sinclair, Barbara. 1983. *Majority Leadership in the U.S. House.* Baltimore: Johns Hopkins University Press.

———. 1990. "Congressional Leadership: A Review Essay and a Research Agenda." In John J. Kornacki, ed., *Leading Congress: New Styles, New Strategies.* Washington, DC: CQ Press.

———. 1992. "The Emergence of Strong Leadership in the 1980s House of Representatives." *Journal of Politics* 54 (August): 658–684.

————. 1995. *Legislators, Leaders, and Lawmaking: The House of Representatives in the Postreform Era*. Baltimore: Johns Hopkins University Press.

————. 1999. "Transformational Leader or Faithful Agent? Principal-Agent Theory and House Majority Party Leadership." *Legislative Studies Quarterly* 24 (August): 421–449.

————. 2000. *Unorthodox Lawmaking: New Legislative Processes in the U.S. Congress*. 2nd ed. Washington, DC: CQ Press.

————. 2002. "Do Parties Matter?" In David W. Brady and Mathew D. McCubbins, eds., *Party, Process, and Political Change: New Perspectives on the History of Congress*. Stanford: Stanford University Press.

Skeen, C. Edward. 1986. "*Vox Populi, Vox Dei:* The Compensation Act of 1816 and the Rise of Popular Politics." *Journal of the Early Republic* 6 (Fall): 253–274.

Skocpol, Theda. 1992. *Protecting Soldiers and Mothers: The Political Origins of Social Policy in the United States*. Cambridge: Harvard University Press.

Skowronek, Stephen. 1993. *The Politics Presidents Make: Leadership from John Adams to George Bush*. Cambridge: Harvard University Press.

Smith, Steven S., and Gerald Gamm. 2005. "The Dynamics of Party Government in Congress." In Lawrence C. Dodd and Bruce I. Oppenheimer, eds., *Congress Reconsidered*. 8th ed. Washington, DC: CQ Press.

Socolofsky, Homer E., and Allen B. Spetter. 1987. *The Presidency of Benjamin Harrison*. Lawrence: University Press of Kansas.

Stagg, J. C. A. 1983. *Mr. Madison's War: Politics, Diplomacy, and Warfare in the Early American Republic*. Princeton: Princeton University Press.

Stanwood, Edward. 1903. *American Tariff Controversies of the Nineteenth Century*. Boston: Houghton Mifflin.

Steely, Mel. 2000. *The Gentleman from Georgia: The Biography of Newt Gingrich*. Macon, GA: Mercer University Press.

Stewart, Charles S., III. 1989. *Budget Reform Politics: The Design of the Appropriations Process in the House of Representatives, 1865–1921*. Cambridge: Cambridge University Press.

————. 2000. "Speakership Elections and Control of the U.S. House, 1839–1859." Paper delivered at the 2000 Annual Meeting of the Midwest Political Science Association, Chicago, IL.

————. 2004. "Architect or Tactician? Henry Clay and the Institutional Development of the U.S. House of Representatives." Paper delivered at the History of Congress Conference, Stanford University (April 9–10).

Stewart, Charles S., III, David Canon, Greg Flemming, and Brian Kroeger. 1995. "Taking Care of Business: The Evolution of the House Committee System before the Civil War." Paper presented at the 1995 Annual Meeting of the American Political Science Association, Washington, DC.

Strahan, Randall. 1989. "Members' Goals and Coalition-building Strategies in the U.S. House: The Case of Tax Reform." *Journal of Politics* 51: 373–384.

————. 2002. " Leadership and Institutional Change in the Nineteenth Century House." In David W. Brady and Mathew D. McCubbins, eds., *Party Process and Political Change: New Perspectives on the History of Congress*. Stanford: Stanford University Press.

————. 2003. "Personal Motives, Constitutional Forms, and the Public Good: Madison on

Political Leadership." In Samuel Kernell, ed., *James Madison: The Theory and Practice of Republican Government*. Stanford: Stanford University Press.

Strahan, Randall, Matthew Gunning, and Richard L. Vining, Jr. 2006. "From Moderator to Leader: Floor Participation by U.S. House Speakers, 1789–1841." *Social Science History* 30 (Spring): 51–74.

Strahan, Randall, Vincent G. Moscardelli, Moshe Haspel, and Richard S. Wike. 2000. "The Clay Speakership Revisited." *Polity* 34 (Summer): 561–593.

Strahan, Randall, and Daniel J. Palazzolo. 2004. "The Gingrich Effect." *Political Science Quarterly* 119 (Spring): 89–114.

Sundquist, James L. 1981. *The Decline and Resurgence of Congress*. Washington, DC: Brookings Institution Press.

Swenson, Peter. 1982. "The Influence of Recruitment on the Structure of Power in the U.S. House, 1870–1949." *Legislative Studies Quarterly* 7: 7–36.

Swift, Elaine K. 1998. "The Start of Something New: Clay, Stevenson, Polk and the Development of the Speakership, 1789–1869." In Roger H. Davidson, Susan Webb Hammond, and Raymond W. Smock, eds., *Masters of the House: Congressional Leaders over Two Centuries*. Boulder, CO: Westview Press.

Swope, Christopher. 1997. "Clinton and the GOP Congress: A Rough Road to Agreement." *CQ Weekly* (May 3).

Taussig, F. W. 1892. *The Tariff History of the United States*. New York: G. P. Putnam's Sons.

Thayer, Nate. 1997. "In Mongolia, a GOP-style Revolutionary Movement; Republican-Inspired 'Contract' Helped End Communist Rule." *Washington Post* (April 6).

Tulis, Jeffrey K. 1987. *The Rhetorical Presidency*. Princeton: Princeton University Press.

Upchurch, Thomas Adams. 2004. *Legislating Racism: The Billion Dollar Congress and the Birth of Jim Crow*. Lexington: University Press of Kentucky.

Valelly, Richard M. 2007. "Partisan Entrepreneurship and Policy Windows: George Frisbie Hoar and the 1890 Federal Elections Bill." In Stephen Skowronek and Matthew Glassman, eds., *Formative Acts: American Politics in the Making*. Philadelphia: University of Pennsylvania Press.

Van Deusen, Glyndon G. 1937. *The Life of Henry Clay*. Boston: Little, Brown.

Vipperman, Carl J. 1989. *William Lowndes and the Transition of Southern Politics, 1782–1822*. Chapel Hill: University of North Carolina Press.

Vobejda, Barbara. 1995. "GOP Outlines Broad Welfare Reform: Proposal Would Replace Federal Programs with Block Grants to State." *Washington Post* (January 7).

Washington Post. 1995. "Details Promised with Budget." *Washington Post* (February 16).

Weaver, R. Kent. 2000. *Ending Welfare as We Know It*. Washington, DC: Brookings Institution Press.

Weingast, Barry R. 1998. "Political Stability and Civil War: Institutions, Commitment, and American Democracy." In Robert Bates et al., *Analytic Narratives*. Princeton: Princeton University Press.

Welch, Richard E. 1965. "The Federal Elections Bill of 1890: Postscripts and Prelude." *Journal of American History* 52 (December): 511–526.

Wellborn, Fred. 1928. "The Influence of the Silver-Republicans." *Mississippi Valley Historical Review* 14 (March): 462–480.

White, Leonard D. 1958. *The Republican Era, 1869–1901: A Study in Administrative History.* New York: Macmillan.

Williams, Dick. 1995. *Newt! Leader of the Second American Revolution.* Marietta, GA: Longstreet Press.

Williams, R. Hal. 1978. *Years of Decision: American Politics in the 1890s.* New York: John Wiley.

Wilson, James Q. 1980. "The Politics of Regulation." In James Q. Wilson, ed., *The Politics of Regulation.* New York: Basic Books.

————. 1995. *Political Organizations.* Princeton: Princeton University Press.

Wirls, Daniel, and Stephen Wirls. 2004. *The Invention of the United States Senate.* Baltimore: Johns Hopkins University Press.

Wolfensberger, Donald R. 2000. *Congress and the People: Deliberative Democracy on Trial.* Baltimore: Johns Hopkins University Press.

Yang, John E. 1996. "Gingrich Reelected GOP Leader: In Conciliatory Speech, House Speaker Vows a Different Approach." *Washington Post* (November 21).

Young, James Sterling. 1966. *The Washington Community, 1800–1828.* New York: Columbia University Press.

Zelizer, Julian E. 1998. *Taxing America: Wilbur D. Mills, Congress, and the State, 1945–1975.* Cambridge: Cambridge University Press.